GOSPEL
SYMBOLISM

GOSPEL
SYMBOLISM

JOSEPH FIELDING MCCONKIE

BOOKCRAFT / Salt Lake City, Utah

Library of Congress Catalog Card Number: 85-72079
ISBN 0-88494-568-5

3rd Printing, 1987

Printed in the United States of America

The things of God are of deep import; and time, and experience, and careful and ponderous and solemn thoughts can only find them out.

—Joseph Smith

Contents

Preface ix
Nonscriptural Abbreviations xiii
Bible Edition Abbreviations xv
1. In Similitude of Christ 1
2. Teaching in Technicolor 12
3. Teaching in Black and White 19
4. Joseph and the Spirit of Prophecy 28
5. An Everlasting Memorial: From Egypt to Sinai 44
6. An Everlasting Memorial: From Sinai to Palestine 60
7. The Law of Moses 76
8. A Temple in the Wilderness 99
9. The Mountain of the Lord's House 118
10. Robes of Righteousness 131
11. Like Unto Me 146
12. Prophets and Pageants 161
13. Names: A Story Within the Story 173
14. Rituals and Righteousness 195
15. Figurative or Literal? 205
16. History of Bible Interpretation 214
17. Interpreting Scripture 231
Glossary of Symbols 250
Bibliography 277
Index 283

Preface

For many within the Church, symbolism is a dead language. The difficulties of interpretation and the barriers posed by scriptural language have discouraged some Saints from feasting upon the inspired word. But those hungering for this greater substance have turned to the scriptures and commenced the struggle to learn the language of revelation. They have discovered that to be fluent in the language of the Spirit one must be fluent in the language of symbolism. It is hoped that this volume will be helpful to that end.

No pretense is made that this work represents an exhaustive treatment of the subject. It does not. What it hopes to be is a helpful introduction to the subject. Further, no claim is made to being the final word. Symbols are the language of feeling, and as such it is not expected that everyone will perceive them in the same way. Like a beautifully cut diamond, they catch the light and then reflect its splendor in a variety of ways. As viewed at different times and from different positions, what is reflected will differ, yet the diamond and the light remain the same. Thus symbols, like words, gain richness in their variety of meanings and purposes, which range from revealing to concealing great gospel truths.

This book was written by a layman for laymen. It seeks no academic plaudits, yet hopes for the quiet approval of the Spirit. It would be a unique book indeed if every expression within it were beyond error. Surely, that will not prove to be the case. I find myself in frequent disagreement with my colleagues on small matters. Such areas of disagreement compel one to more intense study. The net effect is quite positive. It has been wisely observed that they also serve who have the courage to be mistaken.

A brief explanation seems appropriate about the method of interpretation used in this work. The roots of such a discussion are both deep and entangled. My desire is to keep the subject simple. Let it suffice to say that on this matter opinions differ sharply. On the one hand, there are those who argue that unless the interpretation of a symbol is given in the scriptures, any commentary or elaboration is both unwise and unsafe. To give such commentary, it is argued, is to clarify what the Lord has not. At the other end of the spectrum (as we shall see in chapter 16—History of Bible Interpretation), there are those who would allegorize the stories and doctrines of the scriptures to the point that, when they are finished, there is nothing in all of holy writ that can be trusted to be literally true.

Meaningful answers are not found in positions of extreme. If our interpretations were confined exclusively to what is given in the scriptures, symbols would be virtually worthless because, more often than not, the scriptures give no explanation of them. And for the most part they would have to remain unexplained, because little scripture is regarded or recognized as scripture when it is first penned. Did Paul, from whom so much of our symbolic interpretation comes, recognize that he was writing scripture when he interpreted the meaning of Old Testament symbolism? And today we might ask, Are we entitled to interpret the scriptures by the power of that same spirit enjoyed by Paul and the other New Testament writers? One of the great injunctions of this dispensation is that we "deny not the spirit of revelation" (D&C 11:25). Surely the refusal to see or read beyond the literal rendering of a particular verse is to deny that spirit. The warning that those who seek to seal or close the canon of scripture will lose what little understanding they have (2 Nephi 28:30) is as true of chapters and verses as of the book itself. The principle also applies as much to the figurative or symbolic as it does to the literal.

Still the question remains, What sure standard assures that we have not seen angels where there are no angels or found meaning where none was intended? The answer is simple, and appropriately it is given in the scriptures: "Truth embraceth truth" (D&C 88:40). Interpretations in full harmony with truths already revealed are currency backed by the gold of heaven. Conversely, any doctrine relying on the interpretations of a parable, allegory, or symbol must be rejected. Let us state it thus—we do not deduce doctrine from parables; we do not concoct it from allegories; we do not wring it out of symbolic interpretations. But when that doctrine has already been revealed, when it has been clearly stated in the scriptures and by living prophets, then responsible interpretations of parables, allegories, or symbols that sustain the revelation already given are smiled upon by the heavens and may properly wear the label of divine truth.

Thus our gospel understanding must always come first. Before we can understand the symbol, we must understand the truth it is to convey. Understanding the principle must precede understanding the symbol. There is no substitute for good gospel scholarship, and there is no gospel understanding that will not be enriched by an improved knowledge of symbols and their meanings. As preparation and training increase our understanding and enjoyment of art and music, so a knowledge of symbols increases our knowledge and understanding of the scriptures. Indeed, symbols are like music to the soul, and, like inspired music, they raise our feelings to great heights as they testify of eternal truths.

Nonscriptural Abbreviations

The following abbreviations have been used to simplify references in the text of this work. Complete data on each source cited along with other works of interest are listed in the Bibliography.

Answers	Joseph Fielding Smith, *Answers to Gospel Questions*
Biblical Commentary	C. F. Keil and F. Delitzsch, *Biblical Commentary on the Old Testament*
Brieg	James Brieg, "Hell: Still a Burning Question?"
Clarke	Adam Clarke, *Clarke's Commentary*
Concordance	James Strong, *Strong's Exhaustive Concordance*
Cruden	Alexander Cruden, *Cruden's Complete Concordance to the Old and New Testaments*
Customs	James M. Freeman, *Manners and Customs of the Bible*
DCG	James Hastings, *A Dictionary of Christ and the Gospels*
DNTC	Bruce R. McConkie, *Doctrinal New Testament Commentary*
Doctrines of Salvation	Joseph Fielding Smith, *Doctrines of Salvation*
Dummelow	J. R. Dummelow, *The One Volume Bible Commentary*
Edersheim, OT	Alfred Edersheim, *Bible History, Old Testament*
Egypt	Hugh Nibley, *Abraham in Egypt*
ETS	J. C. Cooper, *An Illustrated Encyclopedia of Traditional Symbolism*
Ezekiel 1	Walther Zimmerli, *Ezekiel 1*
Farrar	Frederic W. Farrar, *History of Interpretation*
Garner	David H. Garner, "The Tabernacle—A Type for the Temples"
Girdlestone	Robert Baker Girdlestone, *Synonyms of the Old Testament*
Gleanings	Arthur W. Pink, *Gleanings in Genesis*
HC	Joseph Smith, *History of the Church*

IB	George Arthur Butteric, *The Interpreter's Bible*
IBD	Emory Stevens Bucke, *The Interpreter's Dictionary of the Bible*
Imagery	G. B. Caird, *The Language and Imagery of the Bible*
JD	*Journal of Discourses*
Joseph	Joseph Fielding McConkie, *His Name Shall Be Joseph*
Josephus	Josephus, *Complete Works*
Judaism	Milton Steinberg, *Basic Judaism*
Law	Louis Ginzberg, *On Jewish Law and Lore*
Legends	Louis Ginzberg, *The Legends of the Jews*
Life and Times	Alfred Edersheim, *The Life and Times of Jesus the Messiah*
Messengers	Elle Wiesel, *Messengers of God, Biblical Portraits and Legends*
Midrash	Samuel Rapaport, *A Treasury of the Midrash*
Mormon Doctrine	Bruce R. McConkie, *Mormon Doctrine*
Mortal Messiah	Bruce R. McConkie, *The Mortal Messiah*
Myth	Theodore H. Gaster, *Myth, Legend and Customs in the Old Testament*
Names	Flora Haines Loughead, *Dictionary of Given Names with Their Origin and Meanings*
Offerings	Andrew Jukes, *The Law of the Offerings*
Promised Messiah	Bruce R. McConkie, *The Promised Messiah*
Smith, Dictionary	William Smith, *Dictionary of the Bible*
Tabernacle	Henry W. Soltan, *The Tabernacle: The Priesthood and the Offerings*
Teachings	Joseph Smith, *Teachings of the Prophet Joseph Smith*
Temple History	Hugh Nibley, *What Is a Temple? The Idea of the Temple in History*
Temple Symbolism	John M. Lundquist, "The Common Temple Ideology of the Ancient Near East"
The Temple	Alfred Edersheim, *The Temple*
WDB	Walter Lewis Wilson, *Wilson's Dictionary of Bible Types*
Who's Who	John Comay and Ronald Browning, *Who's Who in the Bible*
Wycliffe BD	Charles F. Pfeiffer and Howard F. Vos and John Rea, *Wycliffe Bible Dictionary*

Bible Edition Abbreviations

JB	Jerusalem Bible
JST	Joseph Smith Translation
KJV	King James Version
LXX	Septuagint
NEB	New English Bible

In Similitude of Christ

Symbols are the timeless and universal language in which God, in his wisdom, has chosen to teach his gospel and bear witness of his Son. They are the language of the scriptures, the language of revelation, the language of the Spirit, the language of faith. They are a language common to the Saints of all generations. Symbols are the language in which all gospel covenants and ordinances of salvation have been revealed. They are a means whereby we enrich, deepen, and enhance understanding and expression. They enable us to give visual and conceptual form to ideas and feelings that may otherwise defy the power of words. Symbols take us beyond the language of words, granting us an eloquence in the expression of feelings.

Symbols are the language of testimony. Such was the language in which the prophets of the Old Testament foretold the birth and ministry of Christ; such was the language in which the atoning sacrifice was foreshadowed and the resurrection foreknown. Nowhere are symbols used with greater effect than in the mortal ministry of the Savior—a ministry that began with his ritual immersion in the waters of Jordan and ended with the rending of the veil of the temple when his work was finished and he gave up the ghost on Golgotha.

All Things Bear Witness of Christ

To be literate in the things of the Spirit is to be fluent in the language of symbols. The Lord told Enoch that "all things have their likeness" and that "all things" were created and made to bear record of him. This he said was true of things both temporal and spiritual, "things which are in the heavens above, and things which are on the earth, and things which are in the earth, and things which are under the earth, both above and beneath: all things bear record of me" (Moses 6:63). To illustrate this principle let us take twelve categories (that being an appropriate number as far as the law of witnesses is concerned), with an example from each category briefly noting how it testifies of Christ. As categories let us use the following: objects, places, personal names, titles, animals, events, feelings, foods, persons, words, rituals, and elements.

Objects. Illustration: an altar. As properly used in the Bible, altars were primarily places of blood sacrifice. They were stages upon which the atoning sacrifice of Christ was enacted. Malachi described them as the "table of the Lord" (Malachi 1:7, 12), suggesting that what was burned on the altar was considered to have been consumed by God, thus attesting that those making the offering were acceptable to him. Classic illustrations of this would be the fire that came from heaven to consume the offering on the altar at the dedication of Solomon's Temple (2 Chronicles 7:1) and the fire that fell from heaven to consume the offering of Elijah in his confrontation with the priests of Baal (1 Kings 18:38). Altars were also understood to be a place of peace and a place where God would manifest himself (Genesis 12:7; 13:18; 26:25; 35:1, 7).

Places. Illustration: the city of Bethlehem. Anciently it was prophesied that Christ would be born in Bethlehem (Micah 5:2). The name means "house of bread." Thus the name seems to testify that it is the place from which the Bread of Life will come (see John 6:35).

Names. Illustration: the name *Jesus.* Both Joseph and Mary were instructed by the angel of the Lord that the Son of God was to be named Jesus (Matthew 1:21; Luke 1:31). That he would bear this name had been known prophetically among the Book of Mormon peoples from the time of Nephi and Jacob (2 Nephi 25:19; Jacob 4:6; Mosiah 3:8). The name *Jesus* (*Joshua* in the Hebrew) means "Jehovah saves." Thus the name of the Savior testified that he was the God of salvation.

Titles. Illustration: the title *Christ.* This is not a given name but rather a title meaning "anointed" or "anointed one." In Old Testament times anointing was the principal and divinely appointed ceremony in the inauguration of prophets, priests, and kings. The anointing was a ritual consecration or setting apart to sacred purposes. The ritual centered in the pouring of pure olive oil upon the head of the one being anointed in a symbolic representation of the Spirit of the Lord that was to be poured out upon him and through him upon the nation of Israel. Under the leadership of her prophets, priests, and kings, Israel was to walk in paths of righteousness, with each prophet, priest, and king being a type or symbolic representation of the Christ who would be the great Prophet, Priest, and King.

Animals. Illustration: a lamb. From the time of Adam to the time of the atoning sacrifice the lamb was a vicarious sacrifice offered by the shedding of its blood as a similitude of the sacrifice that Christ would make for all men. The prophecies of the last days include the promise that the sons of Levi will yet offer this same sacrifice unto the Lord in righteousness (Malachi 3:3; *Teachings*, pp. 172—73). As the priests of the Aaronic Priesthood kneel at the sacrament table to administer the ordinance of sacrament today, so their ancient counterparts in the Aaronic Priesthood were commissioned to make an equivalent offering at the table or altar of the Lord in the form of a lamb without blemish.

Events. Illustration: the Sabbath day. The Sabbath has been consecrated as a day in which to remember and rejoice in the blessings of God. From the days of Adam to the time of the Egyptian bondage the Sabbath commemorated God's resting on the seventh day after the six days of creative labor. From the time of the Exodus to the time of Christ's resurrection the Sabbath commemorated the liberating of the children of Israel from their Egyptian bondage. When Christ came forth from the tomb on the first day of the week, this day was then designated as the Sabbath in remembrance of his atoning sacrifice, his breaking the bands of death, and his extending immortality to all and the privilege of eternal life to those who would diligently seek it.

Feelings. Illustration: the spirit of peace. One of the names or titles by which Christ is known is Prince of Peace (Isaiah 9:6). The title symbolizes the peace associated with his presence and the living of his gospel. Gideon built an altar where the angel of the Lord had appeared to him, and he called the place Jehovah-shalom, meaning "God of peace" (Judges 6:24). Teaching the nature of the spirit of revelation to Oliver Cowdery, the Lord reminded him of the occasions when he had enjoyed that spirit and then asked these questions: "Did I not speak peace to your mind concerning the matter?" and "What greater witness can you have than from God?" (D&C 6:23).

Foods. Illustration: bread. "I am the bread of life," Christ declared, "he that cometh to me shall never hunger; and he that believeth on me shall never thirst" (John 6:35). Israel would have perished in the wilderness were it not for the bread or manna sent down from heaven. That heaven-sent bread symbolized that all men would have perished had it not been for Christ, who came down from heaven as the food or spiritual nourishment of which all must partake or die as to the things of the Spirit.

Persons. Illustration: Christians. Those who follow Christ take upon themselves his name and are adopted into his family. The family resemblance always includes a likeness or similarity of works. Of such Christ said: "In my name they shall do many wonderful works; In my name they shall cast out devils; In my name they shall heal the sick; In my name they shall open the eyes of the blind, and unstop the ears of the deaf; And the tongue of the dumb shall speak; And if any man shall administer poison unto them it shall not hurt them; And the poison of a serpent shall not have power to harm them." (D&C 84:66-72.)

Words. Illustration: those things spoken by Christ. John called Christ "the Word, even the messenger of salvation" (D&C 93:8). Thus Christ becomes both the message and the messenger. The two are inseparable; one cannot profess to accept Christ and reject his doctrines any more than one could profess to accept him while rejecting his example.

Rituals. Illustration: the ordinance of baptism. Paul explained the ordinance of baptism, saying: "We are buried with him by baptism into death: that like as Christ was raised up from the dead by the glory of the Father, even so we also should walk in newness of life. For if we have been planted together in the likeness of his death, we shall be also in the likeness of his resurrection: Knowing this, that our old man is crucified with him, that the body of sin might be destroyed, that henceforth we should not serve sin." (Romans 6:4–6.)

Elements. Illustration: light. Christ, we are told, is the light of truth:

> Which truth shineth. This is the light of Christ. As also he is in the sun, and the light of the sun, and the power thereof by which it was made.
>
> As also he is in the moon, and is the light of the moon, and the power thereof by which it was made;
>
> As also the light of the stars, and the power thereof by which they were made;
>
> And the earth also, and the power thereof, even the earth upon which you stand.
>
> And the light which shineth, which giveth you light, is through him who enlighteneth your eyes, which is the same light that quickeneth your understandings;
>
> Which light proceedeth forth from the presence of God to fill the immensity of space—
>
> The light which is in all things, which giveth life to all things, which is the law by which all things are governed, even the power of God who sitteth upon his throne, who is in the bosom of eternity, who is in the midst of all things. (D&C 88:6–13.)

All things evidence their creators: the watch, the watchmaker; the painting, the artist; the book, its author; the child, its parents; and heaven and earth, the God of heaven and earth. Of Christ, the scriptures say, "All things were made by him, and through him, and of him" (D&C 93:10), and thus all things testify of him. Man, the greatest of God's creations, is in the image and likeness of his Creator—as all things created by him carry within them the evidence of their divine origin, each being a symbol or similitude of the Creator.

INCREASING OUR SCRIPTURAL UNDERSTANDING

Those conversant in the language of symbolism and similitudes enjoy significantly enriched scriptural understanding. Let us briefly illustrate with an example from each of the standard works.

The Old Testament

From the Old Testament let us take as our example Samuel's calling and anointing of David to be the king of Israel. (The story is found in 1 Samuel 16.) The Lord had rejected Saul as the king of Israel because of his disobedience, and Samuel the prophet was directed to fill his horn with oil and go to Jesse the Bethlehemite and find a king from among his sons. When Jesse brought forth his first son, Eliab, Samuel, much impressed with his appearance, thought he should be ordained as Israel's king. Yet when he sought confirmation from the Lord he was told not to judge by the outward appearance of a man, but by his heart. One by one Jesse brought forth seven sons, yet the Spirit identified none of them as the one the Lord had chosen.

Frustrated, Samuel asked Jesse, "Are here all thy children?" and then learned that Jesse had still another son who had been left to tend the sheep. He was sent for, and when he came "the Lord said, Arise, anoint him: for this is he." Samuel then took his horn of oil and anointed David in the midst of his brethren.

Though this is a beautiful story of the anointing of a king, it is also appreciably more than that. The story is what the ancient prophets called a "type and shadow," meaning that it was a replica of future events of even greater importance. Within this story is hidden, for those sensitive to the things of the Spirit and fluent in the language of symbolism, one of the most detailed Messianic prophecies in the Old Testament. Consider how perfectly it foretells both the setting and the events that would surround the coming of Christ.

First, the Messiah was to come at a time when, because of their disobedience, God had rejected those professing the authority and right to rule Israel. He was to come from Bethlehem and be of the lineage of Jesse. He would not be recognized by those looking for outward things or a temporal Messiah, indeed he would be the overlooked one, yet he would be the good shepherd, the boy David (the name meaning "beloved son"), the one destined to be anointed king of Israel. The reader should understand that the term *anointed* as used in the Old Testament, which comes to us from Hebrew manuscripts, when translated into the Greek of the New Testament becomes *Christ*. As David was called forth from the midst of his brethren and anointed Israel's king, he became a type or symbol of the Christ.

The Pearl of Great Price

Let us turn now to the third chapter of the book of Abraham in the Pearl of Great Price as our second illustration. The chapter recounts how Abraham through the use of the Urim and Thummim had the heavens opened to him that he might learn about the glory and revolutions of the sun, moon, and stars. This is the chapter in which we learn about Kolob, the planet nearest the throne of God, and the other great heavenly bodies that are near to it. Midway through the chapter the subject changes and we find ourselves reading about the nature of spirits before they were born into mortality. The chapter concludes with a brief account of the Grand Council in Heaven, at which Satan rebelled.

What is generally missed in the reading of the chapter is the phrase "as, also" in verse 18, which ties the revelation on stars to the revelation on spirits. Here we discover the reason for giving the great patriarch the revelation on stars. The knowledge of astronomy is not essential to salvation, but the knowledge of the order of the government of heaven is. When Abraham was learning about Kolob he was really learning about Christ, for Kolob is the similitude of Christ, and the stars are in the likeness of the spirits. We are told that Kolob was the first created, the nearest to the throne of God, and thus the greatest of all the stars. Kolob is described as being "after the manner" or in the likeness of God, as being first in government, and as governing all those of the same order. Though there are many great ones near it, all receive their light from Kolob and it is Kolob, we are told, that holds the key of power. (Abraham 3; Facsimile 2.) In virtually every detail Kolob is described in the same prophetic language that is used to describe Christ, and the stars are described in language that parallels that used by Abraham to describe the spirits.

The Book of Mormon

Let us turn now to the Book of Mormon and briefly consider an event in the ministry of Christ among the Nephite people. When the Savior introduced the ordinance of the sacrament to the Nephites we are told that he took the bread and gave it to the disciples as the multitude watched and commanded them to eat, which they did until they "were filled." Only after they were "filled" did they give bread to the body of the Church, who also ate until they were "filled." The same ritual was followed with the wine. (3 Nephi 18:4—9.) Scores of times I have asked Book of Mormon students why the Lord would require the nearly twenty-five hundred men, women, and children present in that meeting to wait while the Twelve not only partook of the bread and wine, but had a sacramental meal—that is, actually ate until they were filled. Their response is always the same. The text could not possibly mean that they actually ate until they were filled. Rather, it means that they were filled with the Spirit.

Surely, the experiences of the meeting to that point had been sufficient to fill them with the Spirit. They had already witnessed the descent of Christ from the heavens and heard the voice of the Father introduce him. They had heard as marvelous a gospel discourse as had ever been delivered; they had gone forth one by one to meet the Savior and handle the wounds in his hands, side, and feet; and they had either been healed of infirmities or witnessed loved ones that were. They had already experienced more than we could dare hope for in a lifetime of spiritual experiences. The context of the meeting suggests that they did not have to wait until that point to be filled with the Spirit.

Let us then dare to suppose that the passage means what it says, that they actually ate until they were filled. That is, in this meeting, as in the first sacrament meeting in the Old World, they partook of a sacramental meal. Then let us ask what purpose would be served by their so doing. Obviously, in a meeting of this length (consider the time necessary for all twenty-five hundred to come forth and handle the Lord alone) physical refreshment would be welcome. Yet beyond that, doesn't it seem rather appropriate that the Twelve, these newly called prophets, seers, and revelators, these men through whom the word of the Lord was to come to the people, would symbolically in the sacrament be the first to receive the "bread of life?" Is it not important that the body of the Church learn that there will be those occasions upon which they must patiently wait upon Twelve, for the Twelve cannot give that which they themselves have not yet received? And is it not the Twelve through whom the bread of life both ritually and literally must come to the membership of the Church? The ritual was a perfect teaching device demonstrating the role of the Twelve and their relationship to the body of the Church.

The Doctrine and Covenants

As with our ancient scriptural records, the revelations in the Doctrine and Covenants also take on a greater richness for those conversant with the language of symbols. Since so many of the revelations in the Doctrine and Covenants center in the restoration of the priesthood, keys, and organization of the Church, let us use them as our example. These revelations tell us that the "keys of the kingdom," meaning the authority to preside over the Church, have been held by the Presidency of the High Priesthood in all dispensations (see D&C 81:2). Further we are told that this presidency or presiding quorum has always consisted of three "righteous and holy men" (D&C 107:29). Since we have also been told that the earthly kingdom is patterned after the heavenly kingdom, we then recognize the "righteous and holy men" chosen to stand at the head of the Church on earth as the symbolic representation of the heavenly Presidency of Three, or the Father, Son, and Holy Ghost. By definition, to hold the priesthood is to be the agent of God; it is to have the authority to act in the first person for him.

The New Testament

To complete our survey of the standard works let us now
consider a New Testament type, taking as our example Christ's
cursing of the fig tree. Our story finds Jesus and his associates
walking from Bethany to Jerusalem. It is Monday morning.
Before the week is over Christ's lifeless body will lie in a borrowed tomb for three days, after which an angel will announce,
"He is risen." The group are on their way to the temple, where
Christ, for the second time in his short ministry, will cast out the
money changers and others who have defiled his Father's house.
As they progress to the temple, Christ sees "afar off" a fig tree
"having leaves," to which he then goes in the expectation of
obtaining fruit, doubtless to find refreshment for himself and his
disciples. The tree, however, has no fruit. Mark tells us that "the
time of figs was not yet," simply meaning that it was too early in
the season for figs to have ripened. Christ, finding the tree to be
without fruit, curses it and then proceeds with his company to
the temple. The following morning when he and the Apostles
pass that way again, Peter observes that the cursed tree has
already "withered away." (Mark 11:12–14, 20–24.)

The story has embarrassed some Bible commentators, who
view it as the "least attractive" of the stories about Jesus. These
writers applaud Luke for his wisdom among the synoptic writers
for not having included it in his gospel. Still, Matthew and Mark
mention it, and so they must wrestle with the question of the
common sense and judgment of Christ cursing a fruitless tree
when he knew it was not the season of its fruit.

Viewed with the eye of faith, the incident becomes not only a
great teaching moment but a prophecy as well. All present knew
that fig trees bring forth their fruit before their leaves. All were
equally aware that it would be some weeks before fig trees normally gave fruit. Yet the profusion of leaves on this tree constituted an announcement that it was laden with fruit. Christ was
thus attracted to it. The symbol was perfect—a tree professing
fruits and having none standing in the very shadows of the
temple where a corrupt priesthood professed righteousness and
devotion to Israel's God as they plotted the death of his Son.

How better could Christ have typified the rustling leaves of religious pretense that took refuge within the temple walls? And does not such hypocrisy, be it individual or national, merit the disdain and curse of that very authority it mocks?

The stage was set, the lesson was most timely, and in the false pretense of the fig tree was to be found perfect typecasting. The moment now belonged to the Master Teacher, who used it to dramatize his power over nature and evidence once again his claim to Messiahship, while making the fig tree a prophetic type of what befalls those who profess his authority and fail to bring forth good fruits. Of such he has said, these I will curse "with the heaviest of all cursings" (D&C 41:1).

Our Journey

With the understanding that all things testify of Christ, and that symbols are often the language of that testimony, and with the realization that symbolism is a language common to the revelations of all ages, be they scripture or personal experiences, we proceed on an adventure through scripture and history in the hopes of gaining greater fluency in this the universal tongue. Symbols are a dramatic and effective teaching device for those who have the Spirit, and a stone of stumbling and rock of offense for those who do not. An understanding of gospel symbols enhances both testimony and the ability to bear it. Symbolism is the language of inspired teaching and writing. It has ever been the language of prophecy and prophets. It is the language of the gospel, the means of communication between the Saints of all ages.

2

Teaching in Technicolor

Symbols are to the gospel teacher what pigments are to the artist—the source of color and richness. With them the master teacher can paint word pictures that give breath to thoughts. They are as the morning light that awakens the slumbering soul, bringing with them both warmth and nourishment. Let us acquaint ourselves with the primary colors of the verbal artist—similes, metaphors, and hyperboles—for with these one can create an infinite variety of feelings and enhance ideas of every hue and form.

SIMILES AND METAPHORS

No figurative teaching devices are used more effectively in the scriptures than similes and metaphors. A simile is created by likening one thing to another: "He is like a lion." A metaphor is created by depicting the two things as the same: "He is a lion." Both give confidence and personality to our expression. Similes and metaphors can be strong or mellow, aggressive or serene, but their purpose is always to give depth, color, and warmth to our expressions. They are to words as character is to the individual. Whereas we might say that it is a sad thing for a person to join the Church and then leave it, returning to his old ways, the scriptures evoke more emotion and depth of feeling when they speak of one such as being like a dog who has returned "to his vomit," or like a sow that has been washed only to return to "wallowing in the mire" (3 Nephi 7:8; 2 Peter 2:22). To those professing reverence for the words of dead prophets while demeaning the Prophet Joseph Smith, John Taylor replied, "Rather a live dog than a dead lion."

It was Christ who spoke of Herod as "that fox" (Luke 13:32) and told the Pharisees that they were poisonous snakes. "Ye serpents, ye generation of vipers," he said, and then asked, "How can ye escape the damnation of hell?" He called them "blind guides" who strained at gnats and swallowed camels, and likened them to "whited sepulchres, which indeed appear beautiful outward, but are within full of dead men's bones, and of all uncleanness." (Matthew 23:24, 27, 33.) He warned of "ravening wolves" who came in "sheep's clothing" (Matthew 7:15) and cautioned his disciples against giving that which was holy to dogs or casting their pearls before swine (Matthew 7:6).

Christ's words to the hypocritical hounds that were constantly yapping at his heels tell us something about the soul in which they were forged. Words that are searing hot come from a soul that burns with flaming fire. Words too are living things, created in the image and likeness of those who breathed into them the breath of life. "Give heed to my word," the Lord said to those of our generation, "which is quick and powerful, sharper than a two-edged sword, to the dividing asunder of both joints and marrow; therefore give heed unto my word" (D&C 11:2). Again, the message to those of our day is, "Repent, lest I smite you by the rod of my mouth" (D&C 19:15). Further, we have been told that his word is "true and faithful" (D&C 1:37; 68:34; 71:11). That there is a power innate to the word itself is illustrated in the revelation which states, "For the word of the Lord is truth, and whatsoever is truth is light, and whatsoever is light is Spirit, even the Spirit of Jesus Christ" (D&C 84:45).

The simile and metaphor are miniature parables that can with a quick stroke paint a vivid image or evoke a strong emotion. They can be used to give a feeling of peace or elicit a feeling of tension. The words of the Baptist, "Behold the Lamb of God!" (John 1:36) bring quite a different feeling than the words of the

Revelator as he describes the "great dragon," the "old serpent," "the accuser of our brethren" who was cast out of the heavenly realm (Revelation 12:9—10).

Christ is known to us as "the Branch," "the Bread of Life," "the Door," "the Lamb of God," "the Light," "the Lion of Judah," "the Rock of Heaven," "the True Vine," and the "Living Water." Satan we know as "the Dragon," "the Serpent," or "the Prince of Darkness." We speak of the Holy Ghost descending "like a dove," and one of our favorite hymns announces that the "Spirit of God like a fire is burning." We speak of the "morning stars" who sang together for joy. The righteous we call the "salt of the earth," the faithless are as "salt that has lost its savor." The mortal body is called a "tabernacle of clay," and those coming forth in the morning of the first resurrection are known as the "first fruits."

Effective comparisons are a burst of energy to an idea. They are like sight to the blind or hearing to the deaf—they give a dimension to understanding that otherwise could not be had. Like the rising sun, words can be used to give life and light and warmth to ideas that otherwise we might have missed as travelers in the night.

Parables: To Conceal and Reveal

Parables are similes expanded into short stories. The narrative may be factual or fictional, but it must still represent things according to the nature of the real world. In this sense parables differ from fables, which are fictional stories whose casts of characters include talking animals, trees, and other inanimate objects. An allegory is more of an extended metaphor. Whereas the parable has only one point of comparison, the allegory has many. Somewhat like the fable, the allegory uses inanimate objects for comparison, but it does not involve itself in the fantasy of attributing speech or intelligence to the objects so used. The classical scriptural example is Zenos's allegory of the tame and wild olive trees, in which he prophesies the scattering and gathering of Israel (Jacob 5).

Parables and allegories are much alike, "and it is less important to distinguish between them than it is to distinguish between

allegory, which the author intended, and allegorical embellish-
ment or interpretation, which he did not" (*Imagery*, p. 167). Here
the classic example is Augustine's allegorization of the parable of
the Good Samaritan, in which he held that the man was Adam,
"Jerusalem, the heavenly city; Jericho the moon—the symbol of
mortality; the thieves are the devil and his angels, who strip the
man of immortality by persuading him to sin and so leave him
(spiritually) half dead; the priest and Levite represent the Old
Testament, the Samaritan, Christ; the beast, his flesh which he
assumed at the Incarnation; the inn is the church and the inn-
keeper the apostle Paul" (Ibid., p. 165). Such an interpretation
may have served Augustine's purpose; it most assuredly did not
serve the Lord's.

The use of the parable as a teaching device is greatly misunderstood. Parables have been used in the scriptures both to
conceal and to reveal truth. Christ used them to hide or shield
truth from those seeking to oppose it. Prophets of the Old Testament used parables to expose or dramatically reveal the truth.
Knowing the purpose for which a parable was used is essential to
the proper understanding of it. Let us consider the parable and its
close kin the allegory as they are used to protect prophecy and
sacred truths, and then examine the parable as a device for manifesting and emphasizing truths.

The perspective of the parable's rather limited role is no better
illustrated than in its limited use. No parables were used by
Christ in his visit among the Nephite people. No parables are
found in the entire Book of Mormon. No parables were used by
John in his gospel, which is the gospel written to the Saints. No
parables were used by Paul in his epistles or in any New Testament book save the synoptic Gospels. There are a few parables
used in the Old Testament but they are not used to teach gospel
principles. Similarly, Christ did not teach the Apostles with parables. Matthew and Mark both tell us that Jesus did not begin to
teach regularly in parables until opposition to his teaching developed. (See Matthew 13:10—16; Mark 4:11—12.) After Christ had
taught publicly in parables the disciples came to him privately,
asking, "Why speakest thou unto them in parables?" Notice that
the question was not "Why speakest thou unto us in parables?"
The "them" to whom reference was made were the scribes and

Pharisees; they were the spies sent by the Sanhedrin to find fault;
they were those who had hardened their hearts against Christ.
(See *Mortal Messiah* 2:238—39.) Jesus answered:

> Because it is given unto you to know the mysteries of the
> kingdom of heaven, but to them it is not given.
>
> For whosoever hath, to him shall be given, and he shall
> have more abundance: but whosoever hath not, from him
> shall be taken away even that he hath.
>
> Therefore speak I to them in parables: because they seeing
> see not; and hearing they hear not, neither do they under-
> stand.
>
> And in them is fulfilled the prophecy of Esaias, which
> saith, By hearing ye shall hear, and shall not understand; and
> seeing ye shall see, and shall not perceive:
>
> For this people's heart is waxed gross, and their ears are
> dull of hearing, and their eyes they have closed; lest at any
> time they should see with their eyes, and hear with their ears,
> and should understand with their heart, and should be con-
> verted, and I should heal them. (Matthew 13:11—15.)

As the scriptural example suggests, parables are not appropriately used in teaching members of the Church. The gospel
message ought not be cloaked or veiled to those ready to receive
it in plainness. Further, "Parables are not sources to search to
learn doctrine. They may serve as illustrations of gospel principles; they may dramatize, graphically and persuasively, some
gospel truths; but it is not their purpose to reveal doctrine, or,
standing alone, to guide men along the course leading to eternal
life. Parables can only be understood, in their full and complete
meaning, after one knows the doctrines about which they speak."
(Ibid., p. 241.)

As to allegories, it ought to be observed that they are a form
of prophetic ambiguity, having no meaning apart from their
intended interpretation. They are, as it were, a sealed book until
they have been decoded or translated by the prophet who gave
them or one filled with the spirit of revelation. Once understood
they can be used to effectively sustain the teaching of a particular
doctrine, but they are not the source of doctrine. Unlike the parable, they have no profitable purpose in teaching the nonmem-

ber. They are veiled prophecies to be understood only by those having the spirit of revelation.

Parables to Dramatize Truth

The best known Old Testament parable is the story of the ewe lamb by which Nathan cleverly got David to pronounce his own guilt and punishment for the murder of Uriah. Nathan told David the story of two men, one rich and the other poor. The rich man had great flocks and herds, while the poor man had but one ewe lamb, which he loved and nourished as his own children. When a traveler came to visit the rich man, he took the lamb of the poor man to feed his guest. The story made David very angry and he said to Nathan, "As the Lord liveth, the man that hath done this thing shall surely die: And he shall restore the lamb fourfold, because he did this thing, and because he had no pity." To this Nathan responded, "Thou art the man." He then rehearsed for David the manner in which the Lord had blessed him and how, if that had been too little, the Lord would have given him whatever he desired, and yet he had despised the commandment of the Lord and had had Uriah killed that he might take his wife. Nathan then told David that he had pronounced judgment upon himself. (2 Samuel 12:1—12.)

Another of Israel's prophets used a similar device to get Ahab, the wicked king of the north kingdom, to pronounce judgment upon himself. When the Syrian King Ben-hadad besieged Samaria, the capital of Israel, Ahab routed his army with a surprise attack. Ben-hadad escaped, but later was captured. King Ahab, contrary to the instruction of the Lord, spared Ben-hadad on condition that the Galilee towns that had been occupied by his father be returned and that Israel be given trading rights with Damascus. Wounded and disguised, a prophet waited for Ahab by the roadside. As the king passed he called out to him:

> Sir, I went into the thick of the battle, and a soldier came over to me with a prisoner and said, Take charge of this fellow. If by any chance he gets away, your life shall be forfeit, or you shall pay a talent of silver.

As I was busy with one thing and another, sir, he disappeared. The king of Israel said to him, You deserve to die. And he said to the king of Israel, You have passed sentence on yourself.

Then he tore the bandage from his eyes, and the king of Israel saw that he was one of the prophets.

And he said to the king, This is the word of the Lord: Because you let that man go when I had put him under a ban, your life shall be forfeit for his life, your people of his people. (NEB, 1 Kings 20:39—42.)

Similarly, Christ in speaking to the Pharisees told a parable of a householder who planted a vineyard, hedged it, dug a winepress, and built a tower within it. Then he let it out to husbandmen and went into a far country. When the time of harvest approached he sent his servants to receive its fruits. His servants were beaten and killed. Additional servants were sent with the same results. The householder then sent his own son, and the husbandmen, knowing full well that he was the master's son, killed him also. Now, asked the Savior, "When the lord therefore of the vineyard cometh, what will he do unto those husbandmen?" To which his antagonists replied, "He will miserably destroy those wicked men, and will let out his vineyard unto other husbandmen, which shall render him the fruits in their seasons." Thus they prophesied their own destiny. (Matthew 21:33—41.)

Such parables are not used to conceal but rather to reveal in a clever and dramatic way the justice of God in the affairs of men. Such devices were common among the peoples of the Bible. A touching illustration concerns a young Hebrew mother whose twin sons became ill and died in the absence of their father. Upon his return home the woman told her husband that a few years ago a man had come to her and asked her to care for two precious stones. "Today," she said, "just before you returned, he appeared again. I am loath to part with them. Tell me, must I give them back to him?"

"Of course," the husband responded, "They never really were your property, no matter how long you have held them." Then sensing the quietness of the house he discovered the death of his precious sons. (Milton Steinberg, *As a Driven Leaf*, pp. 132—33.)

3

Teaching in
Black and White

All learning takes place in relationship to what we know. Teachers expand our understanding by comparing or contrasting that which is to be learned to something we already understand. The previous chapter considered how the scriptures teach with comparisons (similes, metaphors, parables, and so on); in this chapter we will consider how the Lord teaches his prophets and people by the use of contrasts. Whereas comparisons give color to ideas, contrasts are most often found in the form of darkness versus light, or scriptural absolutism. Scriptural absolutism is found in an instance where a particular principle is emphasized without showing its relationship to other principles. For instance, one of the commandments given the nation of Israel through Moses was, "Thou shalt not kill" (Exodus 20:13); another was to "utterly destroy" the seven nations that inhabited the land of Palestine (Deuteronomy 7:1—2). No scriptural harmony is provided as a bridge between these two diverse commands; both were given in absolute terms.

A distinctive characteristic of Christ's teaching was the positive and unqualified manner in which he taught. To follow him was and is to travel a "strait and narrow path." There is nothing ecumenical in such statements as: "I am the bread of life" (John 6:35), "I am the light of the world" (John 8:12), or "I am the way, the truth, and the life: no man cometh unto the Father, but by me" (John 14:6). Paul perpetuated that narrowness, declaring that there was but "One Lord, one faith, one baptism" (Ephesians 4:5), as did John Taylor with his motto "The kingdom of God or nothing."

TRUTH AND AUTHORITY

Christ taught "as one having authority, and not as the scribes" (Matthew 7:29). Scribes or rabbis taught by the authority of precedent. They made no claim to the spirit of revelation or to holding priesthood; their authority was conferred by man and consisted of nothing more than the traditions of men. In contrast, Christ spoke as the representative of God. It was at his command that unclean spirits departed and the afflicted were healed. To the man sick of the palsy he said, "thy sins be forgiven thee," and the scribes, knowing that only God could forgive sins, said within themselves, "This man blasphemeth" (Matthew 9:2–3). Again and again in the Sermon on the Mount, he said "that it was said to them of old time" (meaning Jehovah told Moses on Sinai) that they were to do such and such—that is, your revelations tell you this—and then he would add, but I say unto you this and this, and thus he would add to or edit the scriptures. In so doing he forced his listeners to choose between the law he had given Moses and himself as the lawgiver. Such was the authority with which Christ taught.

The system of salvation is the same today. The testimony of the Restoration forces the same choice between the world's profession of loyalty to what God spoke to prophets of ages past and our testimony of what he is speaking to prophets now living. Surely those representing the Savior today should be found teaching the same gospel he taught, and teaching it with the same confidence and authority. Describing Christ's preparatory years, the JST states, "He served under his father, and he spake not as other men, neither could he be taught; for he needed not that any man should teach him" (JST, Matthew 3:25). Similarly, the message of the Restoration is not the result of what men of the world can teach, but that which we know by the spirit of revelation. Thus we find the Lord instructing the missionaries of this dispensation: "Ye are not sent forth to be taught, but to teach the children of men the things which I have put into your hands by the power of my Spirit; And ye are to be taught from on high. Sanctify yourselves and ye shall be endowed with power, that ye may give even as I have spoken." (D&C 43:15—16.)

THE WEAK THINGS OF THE WORLD

The Lord has never chosen to display the majesty of the gospel in worldly trappings. He sought no honor of men, nor would he accept any worldly endorsements. Rather, he said, "I call upon the weak things of the world, those who are unlearned and despised, to thrash the nations by the power of my Spirit" (D&C 35:13). Paul stated it thus: "God hath chosen the foolish things of the world to confound the wise; and God hath chosen the weak things of the world to confound the things which are mighty; And base things of the world, and things which are despised, hath God chosen, yea, and things which are not, to bring to nought things that are: That no flesh should glory in his presence" (1 Corinthians 1:27—29).

Again and again in the scriptures we see the simplicity of faith arrayed against the physical or intellectual powers of the world. We find Gideon and his army of three hundred routing the thousands of Midian; Samson slaying a thousand with the jawbone of an ass; the boy David answering the challenge of the Philistine giant Goliath; Moses and Aaron confronting Pharaoh and the might of Egypt; the Son of God born in a stable; Stephen confounding the Sanhedrin (Israel's greatest scriptural scholars); the unlearned fishermen from Galilee, Peter and John, withstanding the council of the Jews; Paul teaching on Mars Hill, testifying before Agrippa, and appealing to Caesar; and well might we add Joseph Smith, of whom the Lord said, "I raised you up, that I might show forth my wisdom through the weak things of the earth" (D&C 124:1). The power of the gospel is to be kept clearly independent from the "arm of flesh" (D&C 1:19).

HYPERBOLE AND ABSOLUTENESS

A hyperbole is a statement exaggerated for effect. It is a way of verbally underscoring an idea or principle. Hyperbole or overstatement is a figure of speech common to peoples of all ages, and it is natural that the scriptures would abound with it. It can be used in flattery, as in the song of the dancing women: "Saul hath slain his thousands, and David his ten thousands" (1 Samuel 18:7). It is also used in lament: "They were swifter than eagles, they were stronger than lions" (2 Samuel 1:23). It was a device frequently used by Jesus. To the Pharisees he said, you "strain at a gnat, and swallow a camel" (Matthew 23:24). To those who trusted in their wealth he said, "It is easier for a camel to go through the eye of a needle, than for a rich man to enter into the kingdom of God" (Mark 10:25). Literalists suggest to us that the needle's eye was the name for a low gate, like the door into the Church of the Nativity at Bethlehem, but since we find him using exaggerated statements so effectively and frequently one is left to wonder why the fuss in this instance.

The use of hyperbole necessitates at least a modest amount of sense on the part of the listener. The gospel has always been taught in such a manner that those who deliberately want to misunderstand can at least pretend to do so. Since the gospel is positive it is presented in positive or unqualified terms. This is particularly true of the way the Book of Mormon prophets taught. There is no indication in their teachings that they had any knowledge of degrees of glory in the world to come. They speak of paradise and hell, the righteous and the wicked, but no hint is given of a terrestrial or middle kingdom. This absoluteness on their part may represent a strong Old World tie, for it is very much a part of Hebrew and Arab thought and shows itself very markedly in the documents from Qumran. Indeed it has always been common to the way the gospel has been presented. In reading the promises of a patriarchal blessing we do not expect constant reminders that they are predicated on obedience and righteousness. Righteousness is implicit in all promises given by God, and everyone with any Church sense or even the least degree of spiritual maturity knows it. A couple do not receive the promise in the temple that they are married for time and eternity and suppose that it holds irrespective of the way they live. All gospel covenants and promised blessings are conditional. We need not interrupt the beauty of the marriage ceremony to list all the possible sins which would negate the sacred promises being given. That those being married must remain clean and pure, that they must keep their covenants in exactness and honor, has already been taught, and is now symbolized by the robes of righteousness in which they are clothed.

This absolutism finds its expression consistently in the scriptures. For instance, we have Luke recording the Savior as saying, "If any man come to me, and hate not his father, and mother, and wife, and children, and brethren, and sisters, yea, and his own life also, he cannot be my disciple" (Luke 14:26). *Hate* as used here is a hyperbole expressed in terms of gospel absolutism. We have the same idea expressed by Matthew, who records the Savior as saying, "He that loveth father or mother more than me is not worthy of me: and he that loveth son or daughter more than me is not worthy of me" (Matthew 10:37). The meaning of both passages is the same. Salvation is and always has been a family affair. Jesus is merely saying that in the event of conflict between family and the principles of salvation, our loyalty and responsibility must be first to God. Now, keep in mind that the author of this statement is the same who said with absoluteness, that is, without explaining the exceptions, "Honour thy father and thy mother: that thy days may be long upon the land which the Lord thy God giveth thee" (Exodus 20:12). In a different setting Christ rebuked the Pharisees for having perverted this command of Sinai (see Mark 7:9–13).

Hyperboles are helpful in emphasizing gospel principles, and absoluteness is essential in presenting the gospel message. Both, like all other gospel symbols, require sense and judgment in how they are understood.

THE GOD OF LIGHT VERSUS THE PRINCE OF DARKNESS

Among the marvelous scriptural texts restored through Joseph Smith is an account of Moses being taken in the Spirit up into an exceedingly high mountain, where it was necessary for him to be transfigured to abide the glory of God and obtain the revelation that awaited him (see Moses 1:2, 11). Following this experience he was approached by Satan, claiming, as he ever has, that he was the son of God, and commanding Moses to worship him. Moses, who by then had a point of reference, asked: "Where is thy glory, that I should worship thee? For behold, I could not look upon God, except his glory should come upon me, and I were transfigured before him. But I can look upon thee in the natural man." (Moses 1:13—14.) Again he asked: "Where is thy glory, for it is darkness unto me? And I can judge between thee and God." (Moses 1:15.)

The principle established is one of importance to all who seek proper worship and understanding. Earthly power is sufficient for the understanding of earthly things, while the glories of heaven-sent truth can be seen only by eyes that have been anointed by a heaven-sent Spirit. Paul stated it thus: "For what man knoweth the things of a man, save the spirit of man which is in him? even so the things of God knoweth no man, but the Spirit of God." (1 Corinthians 2:11.) The doctrine of the scriptures is that the things of the Spirit must be understood by the power of the Spirit. All other means of understanding are unacceptable to God. (See D&C 50:17—20.)

Moses' experience establishes the pattern. We find it repeated again and again in the experiences of Joseph Smith. In his account of the First Vision, Joseph Smith describes a thick darkness and his near destruction "not to an imaginary ruin, but to the power of some actual being from the unseen world" (JS—H 1:15—16). Joseph's life was saved by the coming of a "pillar of light" and the appearance of two "Personages, whose brightness and glory defy all description" (JS—H 1:16—17). This light-versus-dark experience was repeated again when he went to obtain the plates from which the Book of Mormon was translated. On one occasion while he was being instructed by Moroni the heavens were opened to him and he was allowed to gaze into the heavens, whereupon the angel said to him, "Look!" and as he did so he "beheld the prince of darkness, surrounded by his innumerable train of associates." As this vision passed before him, he was told, "all this is shown, the good and the evil, the holy and the impure, the glory of God, the power of darkness, that ye may know hereafter the two powers and never be influenced or overcome by the wicked one." (*Messenger and Advocate* 2:198.)

Descriptive Contrasts

The manner in which the Lord teaches by contrast is amply illustrated in the great revelation on the degrees of glory. To illustrate the difference between the various kingdoms, Paul likened the greatest to the glory of the sun, the next to the glory of the moon, and finally the lowest to that of the stars (1 Corinthians 15:41). The sequence in which Joseph Smith was granted the same revelation is significant. First, he was allowed to gaze into the celestial realm and to see the throne of God upon which sat the Father and the Son (D&C 76:21—24). This was followed by a revelation of the ultimate destiny of those who become sons of perdition (D&C 76:25—49). Joseph's attention was then returned to a continuation of the revelation of the celestial kingdom (D&C 76:50—70). In this process Joseph Smith was afforded the sharpest contrast that the eternities provide. Note the similarity of this and the experience of Moses; after Moses was carried to the high mountain he was confronted by the prince of darkness and then had the visions of eternity opened to him again.

Following this vision of the celestial kingdom, Joseph Smith was shown the glories of the terrestrial or middle kingdom. He learned that those who inhabit this kingdom will be the "honorable men of the earth," the honest and the upright. He also saw that those whose lives have been touched by the Spirit of the Lord and who have known him and testified of him and yet failed to be fully valiant are to be found here. (D&C 76:71—80.) Thus by contrast Joseph Smith was taught that to inherit the celestial kingdom it is not enough to be honorable and have one's life touched by the Spirit—a full devotion to the gospel cause is necessary. Finally, and by way of further contrast, Joseph was shown the telestial or lowest kingdom. He learned that its citizenry would be made up in large measure of those professing religious devotion of one sort or another while using those professions as an excuse to reject the obligations of citizenry in the Lord's kingdom. (D&C 76:99—101.)

The Doctrine of No Neutrality

There are no neutrals where Christ and the gospel are concerned. "He that is not with me is against me," Christ declared, "and he that gathereth not with me scattereth abroad" (Matthew 12:30). No one taught this principle with greater plainness than Mormon, who told us that "a man being evil cannot do that which is good; neither will he give a good gift. For behold, a bitter fountain cannot bring forth good water; neither can a good fountain bring forth bitter water; wherefore, a man being a servant of the devil cannot follow Christ; and if he follow Christ he cannot be a servant of the devil." (Moroni 7:10.) One cannot march in two armies. We cannot be both an Israelite and a Philistine. Those selling their goods to both will be esteemed an enemy by both. The battle between good and evil, between light and dark, admits no middle ground. Some things we are or we are not. A woman may be pregnant or not pregnant, but hardly undecided. To be indecisive about whether or not we are going to stand for Christ is to remain sitting.

Mormon assured us that "all things which are good cometh of God; and that which is evil cometh of the devil; for the devil is an enemy unto God, and fighteth against him continually, and inviteth and enticeth to sin, and to do that which is evil continually. But behold, that which is of God inviteth and enticeth to do good continually; wherefore, every thing which inviteth and enticeth to do good, and to love God, and to serve him, is inspired of God." Thus the warning that we "do not judge that which is evil to be of God, or that which is good and of God to be of the devil." Nor need we be confused, for Mormon tells us:

> The way to judge is as plain, that ye may know with a perfect knowledge, as the daylight is from the dark night. [This is our doctrine of contrast.]
>
> For behold, the Spirit of Christ is given to every man, that he may know good from evil; wherefore, I show unto you the way to judge; for every thing which inviteth to do good, and to persuade to believe in Christ, is sent forth by the power and gift of Christ; wherefore ye may know with a perfect knowledge it is of God.

But whatsoever thing persuadeth men to do evil, and believe not in Christ, and deny him, and serve not God, then ye may know with a perfect knowledge it is of the devil; for after this manner doth the devil work, for he persuadeth no man to do good, no, not one; neither do his angels; neither do they who subject themselves unto him. (Moroni 7:15—17.)

4

Joseph and the Spirit of Prophecy

No character in the Old Testament should be of greater interest to Latter-day Saints than Joseph of Egypt. Strangely, few if any prophets have been more neglected in our sermons and writings. To Jews, he has been seen as the antitype of his father Jacob, while to Christians he is cited as a near perfect type for the Savior. Bible writers have enumerated more than a hundred points of similarity between Joseph and Christ. Yet, if the life of our father Joseph—for nearly every Latter-day Saint claims descent from him—is intended as a prophetic type, it seems fitting that it be especially such for those of his own family. Perhaps the book of Genesis is hinting that his life is one of prophetic import in that it devotes eleven of its fifty chapters to him. This in a book that recounts the story of the creation and then covers nearly 2700 years of history.

Indeed, no search for treasures within the pages of the Old Testament is more richly rewarding than the story of our ancient father. Let us view the typical Joseph as he is seen in both Jewish and Christian traditions. Then, clothing ourselves with the spirit of prophecy so common to him, let us discover his life as a marvelous prophecy of Joseph Smith and the labors of the tribe of Joseph in the last days.

The Latter-day City of Joseph

Samuel Rapaport in his work *A Treasury of the Midrash* compares the life of Joseph to the history of Zion and Jerusalem. "There is," he said, "a remarkable similarity in the phrases employed in describing the respective events of each whether in their adversity or in their prosperity." Both Joseph and Zion were loved of the Lord and hated of their brethren. Dreams were granted in relation to both and both were destined to rule. As Joseph's brothers contemplated his destruction, so ungodly nations contemplated the destruction of Zion. "Joseph was stripped of his coat of many colours," and concerning Zion the scriptures say, "They shall strip thee also of thy clothes" (Ezekiel 16:39). As Joseph was clothed in grand garments, so the prophecy is "Awake, awake; put on thy strength, O Zion, put on thy beautiful garments" (Isaiah 52). Rapaport continues with a list of more than two dozen such similarities (*Midrash*, pp. 228–30).[1]

The idea of the history of Jerusalem and Zion being foretold in the life of Joseph may have very ancient roots. Moroni, in his commentary on Ether's prophecy of a New Jerusalem to be built by the remnant of Joseph in the last days, announced it as the fulfillment of a type (Ether 13:6). Moroni wrote:

> For as Joseph brought his father down into the land of Egypt, even so he died there; wherefore, the Lord brought a remnant of the seed of Joseph out of the land of Jerusalem, that he might be merciful unto the seed of Joseph that they should perish not, even as he was merciful unto the father of Joseph that he should perish not.

> Wherefore, the remnant of the house of Joseph shall be built upon this land; and it shall be a land of their inheritance; and they shall build up a holy city unto the Lord, like unto the Jerusalem of old; and they shall no more be confounded, until the end come when the earth shall pass away. (Ether 13:7–8.)

Joseph as a Type for Christ

As we have already noted, Christian writers have traditionally treated the life of Joseph as prefiguring that of Christ. As Latter-day Saints we take no issue with this, and in fact with the aid of the restored gospel we can greatly improve upon their efforts to do so. The following list will illustrate:

1. Both were granted a new name. Our ancient father is known in the Bible record by two names—Joseph, the name given by his parents, and Zaphnath-paaneah (Genesis 41:45), the name given him by Pharaoh, king of Egypt. "This later name was given to him by Pharaoh in acknowledgment of the Divine wisdom which was in him. Thus, Joseph may be said to be his *human* name and Zaphnath-paaneah his *Divine* name." (*Gleanings,* p. 344.) Similarly, the Savior's given name was "Jesus," while "Christ" constituted a divinely given title. The remarkable significance of Joseph's names are a matter to which we will return.

2. Both were good shepherds. Like many of our Old Testament types, Joseph was a shepherd. He and his brothers were charged to tend their father's flock. It was in this capacity that he brought his father "their evil report" (Genesis 37:2), and became the recipient of their hatred. In this he can be likened to the Good Shepherd who was hated of the world because he testified that their deeds were evil (John 7:7).

3. Both were known as the most loved of their father. Few verses in the Old Testament seem more strangely inconsistent with the great patriarch Jacob serving as a model to emulate than the announcement that he "loved Joseph more than all his children" (Genesis 37:3) and that Joseph was favored above his brothers. Those lacking spiritual insight have freely criticized Jacob for this behavior, yet it perfectly represents the favoritism shown by the eternal Father to his firstborn, of whom he has repeatedly said, "Thou art my beloved Son" (Mark 1:11; 9:7; 3 Nephi 11:7; JS—H 1:17).

4. Both were clothed in authority and power of their father. The scriptural account tells us that Jacob made Joseph a "coat of many colours" (Genesis 37:3) and that this added to the envy of

his brothers. The marginal reading in our old missionary Bible indicates that "colours" could have been translated "pieces," while more modern translations render it "long, sleeved robe" (NEB) or "coat with long sleeves" (JB), all of which suggests that our story has not been fully told.

Edersheim writes, "But in truth it was not a 'coat of many colours,' but a tunic reaching down the arms and feet such as princes and persons of distinction wore, and it betokened to Joseph's brothers only too clearly, their father intended to transfer to Joseph the right of the first born" (Edersheim, OT 1:144).

Writing about the myths and legends of the Old Testament, Theodore H. Gaster says:

> It seems a pity to strip [Joseph] of so decorative and familiar a vesture, but, like several other elements of popular Bible lore . . . this one too disappears under the searching light of a more exact scholarship. What Joseph received from his father is described in original Hebrew as a "coat of pasaim"—a garment which is said in the story of Amnon and Tamar (II Samuel 13:18—19) to have been worn by the latter and to have been customarily affected by the princesses of royal blood. Now, pasaim is the plural of the word pas, which normally means "length, extension." Literally, therefore, the garment was a "coat of lengths." The Greek Septuagint and some of the other ancient translators took this to mean a garment made out of various lengths of different materials—that is, a kind of quilted or patch work tunic, and it is from this interpretation that the familiar "coat of many colors" is derived. What was really intended, however, was a coat which was extra long and extended to the ankles. (*Myth,* p. 216.)

The late Professor Speiser, however, notes that "the traditional 'coat of many colors,' and the variant 'coat with sleeves' are sheer guesses from the context; nor is there anything remarkable about either colors or sleeves." He, too, traces the Hebrew *pasaim* to its only other Bible usage in the story of Amnon and Tamar and describes the garment as a "ceremonial robe." (*The Anchor Bible Genesis,* pp. 289—90.)

Ginzberg recounts various stories about appearances of
Gabriel to Joseph. One of these appearances was while Joseph
was imprisoned in the pit before his brothers sold him into
slavery. Here it is said that Gabriel placed upon him a special
garment of protection which he wore throughout all his Egyptian
experiences. (*Legends* 2:17.) Ginzberg also records that after
Joseph was reunited with his family in Egypt his father gave him
two gifts, the first being the city of Shechem and "the second gift
was the garments made by God for Adam and passed from hand
to hand, until they came into the possession of Jacob" (ibid.
2:139). "According to the view of later authors, Joseph's coat was
the holy tunic of the priest" (ibid. 5:326).

Like the word *colours*, the word *coat* also bears careful
examination in the story of Joseph. The translation comes from
the Hebrew *kethoneth*, which could have been translated "garment," "robe," or "tunic." Kethoneth finds its first use in the Old
Testament in the account of the "coats of skins" made by God for
Adam and Eve (Genesis 3:21). The King James translators could
just as well have rendered this "garments of skin" or "robes of
skins." Whether intended or not, the phrase "garments of skins"
lends itself to an interesting play on words. The Hebrew word for
skins is *ore*, which has a homonym (*or*) meaning "light." The oral
reading of the phrase "garments of skins" in Hebrew conveys the
meaning "garments of light." Among the Jews, there are a
number of traditions to this effect. Along with the phrase "garments of light," these traditions refer to the garments given by
God to Adam as the "celestial garments," the "priestly garments,"
or "high-priestly garments," which were said to have "supernatural qualities" and to be the garments worn by Adam and his
descendants when offering sacrifices (ibid. 5:103–4). Such
traditions also hold that these were "the priestly garments worn
by the firstborn who performed the priestly service before
Aaron's time" (ibid. 5:283).

Though the story of Joseph's coat is still shrouded in some
mystery, it is evident that it was more than a mere expression of
his father's favoritism. It bespoke Joseph's position of superiority
over his brothers; it apparently announced that the coveted
birthright was to be his. The "coat" given to Joseph by Jacob was

a priesthood garment, and may in some way have been related with Joseph's ability to dream dreams and speak by way of revelation which, in the chronology of the Bible story, he then commenced to do.

5. Both were revelators. Joseph of Egypt dreamed dreams (Genesis 37:5—10), interpreted the dreams of others (Genesis 40; 41), and prophetically described the future to his family (JST, Genesis 50:24—38). Christ, in like manner, taught of future events (Matthew 24; 3 Nephi 20; 21).

6. Both were fully obedient to the will and wishes of their father and responded to their call to serve, saying, "Here am I" (Genesis 37:13; Abraham 3:27). The type is rather remarkable. Joseph's brothers were tending their father's flock, yet they had broken off communication with him. Joseph was sent with word from their father, only to find that they had wandered from Shechem ("the place of the burden") to Dothan. Such was the experience of Christ, who found that those of his brothers charged with tending his Father's flock, the children of Israel, had also wandered far from their original pastures.

7. Both were promised a future sovereignty. It may be worthy of notice that the two recorded dreams of Joseph hinted at a double sovereignty: The first dream concerned "the field" (Genesis 37:7), thus pointing to an earthly dominion; the second dream was occupied with the sun, moon, and stars (Genesis 37:9), suggesting a heavenly rule. This would be in imitation of Christ's ultimate triumph, which will be both temporal and spiritual.

8. Both were betrayed by their brothers. It was essential to the story that Joseph's brothers in their betrayal first strip him of the coat or garment given him by his father. Be it remembered that Christ was also stripped of his seamless coat, which was the symbol of his high priestly office.

9. Both were cast into a pit—Christ to the world of spirits, Joseph into an empty cistern, where he remained according to Jewish tradition for three days and three nights (*Legends* 2:14; Genesis 37:24; Isaiah 24:22).

10. Both were betrayed with the utmost hypocrisy. "Let us sell him to the Ishmeelites," said Joseph's brothers, "and let not

our hand be upon him" (Genesis 37:27). When Pilate told the Jews to take Christ and judge him according to their law they responded, "It is not lawful for us to put any man to death" (John 18:31).

11. Both were sold. It was Judah that sold Joseph for twenty pieces of silver (Genesis 37:26–28), as it was Judas (Greek for Judah) who sold Jesus for thirty pieces of silver (Matthew 26:15).

12. The blood-sprinkled coat of each was presented to his father. "And they took Joseph's coat, and killed a kid of the goats, and dipped the coat in the blood; and they sent the coat of many colours, and they brought it to their father" (Genesis 37:31–32). The blood of Jesus Christ as the blood of a scapegoat, a sin offering, was symbolically presented to the Father.

13. Both blessed those with whom they labored in prison (Genesis 39:21–23; Isaiah 61:1; D&C 138).

14. Both were servants, and as such all that they touched were blessed.

15. Both were tempted with great sin and both refused its enticements (Genesis 39; Matthew 4:1–11).

16. Both were falsely accused: Joseph by Potiphar's wife, Christ by false witnesses. (Christ did not defend himself against the false charges, and there is no record of Joseph doing so, either.)

17. Both stood as the source of divine knowledge to their day and generation. All the wisdom of Egypt had failed to interpret the king's dreams before Joseph was sought and successfully did so. So it was with Christ—in him and him alone were the truths to be found by which man could be saved. Joseph's Egyptian name, Zaphnath-paaneah, means "he who reveals that which is hidden" (see Bible Dictionary, "Zaphnath-paaneah").

18. Both were triumphant, overcoming all.

19. Both were granted rule over all. To Joseph, Pharaoh said, "According unto thy word shall all my people be ruled: only in the throne will I be greater than thou" (Genesis 41:40). Christ, in like manner, was welcomed in the royal courts on high, where he sits on the right hand of the Father with "angels and authorities and powers being made subject unto him" (1 Peter 3:22).

20. Both were thirty years old when they began their life's work. "And Joseph was thirty years old when he stood before

Pharaoh king of Egypt" (Genesis 41:46). And of the time when Christ commenced his public ministry we read, "And Jesus himself began to be about thirty years of age" (Luke 3:23).

21. Both were saviors to their people, giving them the bread of life. The sin of Joseph's brothers turned into the source of their salvation. Through him they were saved. He alone had power to grant to them the bread of life. Further, that same temporal salvation that he offered to trembling Israel was extended to all the nations of the earth. He granted them not only food but seed to sow their fields. How perfect the type! We need but change the name from Joseph to Christ, and the bread of life from the temporal to the eternal, and our story is the same.

22. The rejection of both brought bondage upon the people. "Just as a few years after his brethren had rejected Joseph, they were forced by a famine (sent from God) to leave their land and go down to Egypt, so a few years after the Jews had rejected Christ and delivered Him up to the Gentiles, God's judgment descended upon them, and the Romans drove them from their land, and dispersed them throughout the world" (*Gleanings*, p. 391).

23. Both were unrecognized by their people. When Joseph's brothers came seeking the bread of life, they failed to recognize that it was Joseph who extended the blessing that they sought. Only after he had identified himself did they know him. "I am Joseph," he said. "Come near to me, I pray you . . . be not grieved, nor angry with yourselves, that ye sold me hither: for God did send me before you to preserve life" (Genesis 45:3—5). Do not our scriptures prophesy of that day when the Jews shall look upon the Savior and say: "What are these wounds in thine hands and in thy feet? Then shall they know that I am the Lord; for I will say unto them: These wounds are the wounds with which I was wounded in the house of my friends. I am he who was lifted up. I am Jesus that was crucified. I am the Son of God. And then shall they weep because of their iniquities; then shall they lament because they persecuted their king." (D&C 45:51—53.)

24. Both would be recognized and accepted by their brothers only at the "second time." Such was the testimony of Stephen, who declared to a corrupt Sanhedrin that it was only "at the

second time Joseph was made known to his brethren" (Acts 7:13);
and so it would be with Christ.

25. As Joseph's brothers bowed to him in fulfillment of
prophecy, so all will yet bow the knee to Christ (Genesis
43:26—28; D&C 76:110).

26. Through both, mercy is granted to a repentant people.
As Joseph's brothers sought forgiveness of him, so Christ's
brothers will eventually seek forgiveness of him. In both
instances the mercies of heaven are freely given.

27. After the reconciliation, Israel is gathered. Having
manifest himself to his brothers, Joseph charged them to return
and bring their father and families to Egypt. So it shall be in the
last days. After Israel have returned to their God, they, like
Joseph's brothers, shall be given a change of raiment (Genesis
45:22) and sent to bring all the family of Israel into the kingdom
ruled by Christ.

28. To ailing Jacob, then nearly blind, the Lord said: "Joseph
shall put his hand upon thine eyes" (Genesis 46:4). Through him
you shall see, through him you shall be gathered, through him
you shall be introduced to the king and granted a land from
whence you shall increase endlessly. Such is our story and such is
our type. Again, how perfect: We but substitute *Christ* for *Joseph*
and extend the temporal blessings to the endless eternities, and
our story is one and the same.

THE LATTER-DAY JOSEPH

Joseph's life as a type or prophecy is not limited to the manner
in which it portrays the life of Christ. We have already noticed
that Moroni saw it as foreshadowing that of the New Jerusalem
of the last days. In a discourse by the other Moroni of the Book
of Mormon (the military commander in Alma), there is preserved
for us a prophecy that Joseph's father, Jacob, made shortly before
his death. Having before him a remnant of Joseph's coat, given to
him by his sons when they declared Joseph lost, Jacob noticed
that part of the remnant of that coat had decayed with the
passing of years, while part of the coat's remnant had been preserved. Seeing this, Jacob prophesied, "Even as this remnant of

garment of my son hath been preserved, so shall a remnant of the seed of my son be preserved by the hand of God, and be taken unto himself, while the remainder of the seed of Joseph shall perish, even as the remnant of his garment" (Alma 46:24).

Moroni, in response to dissensions within his own nation, rent his coat and wrote upon it, making of it a memorial to God, their religion, their freedoms, and their families, and then fastened it upon the end of a pole. "He went forth among the people, waving the rent part of his garment in the air, that all might see the writing which he had written upon the rent part, and crying with a loud voice, saying: Behold, whosoever will maintain this title upon the land, let them come forth in the strength of the Lord, and enter into a covenant that they will maintain their rights, and their religion, that the Lord God may bless them" (Alma 46:19—20).

Responding to Moroni's challenge, many came forth "rending their garments in token, or as a covenant, that they would not forsake the Lord their God," and that they would not transgress his holy laws, nor would they be ashamed to take upon them the name of Christ, for should they do so, "the Lord should rend them even as they had rent their garments." Those entering this covenant were reminded by Moroni that they were "a remnant of the seed of Joseph, whose coat was rent by his brethren into many pieces," and that they must keep the commandments of God or their garments would be rent by their brethren and they "be cast into prison, or be sold, or be slain." Rehearsing Jacob's prophecy about the remnant of Joseph that would perish, Moroni, likening the prophecy unto his own people, said, "Who knoweth but what the remnant of the seed of Joseph, which shall perish as his garment, are those who have dissented from us? Yea, and even it shall be ourselves if we do not stand fast in the faith of Christ." (Alma 46:21—27.)

Though we see the shadows of Jacob's prophecy reaching far beyond the circumstances to which Moroni applied them, of greatest interest to the present work is that Book of Mormon and Bible prophets alike saw Joseph's life as a prophetic type. In that same spirit, let it be suggested that its greatest significance to those of our day is as a marvelous foreshadowing of the life of

Joseph Smith, his great labors and those of the tribe of Joseph, of which he effectually stands as the head in this the last dispensation. We know that Joseph of Egypt knew the Prophet Joseph Smith by the spirit of prophecy and revelation, that he described the work that Joseph Smith would do, that he named him by name, and declared that "he shall be like unto me" (2 Nephi 3:15).

Viewing the life of Joseph of Egypt as a type foretelling the destiny of his tribe in the last days as it centers in the experiences of Joseph Smith, the following parallels are suggested:

1. Because they have forsaken the true way, the older brothers (that is, the Christian churches) have lost the spiritual birthright. The great evidence of this is that the Lord no longer speaks to them.

2. The birthright is then given to the youthful Joseph (Joseph Smith and the tribe of Joseph). Evidencing this, the Lord speaks freely to both. The world has never known a more prolific prophet, one who has recorded more revelation, than the prophet Joseph Smith. The tribe of Joseph, as identified by revelation and found within the restored church, are a people familiar with the spirit of revelation.

3. Joseph (both Prophet and tribe) have been clothed in the same coat or robes of authority that Jacob gave his "most loved" son. Thus they go forth seeking others of the family of Israel to clothe in "robes of righteousness" (D&C 109:76) and to endow with "power from on high" (D&C 38:32).

4. The name *Joseph* is itself a prophecy of events of the last days. The etymology of the name is usually given as "the Lord addeth" or "increaser." Though appropriate, such renderings have veiled a richer meaning. In the Bible account wherein Rachel names her infant son Joseph the Hebrew text reads *Asaph*, which means "he who gathers," "he who causes to return," or perhaps most appropriately "God gathereth" (Genesis 30:24; see also the footnote to the LDS edition). No more appropriate name could be given to the prophet of the restoration or to the tribe destined to do the work of the gathering than the name of their ancient father who gathered his family in Egypt.

5. Like their ancient father, Joseph Smith and the tribe of Joseph have had their destiny revealed to them. The dream of the "sheaves in the field," or Joseph's dream of earthly dominion, is matched by the promise given to Joseph of the latter days wherein the Lord has said, "I hold forth and deign to give unto you greater riches, even a land of promise, a land flowing with milk and honey, upon which there shall be no curse when the Lord cometh; And I will give it unto you for the land of your inheritance, if you seek it with all your hearts" (D&C 38:18—19). Joseph's dream of heavenly dominion, that of the sun, the moon, and the stars, finds fulfillment only in the sealing powers of the priesthood. Jacob interpreted Joseph's dream as having reference to himself (the sun), Rachel (the moon), and Joseph's brothers (the stars) bowing down to Joseph (Genesis 37:10). The unanswerable difficulty that this presented to Bible interpreters is that Rachel had died many years before, while giving birth to Benjamin. The context of promises associated with the sealing power and the assurance given Joseph Smith that the keys and authority he held would never be taken from him in this life or "in the world to come" (D&C 90:3) give meaning to Jacob's interpretation. The promise of the continuation of the family and eternal dominions are granted alike to the faithful of all ages.

6. Joseph Smith in his youthful innocence also shared his visionary promises with his "Christian" brothers, only to be severely rebuked. He recounts: "Some few days after I had this vision, I happened to be in company with one of the Methodist preachers, who was very active in the before mentioned religious excitement; and, conversing with him on the subject of religion, I took occasion to give him an account of the vision which I had had. I was greatly surprised at his behavior; he treated my communication not only lightly, but with great contempt, saying it was all of the devil, that there were no such things as visions or revelations in these days; that all such things had ceased with the apostles, and that there would never be any more of them." (JS—H 1:21.) The Joseph Smith story itself appears to be a type or pattern, the individual experiences of Joseph Smith being but representative of the composite experience of the body of the

Church. The rejection in this instance of Joseph's vision typifies the greater rejection by the churches of the world of the testimony of Joseph Smith and the principle of revelation.

7. The thought that Joseph had some promised destiny that was not theirs caused Joseph's brothers anciently to "hate him yet the more." Again our story contains the type or pattern: "I soon found," Joseph Smith said, "that my telling the story had excited a great deal of prejudice against me among professors of religion, and was the cause of great persecution, which continued to increase; and though I was an obscure boy, only between fourteen and fifteen years of age, and my circumstances in life such as to make a boy of no consequence in the world, yet men of high standing would take notice sufficient to excite the public mind against me, and create a bitter persecution; and this was common among all the sects—all united to persecute me" (JS—H 1:22). The popular Jewish author Elie Wiesel in writing of the life of Joseph of Egypt observed: "He aroused hate or love, fear or admiration. Never indifference. Some sought him out, while others avoided him, but nobody failed to notice him. Nobody failed to take stand for or against him." (*Messengers*, p. 129.)

How striking it is that the testimony of both Josephs evoked such reaction! Surely such announcements from obscure boys should have been passed off as youthful prattle, resulting in amusement or perhaps sympathy, but not a murderous hatred. It is truth that kindles the wrath of hell today as it did anciently. Had the Spirit of the Lord found place in the hearts of Joseph's brothers either anciently or in modern times it would have caused rejoicing at the prospect of a divinely appointed leader. Had the brothers disbelieved the prophecies, they certainly had no cause for concern. Their very bitterness in both instances evidenced the truth of the testimony borne.

Joseph's brothers were often quarrelsome, envious, and resentful. One matter alone seems to have united them: that of persecuting their younger brother. Such is the type, and so we find Joseph Smith declaring of his "Christian" brothers, "all united to persecute me," this being but the pattern of a quarrelsome world of churches that can agree upon nothing but to oppose Mormonism.

8. It is of interest that the promise of future destiny was given to Joseph of Egypt when he was seventeen years of age (Genesis 37:2). Similarly, it was when Joseph Smith was seventeen that Moroni appeared to him and unfolded the great destiny that was his and many passages of scripture promising the restoration of Israel in the last days (JS—H 1:33—41).

9. As Joseph's brothers anciently found it impossible to speak "peaceably unto him," so we of the last days can anticipate an endless parade of anti-Mormon literature.

10. Such emotions as noted above constituted the setting in which Joseph of old was sent as a special messenger of his father to his brothers, and such is the setting in which Joseph Smith and his followers are sent as messengers to all the world in the name of the Father.

11. Joseph Smith, like his ancient prototype, obediently responded to the call, knowing full well of his brothers' bitterness toward him.

12. Joseph's brothers, seeing him coming, plotted to betray him. So we find Joseph Smith martyred by those in whom he should have been able to trust, a mob that had in its number leaders of the Christian churches and some who had once been his brothers in the faith of the restored gospel.

13. As Potiphar's wife accused Joseph of her own sins that she might have him cast into prison, so Joseph Smith was accused of the crimes of his enemies who had him cast into prison.

14. "The keeper of the prison" anciently "committed to Joseph's hand all the prisoners that were in the prison" (Genesis 39:22). And so were "committed to Joseph's hand all the prisoners" in the spirit world. As he stands at the head of this dispensation of the gospel on earth, so he stands at its head in the spirit prison.

15. As Joseph was sold into Egypt, so Joseph (the Church in the last days) was forced into the bondage of a desert, where it was assumed that it would perish. As this happened to Joseph when he was seventeen, so it happened to the Church in 1847, or in its seventeenth year.

16. As Joseph interpreted the dreams of those in prison anciently, so Joseph Smith by the power of that same spirit has

been able to interpret revelations given to others (the Bible, the papyrus of Abraham, and so on) in our day. Anciently Joseph was granted the title or name Zaphnath-paaneah, "revealer of that which is hidden," as today Joseph Smith is testified of in all the world as a prophet, seer, and revelator. And as Joseph of Egypt prophesied good to one and evil to another, so Joseph Smith has promised blessings to the obedient and sorrow to those rejecting the message of the restored gospel.

17. To the hungry, Pharaoh, lord of Egypt, said, "Go unto Joseph" (Genesis 41:55). As Joseph was the only source of bread to a starving world, so Joseph Smith, to whom the truths and authority of salvation have been revealed, becomes the only source of the bread of life to a world perishing for want of the truth.

18. As Joseph of Egypt was lifted up and sustained by a foreign power, thus enabling him to restore his family, so Joseph of the last days has been lifted up by a great Gentile nation and granted the power to again restore Israel.

19. Joseph's brothers, the ten tribes, will yet come to him (the Church) seeking the bread of everlasting life (D&C 133:26—32). As Joseph of old was a temporal savior to Israel, Joseph (the Church or the tribes of Joseph) will now be recognized as the source of salvation by gathering Israel, who will bow the knee and acknowledge their younger brother.

20. As Joseph opened his arms and granted his wealth to his family anciently, so will Joseph of the last days receive his brothers as once again the family of Israel will be united.

21. As the whole nation of Egypt was blessed anciently because of Joseph, so the United States and all nations of the earth will be blessed because of the labors of the latter-day Joseph.

22. As Joseph saved his family anciently, so Joseph of the last days will be a savior to Israel (D&C 86:11). As the Lord said to Jacob who was nearly blind, "Joseph shall put his hand upon thine eyes" (Genesis 46:4), so he has said to Israel of the last days: "For his word ye shall receive, as if from mine own mouth, in all patience and faith. For by doing these things the gates of hell shall

not prevail against you; yea, and the Lord God will disperse the powers of darkness from before you, and cause the heavens to shake for your good, and his name's glory." (D&C 21:5—6.)

NOTES

1. Judaism, which revels in reaching into the past, views Joseph's life as an echo of his father, Jacob. "There were many features in the life of Joseph remarkably similar to those of his father," writes Samuel Rapaport in *A Treasury of the Midrash*. "Jacob's mother was for a time barren; so was Joseph's. Jacob's mother had two sons only; so had Joseph's mother. Jacob's brother sought his life; so did Joseph's brothers. Again, each went from Palestine to a foreign land, each had children born in a foreign country, the father-in-law of each were blessed for the sake of their sons-in-law; both Jacob and Joseph went to Egypt; each made his brothers swear to keep the promise made to him, each was embalmed, the bones of each were taken away from Egypt, etc." (*Midrash*, p. 142.)

5

An Everlasting
Memorial:
From Egypt to Sinai

The Old Testament is the canvas upon which the New Testament was painted. Paul describes the experiences of ancient Israel as being symbolic and as having been written "for our admonition" (1 Corinthians 10:11). Their experiences were "types," meaning that they represented or symbolized events that were to take place in the future. To say that a particular story in the scriptures is a type is not to deny the reality of the ancient event, but rather to say that the ancient happening was also a prefiguring or foreshadowing of some future event of even greater magnitude. Paul called such stories shadows; the Book of Mormon prophets called them types or types and shadows. What the prophets seem to be telling us is that the ancient story or event is a "type" that cast its "shadow" into the future, in some instances even to the very end of time. The shadows are in the image and likeness of the initial event, and they may take the form of prophecy, instruction, encouragement, or even solemn warning.

The concept of types and shadows is one of the great teaching devices used by God to ensure the perpetual relevance of ancient scripture. Types and shadows are something akin to a seer stone, for through them we can see both past and future more clearly.

No part of the Old Testament is more rich in types and shadows than that dealing with Moses, the law given through him, and the experiences of the children of Israel in their journey from Egypt to their land of promise. In this and the two chapters that follow we will examine some of the gems in this treasury of prophecy. As we do so it becomes increasingly evident that only by viewing Israel's history as prophecy can we fully understand the importance of our ancient scriptural records. Indeed we might say that the greatest prophecies dealing with Israel are found in her history. The past, as we shall see again and again, is the window to the present and the future.

MOSES AS REDEEMER OF ISRAEL

Let us begin our story as Moses, the shepherd of Midian, returns to lead the Lord's flock out of their Egyptian bondage. We know his return to be a type, for so Stephen filled with the Holy Ghost testified before the Sanhedrin. In his great defense of the faith, Stephen rehearsed Bible history to the council of the Jews, showing that as their fathers had rejected the prophets sent to them, they in like manner had rejected the promised Messiah. He told how Joseph, called of the Lord, was rejected by his brothers, who sold him into bondage, and how they came to him years later seeking corn and still did not recognize him. Stephen's point was that it was "the second time" before they recognized him (Acts 7:13). As it was with Joseph, so it was with Moses. According to Stephen's telling of the story, Moses sought to be the deliverer of Israel while he lived in Pharaoh's court. Yet the children of Israel rejected him, saying, "Who made thee a ruler and a judge over us?" He was not accepted as such until he came the second time. (Acts 7:25–35.) Both Old Testament stories were declared by Stephen to be prophetic types of the rejection of Christ and the fact that his nation would not accept him until the time of his Second Coming.

PRIESTHOOD VERSUS PRIESTCRAFT

In the providence of God the account of Moses' confrontation with Pharaoh has been preserved as a memorial for all generations to witness the difference between the powers of heaven and the priesthoods of the prince of darkness. The majesty of Egypt with its mighty palaces, pyramids, and temples was being challenged by a desert prophet so embarrassed by his own ineptitude of speech that God found it necessary to call another to act as his spokesman. What a spectacle it must have presented as Moses and Aaron, armed with nothing more than a shepherd's crook, stood before the mighty Pharaoh and in the name of Jehovah demanded that he free his slaves to go into the wilderness to worship their God! Mocking, Pharaoh challenged, "Show a miracle that I may know you" (JST, Exodus 7:9). And a God who will not be mocked showed forth his hand and his might that all men, then and in future ages, might know that his name was the Lord.

The miracles, ten in number, carried with them a significance often lost on the modern reader. When Aaron threw down his rod before Pharaoh and it became a serpent, Pharaoh called upon his own magicians to match the miracle and they too cast down their rods, which also became serpents.[1] But as the scriptural account tells us, "Aaron's rod swallowed up their rods" (Exodus 7:12). As rods were a symbol of divine or royal power, the message to Pharaoh—who had demanded the sign—was more plain and eloquent than words could ever be: Moses' power was greater than all of Egypt! Yet Pharaoh hardened his heart.

Miracle followed miracle, each with its special significance. Next came the turning of the Nile and all the waters of Egypt to blood. Consider the shock this must have been to the Egyptian mind, for the Nile was one of their gods. Now its fish, a vital source of life, some of which had been regarded as sacred, were dead, the river stunk, and the Egyptians could not drink its waters. What homage could they pay to a river god who could not save itself, or the life it contained, from the power of these slave prophets? For seven days, according to Moses' command, the river was a source of bitter torment to its Egyptian worshippers, yet if we can rely upon Josephus's account, "it was sweet and fit for drinking to the Hebrews" (Josephus, p. 61).

Then came forth the plague of frogs. They were everywhere —in the Egyptians' food, their beds, and on the people. Among the Egyptians the frog was a sacred animal representing the powers of reproduction. Thus again a sacred symbol became an object of abhorrence (Dummelow, p. 55). The frogs were followed by swarms of flies. That Pharaoh might know that the curse came at the hand of Moses' God, there were no flies in the land of Goshen, where the enslaved Hebrews dwelt. Bible scholars have suggested that the flies were a form of destructive beetle. If their assumption is correct, then this plague was also a double blow, for to the Egyptians the beetle was the sacred emblem of the Sun-god (ibid).

Pharaoh, who would promise Israel freedom until the plagues were stayed again, forsook his promise. The Lord responded by having Moses curse the cattle of the Egyptians so that those in the fields died while the cattle of the Israelites stood unaffected. Once more the utter folly of Egyptian idolatry was manifest, for chief among their gods were sheep, cattle, and bulls. Pharaoh again promised to let Israel go, and again forsook his promise when relief was granted.

A plague of boils and then a hailstorm which fell only upon the Egyptians followed. Pharaoh sent for Moses, saying, "I have sinned . . . the Lord is righteous, and I and my people are wicked" (Exodus 9:27). Again he denied his promise to let Israel go, and again his kingdom was cursed, this time with locusts that ate what herbs and fruit had not been destroyed by the hail. Once more Pharaoh failed to honor his word, and Moses commanded darkness to cover the land. Thick darkness covered Egypt for three days—yet the children of Israel had light in their dwellings. The last vestige of hope was now lost to the Egyptians: Ra the Sun-god and chief object of worship had been rendered powerless.

Before describing the last of the miracles let us observe how completely the God of Israel vindicated himself amid the abominable idolatry of Egypt. It would have been a simple matter for the Creator to immediately free his people from their bondage, but such was not the course of the Master Teacher. He chose the land of Egypt as his classroom to teach a lesson that was to be remembered throughout all generations as a testimony that he was indeed the Lord (Exodus 10:2).

In this confrontation with Moses the priests of Egypt had also turned rods to snakes, changed water to blood, and called forth plagues of frogs. Their ability to work miracles was impressive, yet it must not have been lost upon their people that though they could imitate the plagues they had no power to rebuke them. They had power to further curse their people, but not the power to bless them. When Moses brought forth the plague of lice, their attempts to imitate it failed, illustrating that there are limits to the powers of the kingdom of darkness.

Obvious conclusions growing out of this epic story are: first, that Satan and his associates had the power to perform mighty miracles; and second, that notwithstanding their power to do so, their authority was vastly inferior to that of the priesthood of God. Of greatest importance to us, however, is the realization that there is no reason to believe that Lucifer has lost any power during the past four thousand years since he contested with Moses. He has the same power to work miracles today that he ever had, and we can have every assurance that as it suits his ends and accomplishes his purposes he will manifest that power. And though Pharaoh's course of duplicity and obstinacy seem incomprehensible, his actions and ultimate end must stand as a warning to all of the powerful hold that Satan gains over the hearts of men through their wickedness and his systems of false worship.

THE PASSOVER—A TYPE OF CHRIST

When the chosen people were about to be brought out of Egypt, the word of the Lord came to Moses and Aaron, commanding them to instruct the church to prepare for their departure with a solemn religious ordinance. On the tenth day of the month Abib (March-April) which had then commenced, the head of each family was to select a lamb or a kid, a male of the first year without blemish, to be used as a sacrifice. If the family was too small to eat the entire lamb, they were to invite the nearest neighbor to join them. On the fourteenth of the month the animal was to be killed while the sun was setting. The head of the house was then to take the blood in a basin, and with a sprig of hyssop to sprinkle it on the two side-posts and the lintel of the door of their home. The offering was then to be thoroughly roasted, whole. It was expressly forbidden that it be boiled, or that any bone be broken. Unleavened bread and bitter herbs

were to be eaten with the flesh. No male who was uncircumcised
was to join in the meal. Each man was to have his loins girt, to
hold a staff in his hand, and to have shoes on his feet. They were
to stand as they ate and eat in haste. The number of the party
was to be calculated as nearly as possible, so that all the flesh of
the lamb might be eaten; anything that remained was to be
burned. No morsel of it was to be carried out of the house. All
were told of God's purpose to smite the firstborn of the Egyptians
and that the Passover was to be kept as an ordinance from generation to generation. (Exodus 12.)

Though we do not understand every detail of this ritual, we
cannot misunderstand its essential meaning. Christ is of course
the Lamb, pure and perfect, without spot or blemish, a sacrifice
in the very prime of his life. His death was to come by the
shedding of his blood, yet it was to be accomplished without the
breaking of a single bone. Such, of course, was the case. As he
hung upon the cross and the setting of the sun approached, the
soldiers broke the legs of the two thieves to induce their deaths.
Approaching Christ for the same purpose, they found him
already dead. The blood sprinkled on the doors of the Israelite
homes signified the agony of Gethsemane where the Savior
would bleed at every pore, and the blood that was to gush from
his side at Golgotha when the Roman spear assured his death.
The symbol of his blood assured the Israelites a temporal salvation when the firstborn of the Egyptians died, as the blood
shed by the Lamb of God would yet have power to save the faithful of all ages with an everlasting salvation.

The symbolism associated with the other parts of this ritual
includes the following:

Head of the house: The father or head of the house was to
assume the lead in bringing the household to Christ.

Roasting of the lamb: Fire is the element of purification. The
meat of Christ's sacrifice and his gospel is to be accepted in
purity.

No meat to be left: There is no salvation in partial truths or in
partial acceptance of the truth.

Uncircumcised forbidden: The blessings of the gospel are
reserved for those who join the Church and comply with all ordinances God has given his people.

Bitter herbs: A reminder of their sufferings in Egypt or the world of sin before their liberation.

Unleavened bread: Leaven, which produces fermentation, is in this context the emblem of sin. Symbolically, to put it away is to turn to God with simplicity and uprightness of heart.

Eating in haste with loins girt, staff in hand, and shoes on feet: They were to leave Egypt in haste, as all men should give immediate response to the command of the Lord.

Perhaps of greatest significance is the fact that the sacrifice of the lamb alone did not bring protection from the destroying angel. Safety was promised only to those who properly marked the door of their homes with the blood of the lamb. The symbol is eloquent—all may be saved through the atonement of Christ, if they obey the laws and ordinances of the gospel.

While Jesus and the Twelve were keeping the Feast of the Passover the Lord instituted the ordinance of the sacrament which serves essentially the same purpose. "After the final Passover day and its attendant lifting up upon the cross of the true Paschal Lamb, the day for the proper celebration of the ancient feast ceased" (*Promised Messiah*, p. 431). Paul affirmed this, saying "Christ our passover is sacrificed for us: Therefore let us keep the feast, not with old leaven, neither with the leaven of malice and wickedness; but with the unleavened bread of sincerity and truth." (1 Corinthians 5:7—8.)

THE BODY OF JOSEPH: SERMON AND PROPHECY

When Moses left Egypt, he took the coffin of Joseph with him. It will be remembered that Joseph had the children of Israel promise that when they departed Egypt they would take his bones with them.

> In obedience to his wishes they embalmed his body, and laid it in one of those Egyptian coffins, generally made of sycamore wood, which resembled the shape of the human body. And there, through ages of suffering and bondage, stood the figure-like coffin of Joseph, ready to be lifted and carried thence when the sure hour of deliverance had come.

Thus Joseph, being dead, yet spake to Israel, telling them that they were only temporary sojourners in Egypt, that their eyes must be turned away from Egypt unto the land of promise, and that in the patience of faith they must wait for that hour when God would certainly and graciously fulfill His own promises. (Edersheim, OT 1:189—90.)

As his unburied body was both sermon and prophecy, so we will yet discover hidden within the pages of his life a detailed prophecy of the events of the last days.

THE FIRSTBORN

As Israel marched toward the Red Sea the Lord spoke again to Moses, saying, "Sanctify unto me all the firstborn, whatsoever openeth the womb among the children of Israel, both of man and of beast: it is mine" (Exodus 13:2). To *sanctify* means to consecrate or to set apart from common to sacred use. The firstborn of Israel, both man and beast, having been preserved from death by the grace of God, were now as a token of gratitude to be consecrated to his service. Not only was this divine decree to remind Israel of her redemption from death in Egypt, but it also carried with it the memory of a heavenly council in which the Firstborn of the Father was consecrated as the Lamb to be slain, the servant of all who would believe and obey.

The firstborn of every family was to be consecrated to the service of Jehovah as a priest, while the firstborn of all clean animals were to be offered as a sacrifice. The firstborn of unclean animals were to be redeemed by the offering of a lamb or kid. The law was a constant reminder that all things belonged to God, who had given his own firstborn as the great and last sacrifice. Obviously, it was also a reminder of what the Lord had done in preserving the firstborn of Israel in Egypt. Afterwards the tribe of Levi was consecrated to the priestly service in lieu of the firstborn of all the tribes. Still, the firstborn of the other tribes were released from this bond only by the payment of a redemption tax of five shekels apiece to the priests of the temple. Joseph and Mary complied with this law when they brought the Christ child to the temple forty days after his birth (Luke 2:23—24).

Covenant Breakers Destroyed

Paul, who drew freely upon the experiences of Israel for types to sustain his teachings, reminded the Saints in Corinth that ordinances alone did not save. To illustrate his point he recalled that many who had received gospel ordinances under Moses were later destroyed by the Lord because of their wickedness and rebellion. "All our fathers were under the cloud, and all passed through the sea," Paul said, "And were all baptized unto Moses in the cloud and in the sea; And did all eat the same spiritual meat; And did all drink the same spiritual drink: for they drank of that spiritual Rock that followed them: and that Rock was Christ. But with many of them God was not well pleased: for they were overthrown in the wilderness." (1 Corinthians 10:1—5.) Paul's argument is not against the efficacy of ordinances, but rather that no blessings come from broken covenants. By analogy he is saying that as Israel passed through the Red Sea, leaving the worldliness of Egypt, so their descendants, through baptism, are to forsake the lusts of the flesh and live godly lives; as Israel by passing through the Red Sea committed themselves to follow Moses, so we must leave the world and pass through the waters of baptism and follow Christ.

The full significance of Paul's analogy is denied by sectarian Christianity in its insistence that those of Moses' time could not have known Christ or participated in such ordinances as baptism by immersion for the remission of sins. The Book of Mormon, the Doctrine and Covenants, the Pearl of Great Price, and the Joseph Smith Translation of the Bible all correct this error. The law of Moses itself was the "preparatory gospel, . . . the gospel of repentance and of baptism, and the remission of sins" (D&C 84:26—27).

From Death Came Life

After crossing the Red Sea, Israel traveled three days into the wilderness without finding water. When water was found it proved too bitter to drink. The place was named Marah, meaning "bitterness." The people "murmured against Moses," who in turn sought the Lord and was shown a tree (often translated "a piece of wood") which, when he cast it into the waters, made them sweet. (Exodus 15:22—25.) Surely the story is a type of him who died upon a tree, being cast into the bitter waters of death that they might bring forth the sweet waters of everlasting life. Here Israel entered into a covenant to keep the commandments of the Lord that they might be protected by him.

The Twelve and the Seventy

Following the account of the renewal of covenants at Marah, we read, "And they came to Elim, where were twelve wells of water, and threescore and ten palm trees: and they encamped there by the waters" (Exodus 15:27). Ginzberg states:

> The men of understanding could at this place see a clear allusion to the fortune of the people; for there are twelve tribes of the people, each of which, if it prove God fearing, will be a well of water, inasmuch as its piety will constantly and continually bring forth beautiful deeds; the leaders of the people, however, are seventy, and they recall the noble palm tree, for in outward appearance as well as in its fruits, it is the most beautiful of trees, whose seat of life does not lie buried deep in the roots, as with other plants, but soars high, set like the heart in the midst of its branches, by which it is surrounded as a queen under the protection of her bodyguard (*Legends* 3:10—11).

We are left to wonder if the symbolism of Elim was intended to reach even to our day when the Twelve and the Seventy assume the leading role in the gathering and sustaining of Israel as she leaves the Egypts of the world and returns to God.

Lessons of Need and Greed

Leaving Elim, Israel continued her march into the wilderness of Sin. Having exhausted its food supply, the entire congregation turned on Moses and Aaron, asking if they had been brought into the desert to die of starvation. The Lord said to Moses, "I have heard the murmurings of the children of Israel: speak unto them, saying, At even ye shall eat flesh, and in the morning ye shall be filled with bread; and ye shall know that I am the Lord your God" (Exodus 16:12). In the evening quails came in such numbers that they covered the camp of Israel. Yet the morrow was to see the greater miracle, for as the dew dried up there was in its place manna from heaven, by which Israel would be fed until that day forty years hence when they would eat corn in the land of Canaan.

Great lessons are associated with both quail and manna. We will speak first of the quail. Later on in her desert sojourn Israel would again be fed with quail. This would come after the Lord had brought forth water from a rock, after he had granted them victory over the Amalekites, and after the covenant of Sinai. These children of Moses, always quick to complain, began to murmur once again for the glories of Egypt. "Who shall give us flesh to eat?" was the cry. "We remember the fish, which we did eat in Egypt freely; the cucumbers, and the melons, and the leeks, and the onions, and the garlick: but now our soul is dried away: there is nothing at all, beside this manna, before our eyes." (Numbers 11:4—6.) Moses prophesied that the Lord would send them flesh to eat even for a whole month, until it came out of their nostrils and became loathsome to them, because they despised what the Lord had done for them. From across the sea the wind swept the quail into their camp to the depth of two cubits, extending out a day's journey on each side of the camp. Bushel upon bushel was gathered, "and while the flesh was yet between their teeth, ere it was chewed, the wrath of the Lord was kindled against the people, and the Lord smote the people with a very great plague." And the place was called Kibroth-hattaavah, meaning the "graves of the greedy" or the "graves of lust." (Numbers 11:31—34.)

Thus we see that Israel was to feast twice upon quail. First, as they approached Sinai without food, the Lord opened the heavens and sent forth quail in the evening and commenced the forty-year miracle of manna in the morning. In this way he assured the child Israel that, as at the parting of the Sea and the sweetening of the waters of Marah, a divine providence watched over them. The second instance came after the evidence of the

Lord's protection in their victory over the Amalekites, and the bringing forth of the water from the rock. It came after the covenant of Sinai, to the spoiled child Israel, the child without need to fear or cause for hunger. Israel complained now not out of need but out of greed, only to learn of the sorrows that attend the gratification of lusts.

To Israel of our day the Lord has said, "Whatsoever ye ask the Father in my name it shall be given unto you, that is expedient for you; And if ye ask anything that is not expedient for you, it shall turn unto your condemnation" (D&C 88:64—65).

THE BREAD OF LIFE

It is in the great Bread of Life sermon of the Savior that we find the richness of the manna as a type unfolded. Having miraculously fed five thousand from five loaves of bread and two small fishes, he reminded them that Moses gave their fathers "bread from heaven" while they were in the desert. But it was they who had been given the "true bread from heaven. For the bread of God is he which cometh down from heaven, and giveth life unto the world. . . . I am the living bread which came down from heaven," he testified, and then promised, "If any man eat of this bread, he shall live for ever: and the bread that I will give is my flesh, which I will give for the life of the world." (John 6:31—58.)

To the membership of the Church the Lord said, "To him that overcometh will I give to eat of the hidden manna, and will give him a white stone and in the stone a new name written, which no man knoweth saving he that receiveth it" (Revelation 2:17). Explaining this passage, the Lord told Joseph Smith that "the white stone mentioned in Revelation 2:17, will become a Urim and Thummim to each individual who receives one, whereby things pertaining to a higher order of kingdoms will be made known; And a white stone is given to each of those who come into the celestial kingdom, whereon is a new name written, which no man knoweth save he that receiveth it. The new name is the key word." (D&C 130:10—11.)

It appears that the passage just quoted was intended to take the symbolism of manna even beyond that of a daily sacramental meal to remind Israel that salvation was in Christ and none else. Perhaps there is something suggested in the exchange between the people and Moses their mediator which is hidden to the eyes of the unendowed. When the children of Israel first saw their heaven-sent bread without knowing what it was, they asked, "What is this?" Moses responded, "This is the bread which the Lord hath given you to eat," meaning that this is the Son of God whose life will be shed that you might enter again into his presence (Exodus 16:15).[2]

Leaving the desert of Sin, Israel came in the course of their journey to the plain (Rephidem) where there was no water. Once more they manifested their distrust in the Lord, murmuring against his prophet. Moses sought the Lord, who directed him to leave the people, taking with him his rod and certain of the elders. His destination was a particular rock to be identified by the Lord, which he was then to smite with his rod that it might bring forth water.

Paul assures us the story is a type and identifies the rock as Christ (1 Corinthians 10:4). Edersheim writes, "And from the river side of the parched rock living waters flowed," suggesting to our minds the image of Christ upon the cross, his side pierced with a Roman spear giving forth blood and water that all might live (Edersheim, OT 2:101; John 19:34). In any event, the story illustrates our constant dependence on the Lord. Nor is it without significance that Moses and a few special witnesses were separated from Israel, who being unworthy to approach the Lord were required to drink of the waters of salvation downstream. The place was named Massah (meaning testing or proving) and Meribah (meaning strife or complaint). (Exodus 17:1–7.)

A Type Describing Israel's Enemies

As Israel witnessed the miracle of the Smitten Rock, the Amalekites swept down upon them. This army that "feared not God" attacked from the rear, hoping to find advantage among the stragglers, those most "feeble," "weary," and "faint" among the hosts of Israel. (Deuteronomy 15:17—19.) Moses directed Joshua to "Choose us out men, and go out, fight with Amalek," saying, "tomorrow I will stand on the top of the hill with the rod of God in mine hand." Joshua did so, and the following morning as he led his troop to battle Moses ascended the hill with Aaron and Hur at his side. As Moses stood upon the hill with his arms extended to the heavens holding aloft his rod, the army of Israel was victorious, but as his arms wearily ebbed to his side the army of Amalek prevailed. Aaron and Hur took a large stone and put it under Moses for him to sit upon, and then, standing one on each side of him, they held his arms heavenward. Joshua's forces were thus victorious "and the Lord said unto Moses, Write this for a memorial in a book," rehearse it to Joshua, and remember that "I will utterly put out the remembrance of Amalek from under heaven." Commemorating the event, Moses built an altar, which he named Jehovah-nissi: "For he said, Because the Lord hath sworn that the Lord will have war with Amalek from generation to generation." (Exodus 17:8—16.)

A story more obviously intended as a type would be difficult to imagine. Certainly there was no advantage extended to Israel's army by the place where Moses stood, the manner in which he held his arms, what he held in his hands, or who stood at his side, unless some greater purpose is found in those actions. Let us rehearse the story again with such an idea in mind. First we observe that the attack by the Amalekites was without provocation. No justification can be given for these descendants of Esau attacking their kin, Jacob's sons. Reason is found only in the statement that they "feared not God." Their antagonism, it appears, was more with the idea of a chosen people than with the people that were chosen. The Amalekites aptly represent the hostility of the world toward the kingdom of God. Those professing to "fear not" are in fact "afraid of" what that kingdom represents. They find it necessary to constantly test themselves in unprovoked attack—not in frontal attack, be it noted, but from the rear where they find victory among the spiritual stragglers, the feeble, weary, and faint. The corresponding oath that their treachery be remembered throughout all generations and that the Lord would war against them is the recompense of all who fight against the Lord and his people. "Wo unto all those that discomfort my people," the Lord said in our dispensation, "and drive, and murder, and testify against them, saith the Lord of Hosts; a generation of vipers shall not escape the damnation of hell. Behold, mine eyes see and know all their works, and I have in reserve a swift judgment in the season thereof, for them all; For there is a time appointed for every man, according as his works shall be." (D&C 121:23—25.) Such will always be found assailing the nation of God until that time when all ungodly powers have been arrested and the millennial reign established.

In some stages of Israel's history the battle will be one of words, a war of opinions, but there are also occasions enough when the battle will be one of cold steel. In either case Israel must take up her arms and fight. It must always be remembered that though Israel fights, the victory is the Lord's. Their dependence is always upon him. The name of Moses' altar, *Jehovah-nissi,* interpreted is "the Lord my banner," for it is under such that Israel must march. Nor does our type end here, for Joshua, which is the Hebrew form of the name Jesus, is their appointed leader. He in turn is to choose those that are to march at his side, as in the meridian Jesus said, "ye have not chosen me, but I have chosen you" (John 15:16). As Israel marches to battle, Moses ascends the hill where he will raise his arms to heaven in mighty prayer, holding aloft his rod as a symbol of that power which comes only from the divine presence. Such is the source of Israel's strength, and when Moses' arms sag in weariness, victory flees from his army. Aaron and Hur as counselors in this presidency of three then recognize their role and step forth to sustain the prophet with their own strength, holding his arms heavenward. Thus we see that in all its conflicts with the ungodly powers of the world, Israel must find its strength for victory under the banner of Jehovah, marching in unity and faith.

TEACHING CORRECT PRINCIPLES

As the company of Israel continued their journey into the wilderness of Sinai toward the mountain of the Lord, they were joined by Jethro, Moses' father-in-law, who brought with him

Zipporah, Moses' wife, and his two sons. Jethro thus became the source of wise counsel to Moses and all who would in some future time be called to lead Israel. Observing that Moses sat alone upon the judgment seat from morning to night to judge among the people, Jethro said, "The thing that thou doest is not good." Not only was Moses exhausting himself, but the very system of administering justice was exhausting the patience of his people. Jethro instructed Moses that his role was to teach the children of Israel correct principles that they might govern themselves, for surely the teacher of the law is greater than the administrator of the law. He said: "Thou shalt teach them ordinances and laws, and shalt shew them the way wherein they must walk, and the work that they must do. Moreover thou shalt provide out of all the people able men, such as fear God, men of truth, hating covetousness; and place such over them, to be rulers of thousands, and rulers of hundreds, rulers of fifties, and rulers of tens." (Exodus 18:17—21.) Thus only the great matters would be brought to Moses and the people would be strengthened as they learned to govern themselves.[3]

NOTES

1. There is some justification in the root word to render this *crocodile* instead of *serpent*. Such would be most fitting since the crocodile was so reverenced in Egypt. (The JST leaves it *serpent*.)

2. This dialogue is poorly translated in the King James Version. *Manna* (man-hu) in Hebrew means "What is this?" or "What is that?" The NEB translates the verse thus: "When the Israelites saw it, they said one to another, 'What is that?,' because they did not know what it was."

3. The same principle was revealed anew to the modern Moses, Brigham Young, as he prepared the Saints for their westward trek. The revelation reads: "The Word and Will of the Lord concerning the Camp of Israel in their journeyings to the West: Let all the people of The Church of Jesus Christ of Latter-day Saints, and those who journey with them, be organized into companies, with a covenant and promise to keep all the commandments and statutes of the Lord our God. Let the companies be organized with captains of hundreds, captains of fifties, and captains of tens, with a president and his two counselors at their head, under the direction of the Twelve Apostles." (D&C 136:1—3.)

6

An Everlasting Memorial: From Sinai to Palestine

As the journey from Egypt to Sinai was replete with types and shadows, so the journey from Sinai to the land of promise was filled with timeless teaching moments. As with the stories heretofore told, not only are such experiences marvelous teaching devices to which we can liken the present, but they prophetically prefigure and foreshadow events of far greater importance in the destiny of Israel than those of the moment of their occurrence.

It is one thing to possess a valued book and quite another to know of its value. Let us resume our journey with Israel through its wilderness wanderings, watching closely as we do so for those things of greatest worth.

A HOLY NATION, A KINGDOM OF PRIESTS

After Moses had brought the nation of Israel into the wilderness of Sinai, he again ascended the holy mountain, where the Lord told him of the covenant he desired to make with his people. "If ye will obey my voice indeed, and keep my covenant," the Lord directed Moses to tell Israel, "then ye shall be a peculiar treasure unto me . . . a kingdom of priests, and an holy nation." When Moses presented this covenant to Israel they responded, "All that the Lord hath spoken we will do." Moses returned and reported to the Lord. (Exodus 19:5—8.) He was then instructed to sanctify Israel that the Lord might "come down in the sight of all the people upon mount Sinai" and give them his law. The cleansing process included the washing of their clothes. (Exodus 19:10—11, 14.) Jewish tradition holds that they were baptized at this time (*Legends* 3:88). If the allegory of Ezekiel about the covenant that God made with Israel is interpreted to begin at this point, then the sanctification ritual consisted of washing and anointing (Ezekiel 16:8—10). The Doctrine and Covenants affirms that the children of Israel at the time of Moses practiced the rituals of baptism, washings, and anointings (D&C 84:26—27; 124:37—40). However one chooses to interpret the ritual by which Israel was prepared to see their God, of this we can be certain: The physical cleansing mentioned in the scripture assumes meaning only as it is an emblem of the necessary spiritual cleansing.

The covenant that the Lord sought to make with Israel was one in which they would become a "kingdom of priests, and an holy nation" (Exodus 19:6). "Early commentators, both Jewish and Christian, and also in the ancient versions," understood this to mean that they would be "priests and kings" (*Biblical Commentary* 2:96—97). That accords with the expectation of the New Testament Saints (Revelation 1:5—6; 5:9—10) and is the same promise made to the Saints of our day (D&C 76:56).

The covenant that Israel would become a "kingdom of priests" meant that they were to be a nation in which their citizens were to be priesthood holders. The priesthood that they held would have been the higher or Melchizedek Priesthood. The Aaronic or Levitical Priesthood had not yet been revealed. These priesthood holders were to possess a royal power and dignity. A priest is an intermediary between God and man; thus Israel would become the dispenser of the knowledge of God and the ordinances of salvation to all the nations of the earth. They were to be called and chosen according to the promise the Lord had made with Abraham—that is, to bear the ministry and priesthood to all nations that all might have the opportunity to receive the "blessings of the Gospel, which are the blessings of salvation, even of life eternal" (Abraham 2:9—11). Such was the desire of God, but as we shall see, such was not the propensity of Israel.

SINAI WAS ISRAEL'S FIRST TEMPLE

Sinai served as a temple for Moses and the children of Israel. All that took place on the holy mount we will yet see embodied in the tabernacle and the temples of the Bible. Sinai, like the temple, was the place where God and man were to meet. It was now to become the place where covenants are made. Nor is it without significance that purity was a prerequisite to participate in its blessings. Israel had been washed and sanctified in preparation for the appearance of the Lord, and Moses was instructed to establish bounds around the holy mount beyond which the children of Israel were not to go. None were to go up to the mount or even touch the border of it. Any doing so, be they man or beast, were to be killed. (Exodus 19:12–13.) The glory of the Lord would occupy the top of the mountain; Moses alone, Israel's high priest, would be allowed to part the veil and enter here. Later Aaron and the seventy were permitted to advance some way up the mountain, while the people were only permitted to come up to its base (Exodus 24:9–11). These bounds were a type for the order of the tabernacle, which would be divided into three parts: the outer court, into which the people could enter; the Holy Place, into which the priests could enter; and the Holy of Holies, into which only the high priest could enter. Moses, as the lawgiver, was to receive the statutes and judgments from God's mouth; Aaron and the elders were to receive them from Moses and in turn were to teach them to the people. The positioning of each group dramatized the order of the kingdom. Yet for all there were bounds or limits within which they must remain or be destroyed. Thus we learn that every office in the kingdom of God has its bounds and limits, as do appetites. To exceed those limits is to invite destruction.

ISRAEL FEARS THE VOICE OF THE LORD

On the third day, according to his promise, the Lord descended upon mount Sinai amid fire and smoke while the mount "quaked greatly." Moses was summoned to enter the cloud resting on the top of the mount. He had hardly entered the divine presence when the Lord told him to return and warn his people "lest they break through unto the Lord to gaze, and many of them perish" (Exodus 19:21). Then from the heights of Sinai the Lord gave the "ten words" or commandments. "All the people saw the thunderings, and the lightnings, and the noise of the trumpet, and the mountain smoking: and when the people saw it, they removed, and stood afar off. And they said unto Moses, Speak thou with us, and we will hear: but let not God speak with us, lest we die." (Exodus 20:18—19.) "For who is there of all flesh, that hath heard the voice of the living God speaking out of the midst of the fire, as we have, and lived?" (Deuteronomy 5:26).

It was a well-established principle among Old Testament peoples that no unclean thing could endure the presence of God or his angels. Hagar, when instructed by the angel of the Lord to return to Sarai, manifested surprise, saying, "I have indeed seen God and still live after that vision" (NEB, Genesis 16:13). After the angel of God had appeared to Manoah and his wife, Manoah exclaimed, "We shall surely die, because we have seen God" (Judges 13:22). The principle has been announced in our dispensation in this language: "For no man has seen God at any time in the flesh, except quickened by the Spirit of God. Neither can any natural man abide the presence of God, neither after the carnal mind." Then to those to whom the revelation was being given the Lord said, "Ye are not able to abide the presence of God now, neither the ministering of angels; wherefore, continue in patience until ye are perfected." (D&C 67:11—13.)

ISRAEL COVENANTS WITH HER GOD

Hearing Israel's fear of his presence, the Lord directed Moses to have them return to their tents. He then revealed his commandments, statutes, and judgments to Moses. Moses recorded them in the book of the covenant, read them to Israel, and placed the people under covenant to abide by them. As a symbol of their covenant Moses built an altar at the foot of Sinai with twelve pillars, one representing each of the tribes. On it were offered burnt offerings and peace offerings of oxen. Moses sprinkled half of the blood of the oxen on the altar and half of it on the people.

This represented the sacred fellowship or unity of God and man in the covenant. Having thus been consecrated with the blood of the covenant, the Israelites were qualified to ascend the mountain, where they would behold their God. In this instance Moses, Aaron, Aaron's two sons, and the seventy elders of Israel ascended the mountain, where they saw God. The Lord then invited Moses to come further up the mountain to receive the tables of stone containing the law and commandments which the Lord had written. This Moses did, being absent from Israel for forty days and forty nights. (See Exodus 24.)

MOSES AS ISRAEL'S ADVOCATE

Upon returning to the presence of the Lord, Moses was instructed in the necessity of making a sanctuary so that there would be a suitable place, howbeit temporary, for Him to dwell among them. In labored detail Moses was given the pattern for the tabernacle and "all the instruments thereof" (Exodus 25:8—9). He was further instructed in the manner in which Aaron and his sons were to minister as priests. When Moses was fully instructed the Lord wrote the Law upon two tables of stone with his own finger. Then he said to Moses, "thy people . . . have corrupted themselves: They have turned aside quickly out of the way which I commanded them: they have made them a molten calf, and have worshipped it, and have sacrificed thereunto, and said, These be thy gods, O Israel, which have brought thee up out of the land of Egypt" (Exodus 32:7—8). The Lord's anger was kindled and he told Moses that he would destroy Israel and raise up a new nation from Moses' seed. At this point in our story, Moses, whom the scriptures tell us was in the similitude of Christ (Moses 1:6), assumed the role of a mediator and pleaded for his people. His argument was threefold: first, that they were God's people, he having brought them out of Egypt by his own power; second, that God's glory was thus involved and would be shamed in the sight of Israel's enemies; and third, that he had covenanted with Abraham, Isaac, and Jacob to raise up a mighty nation from their seed. Though the Old Testament account of this story is garbled, it has been clarified in the Joseph Smith

Translation. There we read of Moses saying: "Turn from thy fierce wrath. Thy people will repent of this evil; therefore come thou not out against them. . . . And the Lord said unto Moses, If they will repent of the evil which they have done, I will spare them, and turn away my fierce wrath; but, behold, thou shalt execute judgment upon all that will not repent of this evil this day. Therefore, see thou do this thing that I have commanded thee, or I will execute all that which I had thought to do unto my people." (JST, Exodus 32:12, 14.)

A Broken Covenant

Moses returned to his people and, seeing their wickedness, was so angered that he broke the tablets of the law even as Israel had broken their covenant and the law. Swift retribution followed in the camp of Israel. Moses took the golden calf and burnt it—then, grinding it to powder, he sprinkled it on water and made the Israelites drink it, as a symbol that "each one must receive and bear the fruits of his sins" (Edersheim, OT 2:129) Many resisted Moses, but the tribe of Levi stepped forward to sustain him. At their hand nearly three thousand Israelites were slain that day. Though not stated, it appears that those who died were the rebellious and unrepentant of Israel.

Moses as Israel's Mediator

Having received an errand from the Lord, Moses was required to return and report. The honor of the Lord having been avenged, Moses returned to give an accounting and receive further instruction. In this obvious type for Christ, Moses departed from Israel, saying, "I shall make an atonement for your sin" (Exodus 32:30). To the Lord he said, "Blot my name from the book of life if you will not forgive them." The Lord responded that those who had sinned would be blotted from that book but that Moses was to lead his people to the land of promise and that an angel would go before them. Further, the Lord said, "When I visit I will visit their sin upon them" (Exodus 32:34). Israel could not escape from the responsibility of her sins. Though the nation would be preserved and yet lay claim to the land promised, the covenant relationship was not to be restored in full, for as one scholar noted: "Though grace may modify and soften wrath, it cannot mar the justice of the holy God" (*Biblical Commentary*, 2:232).

A LESSER LAW GIVEN

Israel was now promised the presence of an angel but not that of the Lord himself, for the Lord said, "I will not go up in the midst of thee; for thou art a stiffnecked people: lest I consume thee in the way" (Exodus 33:3). When the people heard this they mourned, and as a manifestation of their sorrow we are told that they "stripped themselves of their ornaments by the mount Horeb" (Exodus 33:6). The Septuagint reading of this passage is especially interesting: "The people, having heard this sad declaration, mourned with lamentations. And the Lord said unto the children of Israel, Now, therefore, put off your robes of glory, and your ornaments, and I will show you the things I will do unto you. And the children of Israel put off their ornaments and robes by the mount, by Horeb." In his commentary Clarke suggests that that which they took off was "emblematical of spiritual things," because they were no longer entitled to these emblems of "Divine protection" (Clarke 1:470).

To further illustrate that he would no longer be in the midst of Israel, the Lord directed Moses to place the tabernacle of the congregation outside the camp, where he would then come to converse "face to face" with Moses. Shortly thereafter the Lord instructed Moses, "Hew thee two other tables of stone, like unto the first, and I will write upon them also, the words of the law," but we learn from the Joseph Smith Translation that it would "not be according to the first," for the Lord said, "I will take away the priesthood out of their midst; therefore my holy order, and the ordinances thereof, shall not go before them; for my presence shall not go up in their midst, lest I destroy them." The law they were then given was to "be after the law of a carnal commandment." (JST, Exodus 34:1–2.) From the Doctrine and Covenants we learn that the Melchizedek Priesthood holds the "key of the mysteries of the kingdom, even the key of the knowledge of God." The revelation then states that it is in the "ordinances" of that kingdom that the "power of godliness is manifest. And without the ordinances thereof, and the authority of the priesthood, the power of godliness is not manifest unto men in the flesh; For without this no man can see the face of God, even the Father, and live." Such were the privileges forfeited by Israel in her rebellion and apostasy. "This Moses plainly taught to the children of Israel in the wilderness, and sought diligently to sanctify his people that they might behold the face of God; But they hardened their hearts and could not endure his presence; therefore, the Lord in his wrath, for his anger was kindled against them, swore that they should not enter into his rest while in the wilderness, which rest is the fulness of his glory. Therefore, he took Moses out of their midst, and the Holy Priesthood also." (D&C 84:19–25.)

A WARNING AND A PROMISE TO MODERN ISRAEL

Our ancient text is a sober warning to modern Israel, for we too have been invited to be a "peculiar treasure" unto the Lord, a "kingdom of priests, and an holy nation." We too must be sanctified and so live as to enter the presence of the Lord, even while in the flesh. And we too, if we turn to worship the idols of the world and fail to honor our covenants, will have that priesthood, its power, its blessings, and its ordinances taken from us by a God who is the same yesterday, today, and forever. If the Lord is to be in our midst, as he has promised, we must live for that privilege. Teaching this same principle to the meridian Saints, Paul said: "For unto us was the gospel preached, as well as unto them [Moses and the children of Israel]: but the word preached did not profit them, not being mixed with faith in them that heard it. . . . And they to whom it was first preached entered not in because of unbelief." (Hebrews 4:2, 6.)

To the faithful of Israel in our day the Lord has promised:

Therefore, I will raise up unto my people a man, who shall lead them like as Moses led the children of Israel.

For ye are the children of Israel, and of the seed of Abraham, and ye must needs be led out of bondage by power, and with a stretched-out arm.

And as your fathers were led at the first, even so shall the redemption of Zion be.

Therefore, let not your hearts faint, for I say not unto you as I said unto your fathers: Mine angel shall go up before you, but not my presence.

But I say unto you: Mine angels shall go up before you, and also my presence, and in time ye shall possess the goodly land. (D&C 103:16—20.)

PILLARS OF FIRE AND OF THE CLOUD

When the sanctuary was completed, the cloud which had evidenced the protection and presence of the Lord from the beginning of their wilderness march filled the dwelling. When the Israelites were fleeing Egypt this same cloud moved from its position in leading Israel to the rear of their camp to separate them from their enemies. This phenomenon was a cloud of darkness to the Egyptians while giving light to the camp of Israel. (See Exodus 14:19—20.) So glorious was the cloud in filling the tabernacle that even Moses was unable to enter the sanctuary. The cloud afterwards drew back into the most holy place, to dwell there above the outspread wings of the cherubim of the ark of the covenant, so that Moses and (eventually) the priests were able to enter the holy place and perform the required service there without violating the sacredness of the Holy of Holies.

So long as the cloud rested upon the tabernacle the children of Israel remained encamped; when it ascended, they broke up the encampment to proceed onward. Thus the cloud by day or the pillar of fire by night became the sign for camping and for breaking camp and moving forward until the time their wilderness journey ended. (Exodus 40:34—38.) Such was the symbol of the divine presence. Their path could only be that path in which he led them, and it must be in the patience of faith that they waited upon him. "Whether it was by day or by night . . . , whether it were two days, or a month, or a year," they journeyed or rested at his command (Numbers 9:21—22). Further, the cloud was a symbol of his presence and their right to appear before him and seek his blessings. Yet they were still forbidden to go directly to his throne. The barrier which sin had erected between the Holy One and this unholy nation was not yet taken away. To this end a law had been given, a law to remind them that no unclean thing could enter his presence.

THE ARK OF THE COVENANT

When Israel marched they were instructed that the ark of the covenant was to go before them; otherwise it was to occupy the most holy place within the sanctuary. As with the pillar of fire and the cloud, the ark was a symbol of the presence of the Lord. It will be remembered that those who rebelled at Kadeshbarnea and attempted to possess the land of promise without the ark fell by the sword (Numbers 14:40—45). In contrast, when the soles of the feet of the priests carrying the ark touched the water of the Jordan River, it parted so that all of Israel could walk through on dry ground (Joshua 3:13—16).

REBELLION AND SPIRITUAL DEATH

Other than Moses, none were held in higher esteem among the camp of Israel than his sister, Miriam the prophetess, and his brother, Aaron the high priest. Both had been richly endowed with spiritual gifts and both had spoken and prophesied in the name of the Lord (Numbers 12:2). It appears that both drank too deeply of the sweet wine of pride, the dregs of which leave the bitter aftertaste of jealousy. Intoxicated by such foolish spirits, they brought accusation against Moses and claimed themselves his equal. This strange story has its counterparts in our day. It will be remembered that Oliver Cowdery, in the very early days of the Church, commanded Joseph Smith to erase certain words from a revelation that he had received (HC 1:104—5). And William McLellin thought himself quite capable of writing revelations the equal of Joseph Smith's, at least until he attempted to do so (HC 1:226).

That Miriam was the instigator of this rebellion needs no other proof than the punishment God inflicted upon her, though her role is hinted at by the placing of her name before Aaron's in the Bible story (Numbers 12:1). Together they could do no better for an accusation against Moses than that of his having "married an Ethiopian woman," a marriage he had entered into long before he had been called of God.

Moses in perfect humility made no response, though the Lord was not slow to speak. The three children of Amram were immediately summoned to appear together before the judgment seat, to which the Lord had descended in a pillar of cloud. Aaron and Miriam were called to come forward. To them the Lord said: "If there be a prophet among you, I the Lord will make myself known unto him in a vision, and will speak unto him in a dream. My servant Moses is not so, who is faithful in all mine house. With him will I speak mouth to mouth, even apparently, and not in dark speeches [riddles]; and the similitude of the Lord shall he behold: wherefore then were ye not afraid to speak against my servant Moses?" (Numbers 12:6—8.) Moses was the dispensation head; until the day of Christ all other prophets would but echo that which had been revealed through him.

The matter did not end with this expression of the Lord. He was still angry, and immediately upon his departure Miriam was stricken with leprosy. Seeing his sister thus smitten, Aaron, fully aware of his own guilt, sought Moses to heal her. Moses importuned the Lord to do so and was told that she was to remain outside of the camp of Israel for seven days before she was to be admitted again (Numbers 12:14).

As we shall see in the chapter that follows, leprosy was a symbol to ancient Israel of the corruption of sin. Because it was contagious, lepers were banished from the camp of Israel. The afflicted were thought of as dead. Thus this loathsome and dreaded disease provided the perfect type to represent spiritual death. Dramatically, Miriam and those of all future generations were here warned that jealousy and evil speaking of those the Lord has called place the accuser in jeopardy of contracting the most loathsome of spiritual diseases, banishment from the society of his people, and ultimate spiritual death.

THE TWELVE SPIES

After Miriam had been cleansed and readmitted to the camp of Israel they marched into the wilderness of Paran. It was here that the Lord commanded Moses to send men to search the land of Canaan. Moses formed the group by choosing one of the chief rulers from each of the tribes. Oshea of the tribe of Ephraim was apparently designated to be their leader. Not satisfied with Oshea's name, however, Moses changed it to Joshua (Numbers 13:16). Thus Moses chose twelve men, the "heads of the children of Israel," to act as guides to show Israel the way from their wilderness wanderings to their promised land. He set one at their head and specified that he was to be called Joshua. As earlier noted, Joshua is the Hebrew form of the name Jesus. The story is an obvious type, saying to Israel of all future generations that the only way they can escape the wilderness of life and obtain the eternal inheritance promised them is to follow Jesus and the Twelve.

AN ATTEMPT TO USURP PRIESTHOOD

Among the epic lessons of the wilderness years, none is of greater interest than the Korah rebellion (Numbers 16). Korah, a Levite, along with Dathan and Abiram of the tribe of Reuben, led two hundred and fifty of the leaders of the church, all "men of renown," to challenge the authority of Moses and Aaron. From a restoration of text in the Joseph Smith Translation we learn that Korah, who held the Aaronic Priesthood, desired to hold the higher or Melchizedek Priesthood held by Moses and Aaron (JST, Numbers 16:10). The Reubenites involved in this sedition may have been seeking that same authority. Theirs would have been the birthright tribe had it not been for the sin of their ancestral father. Our story finds them seeking the authority to officiate in the sacred rituals of the tabernacle.

Moses responded first to Korah and his company, suggesting a test that would afford a sure answer as to whom the Lord desired to function in the priestly office. He invited the rebels to appear on the morrow in the holy place of the tabernacle with censers to perform the sacred priestly function. There the Lord could manifest his approval of or displeasure with their action.

The test was fairly put. All Israel knew that no unclean thing could stand in the presence of the Lord and live. Further, all knew that Aaron's sons Nadab and Abihu had been devoured by fire when they improperly attempted to perform the same ordinance (Leviticus 10:1—3).

Moses also sought to counsel with Dathan and Abiram, but they bitterly refused to speak with him. The following morning the two hundred and fifty princes of Israel took their censers, entered the holy place, and functioned in the stead of the authorized priests. In the meantime Moses stood before the tents of Korah, Dathan, and Abiram, and said: "Hereby ye shall know that the Lord hath sent me to do all these works; for I have not done them of mine own mind. If these men die the common death of all men, or if they be visited after the visitation of all men; then the Lord hath not sent me. But if the Lord make a new thing, and the earth open her mouth, and swallow them up, with all that appertain unto them, and they go down quick into the pit; then ye shall understand that these men have provoked the Lord." Immediately the earth opened and swallowed Moses' three chief antagonists "and all that appertained to them." At the same time a fire from the Lord consumed the two hundred and fifty men that had offered incense. (Numbers 16:28—35.)

The judgment on Korah, his company, and the would-be priests filled the camp of Israel with terror, yet it did not change the hearts of those in rebellion. The next morning the whole congregation began to murmur against Moses and his brother, accusing them of having killed the people of the Lord. Their murmurings were met with a wrathful judgment; a deadly plague immediately began to spread among the people. Moses directed Aaron to go quickly with his censer, coals, and incense to the holy place and make expiation for the congregation. Thus the plague was stayed (though not until 14,700 were to die) and it was abundantly evident to Israel that it was God's wrath that had opened the earth and brought forth the fires of heaven the previous day, not some occult powers of Moses and Aaron.

Further, Israel then understood that only by the intervention of one who held the proper authority could the ravages of the plague be stayed. The temporal salvation granted by Aaron's ministration typified the power of him who as the great high priest would yet save all mankind from an endless death.

Moses and his people were once more reconciled.

THE ROD OF AARON

The Lord's acceptance of Aaron and his house as his priestly ministers, as evidenced by the staying of the plague when Aaron made the high-priestly offering, was immediately confirmed for all the families of Israel. Moses was directed to have each tribe bring a rod with its tribal name written upon it. These twelve rods were then taken and placed before the Lord in the Holy of Holies within the tabernacle.

Moses had been told that the rod representing those chosen to minister for the Lord would be made to blossom. In this manner the Lord could indicate if the sacred dignity of this office was to be shared by all the tribes, and if not, to which tribe or tribes it should be extended. The following morning when Moses went to the sacred place he found the rod of Aaron covered with buds, blossoms, and even mature almonds. The other rods remained as barren as before. (Numbers 17.)

The symbolism associated with this test was most deliberate: A rod, or branch, had been chosen to represent each of the twelve tribes or families of Israel, each had its name carefully placed upon it. By tradition the rod, as a staff or sceptre, represented one's position and authority. Together all were presented before the Lord. By making Aaron's rod bud, blossom, and put forth fruit, the Lord demonstrated once again that it was for him to choose those who will stand in his stead, be filled with his power, and bring forth his fruits.

God then commanded that Aaron's rod be taken back into the sanctuary and preserved as "a token against the rebels," that they murmur not, lest "they die." The preservation of the rod before the ark of the covenant, in the immediate presence of the Lord, was a pledge to Aaron of the continuance of his call and the permanent duration of his priesthood.

Water Flows from a Rock

In the fortieth year of their wanderings the camp of Israel found themselves in Kadeshi, the very place where the ban had been passed thirty-seven and a half years earlier forbidding that generation from entering the land of promise. As our wilderness story concludes, once again the children of Israel find themselves without water, and once again we find them murmuring against their prophet. Moses sought direction of the Lord and was told to take his rod (not to be confused with the rod of Aaron), gather the assembly of Israel, and in their presence command a rock to bring forth water. This Moses did, saying, "Hear now, ye rebels; must we fetch you water out of this rock?" He then smote the rock twice with his rod "and the water came out abundantly." (Numbers 20:10—11.)

Thereupon the Lord said to Moses, "Because ye believed me not, to sanctify me in the eyes of the children of Israel, therefore ye shall not bring this congregation into the land which I have given them" (Numbers 20:12). It is often concluded that Moses sinned in not speaking to the rock but striking it instead. The Psalmist recorded that Moses' error was in speaking "unadvisedly," the inference being that he and Aaron were improperly taking credit for the miracle by saying "we" fetch you water (Psalm 106:32—33). Such would accord with the expression of the Lord to our dispensation wherein he said, "In nothing doth man offend God, or against none is his wrath kindled, save those who confess not his hand in all things, and obey not his commandments" (D&C 59:21).

Though the precise nature of Moses' transgression is not clear, this event perfectly illustrates that everyone, irrespective of office or position, from Moses and Aaron to the least of Israel, must endure in faith and obedience to the end of life's journey if he is to be privileged to obtain his land of promise.

The Brazen Serpent

As Israel circled Edom en route to the point at which they would cross the Jordan, they found the way hard and again became greatly discouraged. Once more we find them speaking against God and against Moses. "Wherefore have ye brought us up out of Egypt to die in the wilderness? for there is no bread, neither is there any water; and our soul loatheth this light bread," they complained. Their thankless grumbling was properly rewarded with a plague of fiery flying snakes, whose venom was as poisonous to the body as their evil words were to the soul. Many died of their bite.

Realizing they had brought this curse upon themselves, a repentant people pleaded with Moses to persuade the Lord to remove the snakes from them. Moses was commanded to make a serpent of brass and raise it as a standard, with the promise that any bitten by the serpents could by looking upon it in faith be healed. (Numbers 21:4—9.)

The incident is one of the best known of the Old Testament types. Christ interpreted it, saying: "As Moses lifted up the serpent in the wilderness, even so must the Son of man be lifted up: That whosoever believeth in him should not perish, but have eternal life" (John 3:14—15). Nephi told us that still there were many of their number who refused to look upon the brazen serpent because of "the simpleness of the way, or the easiness of it," and thus they died (1 Nephi 17:41). Well may we suppose that it will ever be that in like manner men will eschew faith in Christ, repentance from sin, and the healing waters of baptism, because of the "simpleness of the way," and die in the anguish of their sins.

We end our brief account of the wilderness journey with the story of the brazen serpent and its testimony of the coming of Christ, for it reflects the meaning and purpose of all that has preceded it.

7

The Law
of Moses

The gospel in its fulness was on the earth from the time of Adam to the time of Moses. Because of their rebellion, as we have seen in the two preceding chapters, the children of Israel lost the right to that gospel, its ordinances, and its priesthood. Responding to the question, Was the Melchizedek Priesthood taken when the Lord took Moses from the midst of Israel? Joseph Smith said, "All Priesthood is Melchizedek, but there are different portions or degrees of it. That portion which brought Moses to speak with God face to face was taken away; but that which brought the ministry of angels remained." (*Teachings,* p. 180.) In keeping with the statement of the Prophet that there is but one priesthood, it ought also to be said that there is but one gospel, one plan of salvation, and one Christ. As the Aaronic or Levitical Priesthood is to the Melchizedek, so the law of Moses is to the fulness of the gospel. We do not understand it to be another gospel, for there can be no other gospel; it is rather a partial manifestation of that gospel to which were added performances, ordinances, and restrictions designed to keep Israel in constant remembrance of God and their duty to him.

In its weakness Israel was given a law of carnal commandments (D&C 84:27; JST, Exodus 34:2). The concept of carnal commandments does not refer to the lusts of the flesh alone, but rather to all that is worldly as contrasted with the things of the

Spirit. The law was replete with daily reminders that Israel was to be a people set apart and consecrated to the Lord and that in all things they must keep themselves clean and pure. Virtually all aspects of their lives were drawn upon as types or reminders of who and what they were to be. Birth and death, seedtime and harvest time, their diet, the manner in which food was prepared, their Sabbaths and feast times, even diseases and restoration to health, were all used to typify their obligations to God. The law also contained a host of sacrificial rituals that served to keep constantly before them their dependence on the great sacrifice yet to be offered by the Son of God.

In addition to the carnal law, Israel enjoyed a portion of the gospel law, including the invitation to exercise faith in Christ, repent, and be baptized by immersion for the remission of sins. Further, they held the keys of the administration of angels through those of the tribe of Levi, who held the lesser or Aaronic Priesthood. (D&C 84:26–27; 107:20.) Together the carnal law and the lesser portion of the gospel law enjoyed by Israel constituted a "preparatory gospel," its purpose being to prepare them to accept Christ and receive once again the gospel in its fulness.

DIFFICULTIES IN UNDERSTANDING THE MOSAIC LAW

1. The Mosaic system was a mixture of carnal and eternal laws. Until more has been revealed, one unsolvable difficulty facing the student of the Mosaic system is untangling the carnal portion of the law from that which is a part of the fulness of the gospel. Some rituals that were included in the Mosaic system, such as animal sacrifice, were had from the time of Adam and will yet be a part of the restoration of all things. All other portions of the law—that is, the carnal portions—were done away in Christ. Teaching this principle, Joseph Smith said,

> It is generally supposed that sacrifice was entirely done away when the Great Sacrifice, the sacrifice of the Lord Jesus was offered up, and that there will be no necessity for the ordinance of sacrifice in future; but those who assert this are certainly not acquainted with the duties, privileges and authority of the Priesthood, or with the Prophets.

The offering of sacrifice has ever been connected and forms a part of the duties of the Priesthood. It began with the Priesthood, and will be continued until after the coming of Christ, from generation to generation. We frequently have mention made of the offering of sacrifice by the servants of the Most High in ancient days, prior to the law of Moses; which ordinances will be continued when the Priesthood is restored with all its authority, power and blessings. (*Teachings*, p. 172.)

It is to be remembered that Malachi foretold a day when the sons of Levi would offer an offering unto the Lord in righteousness and that such could happen only after they had been purged and purified. "Then," he said, "shall the offering of Judah and Jerusalem be pleasant unto the Lord, as in the days of old, and as in former years" (Malachi 3:3—4). Nothing even resembling the fulfillment of this prophecy took place in the ministry of Christ. It remains to be fulfilled, and to that end on May 15, 1829, John the Baptist appeared to Joseph Smith and Oliver Cowdery on the banks of the Susquehanna River, near Harmony, Pennsylvania, and restored the priesthood of Aaron with all the keys and authority had anciently. This priesthood, he said, "shall never be taken again from the earth, until the sons of Levi do offer again an offering unto the Lord in righteousness" (D&C 13). This offering is to be made by literal sons of Levi and should not be confused with the offering to be made by the adopted sons of Moses and Aaron which will involve genealogical and temple work (D&C 84:31—32; 128:24).

Joseph Smith indicated that certain sacrifices,

as well as every ordinance belonging to the Priesthood, will, when the Temple of the Lord shall be built, and the sons of Levi be purified, be fully restored and attended to in all their powers, ramifications, and blessings. This ever did and ever will exist when the powers of the Melchizedek Priesthood are sufficiently manifest; else how can the restitution of all things spoken of by the Holy Prophets be brought to pass. It is not to be understood that the law of Moses will be established again with all its rites and variety of ceremonies; this has never been spoken of by the prophets; but those things which existed prior to Moses' day, namely, sacrifice, will be continued. (*Teachings,* p. 173.)

2. The Melchizedek Priesthood was never fully taken. The difficulty of untangling the pre-Mosaic ritual from that which was given as a part of the carnal law is further complicated by the fact that the Melchizedek Priesthood, though taken from the people generally, was always had in Old Testament times. Joseph Smith said, "All the prophets had the Melchizedek Priesthood and were ordained by God himself" (*Teachings,* p. 181). Moses, Aaron, and at least the quorum of the seventy all held that priesthood. Certainly Joshua held the Melchizedek Priesthood when he succeeded Moses as prophet, seer, and revelator. When Lehi and his sons left the Old World they held the Melchizedek Priesthood, though they were fully obedient to the demands of the Mosaic system. Nephi explained, "Notwithstanding we believe in Christ, we keep the law of Moses, and look forward with steadfastness unto Christ, until the law shall be fulfilled. For, for this end was the law given; wherefore the law hath become dead unto us, and we are made alive in Christ because of our faith; yet we keep the law because of the commandments." (2 Nephi 25:24—25.)

The law of Moses was faithfully observed by the Saints in the Americas before the coming of Christ. Alma explained, "For it was expedient that they should keep the law of Moses as yet, for it was not all fulfilled. But notwithstanding the law of Moses, they did look forward to the coming of Christ, considering that the law of Moses was a type of his coming, and believing that they must keep those outward performances until the time that he should be revealed unto them." (Alma 25:15.) Obviously there were those in the Old World, like those in the New, who had the fulness of the gospel while rendering obedience to the law of Moses.

From revelations given to Joseph Smith we also learn that at least some temple ordinances, including washing and anointing, were administered to the children of Israel in the tabernacle in the wilderness (D&C 124:37—39).

3. Another of the primary difficulties in understanding the law of Moses is the loss of Bible texts. Nephi prophesied that

"many parts" of the Bible record "which are plain and most precious; and also many covenants of the Lord" would be taken from it (1 Nephi 13:26). By revelation we know that the doctrines of faith, repentance, and baptism were had from the beginning, and that they were a fundamental part of the law of Moses. Since they have been taken from the Old Testament the Christian world has falsely supposed that they were not had until the time of Christ, and that the Old Testament represents a system of evolving religious ethics that reached its zenith with Christ. Because of the things taken from the Bible a full understanding of the Mosaic code will have to wait until those things are restored.

4. Changing circumstances brought some changes in the law. Some changes were made in the manner of observance and in the ritualistic performances from time to time according to the circumstances and needs of the people. For instance, the Passover was conducted differently in Palestine than it was in Egypt.

5. Hosts of uninspired things were added to the law. Many additions and perversions of the Mosaic system were evident in Christ's day. Christ, who gave the law, rendered perfect obedience to it and yet was constantly accused by the Pharisees of violating it (*Teachings,* pp. 276–77). The law had become so encumbered with rabbinic restrictions that Christ told his accusers, you have "made the commandment of God of none effect by your tradition" (Matthew 15:6). The law of the Sabbath, as an illustration, had been hopelessly lost in a forest of rabbinic tradition.

6. The traditions of the Jews are of little or no help in our attempt to understand the Mosaic system. Had they understood their own law it would have led them to Christ. Since the destruction of the temple in Jerusalem, nearly two thousand years ago, there have been no sacrificial rites practiced among them. Even in their system of synagogue worship no pretense is made to having priesthood or of complying with the complexities of the Levitical order. Surely this is but a silent admission that both the knowledge and the authority of the ancient system are lost to them.

Were it essential for us to fully understand the Mosaic system it would be fully restored to us. The carnal law has served its purpose and was done away in Christ. Those parts of the law that are essential to salvation have been restored along with the necessary keys, authority, and instructions.

Yet among the fragments of the law preserved for us we may freely glean. Indeed we are obligated to do so, not with the idea of reinstituting any of its rituals, feasts, or provisions, for such would be a mockery of the Atonement and a dead work, but rather for the purpose of identifying the timeless and eternal principles that the ancient system was given to teach. The effort to do this is marvelously rewarding, as we shall shortly see.

The Authority of the Mosaic Law

We must clearly understand that the law of Moses was a divinely ordained system. God was its author, Moses was its mediator, heaven was its origin, and eternal truth was its substance. If Jesus of Nazareth was not the Christ, then the provisions of the law of Moses would still be in effect and all faithful souls would render obedience to it. There was more truth and authority in the law of Moses than can be found in the combination of all the churches of the world. Its priesthood and laws were the offspring of a heavenly system and bore its image and likeness. Every detail of its ritual was dictated by the heavens. It was God's system, not man's. Israel was to be God's vineyard and the fruits his. How timeless the declaration, "Ye have not chosen me, but I have chosen you, and ordained you, that ye should go and bring forth fruit" (John 15:16).

Symbols, Similitudes, and Substitutes

As every doctrine in the fulness of the gospel grows out of or is an appendage to the Atonement, so every ritual of the Mosaic law pointed to Christ and his atoning sacrifice. "This is the whole meaning of the law," Amulek explained, "every whit pointing to that great and last sacrifice; and that great and last sacrifice will be the Son of God, yea, infinite and eternal" (Alma 34:14). Further, the entirety of the law of Moses was symbolic. It was a system of vicarious ordinances, all of which had as their purpose to center attention and faith in the great vicarious ordinances that brought life and hope of salvation to all who would believe. The doctrines of atonement, redemption, punishment, and forgiveness were all taught through vicarious offerings. The bullock, lamb, goat, ox, and dove were all substitutes, the lifeblood of each being offered in behalf of the one sacrificing. The whole system was one of vicarious ordinances and proxies, all pointing to the great vicarious sacrifice and the great proxy for us all.

THE DAY OF ATONEMENT

The concept of substitution or vicarious ordinances is perhaps best seen in Israel's annual commemoration of the Day of Atonement. In the fall of each year on the tenth day of the seventh month, Israel observed its Sabbath of Sabbaths, its most holy day, one which signified that the sins of Israel had been atoned for and that the nation and its people were restored to a state of fellowship with God. It was a day replete with types and shadows, a day of cleansing and a day of renewal. It was upon this day, and this day alone, that Israel's high priest entered the Holy of Holies, where he made atonement for the sins of the people.

Upon this day the high priest, he who held the office and position once given to Aaron, was to preside. He alone could stand as mediator for the people. Both a cleansing and a sacrificial ritual preceded his entrance into the Holy of Holies. He was first required to cleanse himself, then to clothe entirely in white linen garments (this in distinction to the golden garments which he otherwise wore). On this day he was to make a sin offering (a young bullock) and a burnt offering (a ram) for himself and his own family. These were to be purchased with his own money. From the public treasury he was to purchase two young goats for a sin offering, and a ram for a burnt offering. These he sacrificed in behalf of the people. By lot one of the goats was to be designated as the goat of the Lord, the name Jehovah being placed upon him. (*Promised Messiah*, p. 436.) The other goat was to carry the name Azazel, the root of which means "wholly to put aside," or "wholly to go away" (*The Temple*, p. 324). This was the scapegoat. The goat of the Lord was to be offered as the sin offering. When the high priest entered the Holy of Holies he would take the blood of this goat and sprinkle it on the lid of the ark of the covenant. Later he would lay his hands on the head of the live goat and confess all the sins and iniquities of his people. This goat was then led off into the wilderness. (See Leviticus 16.)

In his epistle to the Hebrews, Paul shows how the law of Moses and particularly the ritual associated with the Day of Atonement was an outward ordinance or type that was fulfilled in Christ. He described the tabernacle as "a worldly sanctuary" where the sacrificial ordinances performed on the Day of Atonement prefigured the atoning sacrifice of Christ. These ordinances were to remain "until the time of reformation," when Christ should come as a high priest of "a greater and more perfect tabernacle," to prepare himself and all men, by the shedding of his own blood, to obtain "eternal redemption for us." Paul described the Mosaic covenant as a "shadow of good things to come, . . . for it is not possible that the blood of bulls and of goats should take away sins. . . . But this man, after he had offered one sacrifice for sins for ever, sat down on the right hand of God." (Hebrews 9 and 10.)

"Knowing, as we do, that sins are remitted in the waters of baptism; that baptisms were the order of the day in Israel; and that provision must be made for repentant persons to free themselves from sins committed after baptism—we see in the annual performances of the Day of Atonement one of the Lord's provisions for renewing the covenant made in the waters of baptism and receiving anew the blessed purity that comes from full obedience to the law involved. In our day we gain a similar state of purity by partaking worthily of the sacrament of the Lord's supper." (*Promised Messiah*, p. 436.)

In his epistle to the Hebrews, Paul shows how the law of Moses and particularly the ritual associated with the Day of Atonement was an outward ordinance or a type which was fulfilled in Christ. Israel, Paul explained, had her tabernacle with its altar, ark, veil, and holy of holies, in which sacrifices and cleansing ordinances were performed. All of these the Holy Ghost manifested were in similitude of the coming ministry of the Son of God. Through those ordinances Israel anciently gained a forgiveness of sins because of their faith in the future coming of Christ, which the ordinances foreshadowed. That Christ, Paul testified, had now come, and in fulfillment of the ancient type had shed his own blood and entered into the eternal Holy of Holies, and thus those who embraced and served him in faith could also receive a remission of sins. (See Hebrews 9.)

THE FIRSTFRUITS

Another ritual of the Mosaic system laden with symbolism was that of the offering of the firstfruits. These offerings were essentially of two kinds: those offered by an individual or family, and those offered for the entire nation of Israel. The offering made for both the individual and nation shared meaning in that both constituted an acknowledgment of Israel's indebtedness to God and that all blessings both temporal and spiritual come from him. The yearly presentation of their firstfruits in the temple manifested their relationship with God as one in which they gratefully received at his hand all that they enjoyed, and solemnly dedicated it and themselves to him. The ritual was an acknowledgment that the Lord was master and that they sought only to be wise stewards of his property. Their daily bread they would seek and receive only at his hand, use it with thanksgiving, and employ it in his service—and this, their dependence upon God, was their joyous freedom, in which Israel declared itself the redeemed people of the Lord.

As a family feast the presentation of the firstfruits would enter more than any other rite into family religion and family life. Not a child in Israel—at least of those who inhabited the Holy Land [for only that grown in the Holy Land was thus sacrificed]—could have been ignorant of all connected with this service, and that even though it had never been taken to the beautiful "city of the Great King," nor gazed with marvel and awe at the Temple of Jehovah. For scarcely had a brief Eastern spring merged into early summer, when with the first appearance of ripening fruit, whether on the ground or on trees, each household would prepare for this service. The head of the family . . . accompanied by his child, would go into his field and mark off certain portions from among the most promising of the crop. For only the best might be presented to the Lord, and it was set apart before it was yet ripe, and solemn dedication being, however, afterwards renewed, when it was actually cut. Thus, each time any one would go into the field, he would be reminded of the ownership of Jehovah, till the reapers cut down the golden harvest. (*The Temple*, pp. 380–81.)

Jeremiah explained the type. Israel was the Lord's firstfruits and as such had been consecrated to him; all that sought to devour Israel sought that which was the Lord's, and evil would come upon them (Jeremiah 2:3).

There were two firstfruit offerings that were public or national. The first was associated with the Passover and involved a sheaf of grain; the second took place at Pentecost using loaves of bread. At the time of Christ the sheaf offering was accomplished as follows: The wave-sheaf was to be taken from the neighborhood of Jerusalem. Deputies from the Sanhedrin went out on the eve of the festival, and tied the growing stalks in bunches. In the evening of the festival day the sheaf was cut with all possible publicity, and carried to the Temple. It was there threshed, and an omer of grain after being winnowed, was bruised and roasted: after it had been mixed with oil and frankincense laid upon it, the priest waved the offering in all directions. (*The Temple*, pp. 256–59.) The waving of the sheaf of the firstfruits took place "on the morrow after the sabbath," immediately following the Passover (Leviticus 23:11), this being the very time of year when Christ actually burst the bonds of death.

The offering made at the feast of the Pentecost was a thanksgiving offering noting the conclusion of the wheat harvest. It consisted of two loaves of new flour baked with leaven, which were waved by the priest as were the sheaves at the Passover. These first loaves appear to be a type for the firstfruits of those gathered by Christ in the gospel harvest, who were on that day filled with a marvelous outpouring of the Holy Ghost as they commenced their labors among those of all nations. (Acts 2.)

The Law of Sacrifice

Nothing was more basic to the Mosaic system than the law of sacrifice. The variety of sacrifices included offerings of cereals (rendered "meat offerings" in the KJV) and various animal offerings. There were public sacrifices, offered by the priests on behalf of the whole community, and also private offerings made by individuals or families. Five basic offerings are described in the book of Leviticus: the burnt offering, the meal offering, the peace offering, the sin offering, and the trespass offering. Let us briefly examine each.

The burnt offering

The burnt offering involved the presentation of a male animal (bull, ram, goat—if fowls, either turtledoves or young pigeons) without blemish at the door of the congregation. The one offering the sacrifice would then place his hands upon the head of the animal, thus dedicating it to God as a vicarious representation of himself or those for whom the ordinance was being performed. The sacrificer would then slaughter the animal. The priests would take its blood and sprinkle it upon the altar, and after properly preparing the animal they would place it upon the altar, where it was to be entirely consumed. (See Leviticus 1:1—3.) Because this offering could only be accepted from one either sinless or already purified from sin, it was always preceded by a sin offering (*Offerings*, pp. 61, 138).

Apparently this is the same ordinance had from the time of Adam (Moses 5:7). As such, it is not properly thought of as a part of the Mosaic system. It also appears that it will be this same offering that will be offered by the sons of Levi in fulfillment of the prophecies of Malachi and John the Baptist, and the promise of Joseph Smith (Malachi 3:3—4; D&C 13; *Teachings*, pp. 172—73).

Adam was told that this sacrifice was in similitude of the atoning sacrifice of Christ (Moses 5:7). In the Mosaic system, Christ can be seen as the sacrificial offering, the priest, and the offerer. That he is vicariously represented by the male animal without blemish is most obvious. In the entirety of the Mosaic system the priest is to be seen as the mediator standing between God and man. Hence the Levitical priest was always to be seen as the representation of Christ. Nor has that order changed, for it is the priest in the Aaronic or Levitical Priesthood who kneels at the sacramental altar to bless both bread and water in our weekly sacramental ritual (D&C 20:46). In the instance of the burnt offering Christ can also be seen as the offerer, at least in the sense that he, above all, must comply with all ritual "to fulfill all righteousness."

It should be observed here that no single type can adequately represent Christ. Thus the necessity for many emblems and the propriety of these emblems carrying a multiplicity of meanings. As with the shadows cast by light, these spiritual reflections cast various shapes and figures according to the position from which they are viewed. Though gospel principles do not vary, we can constantly expand our perspective of them. None can properly say of their understanding of gospel principles, "We have enough" or "We understand in full."

Among the offerings, only the burnt offering was to be entirely consumed. This was a type connoting the necessity of complete submission to the will of God, with the attendant idea of total dedication to his service. When we covenant to live the law of sacrifice we are announcing that our sacrifice will in like manner be one of complete submission and total dedication. Our commitment is to give all our heart, might, mind, and strength. Further, the burnt offering was acceptable only when preceded by a sin offering. As a "sweet savor" offering, it, like proper service to God, must be offered in righteousness and purity. It was an offering seeking acceptance rather than expiation for sin.

The meat offering

Like the burnt offering, the meat offering was a "sweet savor" offering. It is not associated with the idea of sin but is rather the representation of man in perfect obedience giving to God that which is acceptable and pleasing to Him. Unlike the burnt offering, it did not represent the giving of life. The ingredients were "fine flour," oil, and frankincense. It was to be burnt upon the altar but not entirely consumed. That which was not burned was to be eaten by Aaron and his sons. No leaven or honey was to be used in the offering, while every oblation was to be seasoned with salt. (See Leviticus 2.)

As would be anticipated, the ritual is rich with symbolism. This bread offering obviously represented Christ as the bread of life. The fine flour, or bruised corn as Isaiah called it (Isaiah 28:28), represented Christ in the deepest of suffering. It may also betoken that there is no unevenness in him. The oil was the constant emblem of the Holy Spirit. As the oil was poured on the flour, so the Holy Ghost would descend upon the Messiah or Anointed One as he commenced his ministry. Frankincense brought to the offering sweetness and fragrance. All were inseparably mixed together. Honey and leaven were forbidden, for these are agents of corruption, and none such were to touch the symbol of our salvation. The last ingredient was salt, which stood in opposition to honey and leaven, as the agent of preservation.

The peace offering

The peace offering was given either in thanksgiving or as a vow offering. It was an offering of the flock, either male or female without blemish. It too was a "sweet savor" offering, meaning that it was not associated with atonement for sin but with the desire to be fully acceptable to the Lord. It was a giving of that which was sweet and pleasant to the Lord. The ritual of presentation, laying on of hands, and slaughtering of the animal were the same as in the burnt offering. (See Leviticus 3.)

The symbolism is much the same as that of the burnt offering, differing, however, in that the peace offering was not entirely consumed on the altar. Both offerer and priest were fed upon that which was not symbolically consumed by God. In this respect it differed from all other offerings. God, man, priest, and even his family were all to partake of this offering and find satisfaction in it. However, none of the priest's family could eat of the offering unless they were clean (Leviticus 7:20). Such is the peace enjoyed only by those who can feast together in perfect unity and harmony.

The sin offering

The sin offering could be either a male or female animal or fowl without blemish. It involved the expiation of sin and as such was not a "sweet savor" offering. The offering was not entirely consumed by fire, but like the peace offering was eaten in a sacrificial meal as a part of the ritual. (See Leviticus 4.) The offering was for the forgiveness of sins committed in ignorance or in violation of covenants. It constituted a renewal of covenants much as we do in the partaking of the sacrament.

The sin offering apparently was burnt without the camp (Leviticus 4:12, 21). The other offerings were burnt on the altar in the tabernacle. The fulfillment of this type was found in the crucifixion of Christ. Paul announces its fulfillment in this language: "Wherefore Jesus also, that he might sanctify the people with his own blood, suffered without the gate" (Hebrews 13:12).

The trespass offering

As the name implies, the trespass offering, like the sin offering, is not one of "sweet savor." Of necessity the trespass offering had to be preceded by the sin offering (Leviticus 5:8). The trespass offering seems to differ from the sin offering in that it centers in overt acts, acts that wrong another and for which justice demands that restitution be made. The trespass offering required not only the life of the sacrificial animal but a payment to the injured party, the valuation of which was to be made by the priest and paid in shekels of the sanctuary. Then, in addition to this, a fifth part more, in shekels also, was added to the sum determined by the priest. All was given to the person trespassed against by the offender. (See Leviticus 5.) The sin offering centered on what one was, while the emphasis of the trespass offering centered on what one had done. The primary principle being taught was that of restitution.

Though the nature of the sacrificial laws was varied and complex, the principles upon which they operated were common to every gospel dispensation and are an inseparable part of the doctrine of salvation. Under the law no sacrifice was acceptable unless it was offered as God required. The offering, the place, the mode of sacrifice—all were specified in laborious detail. All were of God's design and of his choice. Anything other than exact compliance with these requirements as God had established them could not, by its very nature, be regarded as a true sacrifice. It is not for man to suggest alternatives to the partaking of the bitter cup, nor could the ordinances comply with their preordained types. One must comply with the letter in order to obtain the spirit. It was Nephi who observed that Christ, notwithstanding his holiness, rendered obedience to the outward ordinances of the law in order that he might "fulfill all righteousness. . . . How much more need have we, being unholy, to be baptized." (2 Nephi 31:5.)

It must also be observed that, according to the ancient system, no offering was regarded as efficacious unless it was sustained by righteousness. Without repentance there was no atonement made. The Psalmist wrote, "The sacrifices of God are a broken spirit: a broken and a contrite heart," for all others would God despise (Psalm 51:17). Sacrifice of an unrighteous man was declared to be mockery, for the "Most High is not pleased with the offering of the godless, nor do endless sacrifices win his forgiveness" (NEB, Ecclesiastes 34:18–19). Speaking to an apostate Israel through the Prophet Amos, the Lord said: "I despise your feast days, I will not smell in your solemn assemblies [I will not take heed of your sacrifices]. Though ye offer me burnt offerings and your meat offerings, I will not accept them: neither will I regard the peace offerings of your fat beasts. Take thou away from me the noise of thy songs; for I will not hear the melody of thy viols. But let judgment run down as waters, and righteousness as a mighty stream." (Amos 5:21–24.)

Righteousness was the lifeblood of every Old Testament sacrifice, and, as Paul said, without blood there is no sacrifice. All who see and read with an honest heart must acknowledge that this near-endless array of Old Testament types all bespeak the same truth—that man is saved by the grace of another's sacrifice *only* if he has sustained his faithful offering with works of righteousness!

PURIFICATION AND CONSECRATION

The Mosaic system consisted of a host of ritualistic reminders to Israel that they were a nation set apart, a nation consecrated to God and his service—and that as such they needed to be pure. Only that which was clean could enter into his presence. This was the purpose of their dietary laws, which delineated at great length between those animals which they were permitted to eat, designated as "clean," and those forbidden to them, designated as "unclean."

The Hebrew word for *clean* used in the dietary law reached far beyond that of physical cleanliness. Synonyms include *pure, unadulterated, uncontaminated, innocent,* and *holy.* a Jewish writer explaining these dietary laws observed:

> A hog could be raised in an incubator on antibiotics, bathed daily, slaughtered in a hospital operating room, and its carcass sterilized by ultra-violet rays, without rendering kosher the pork chops that it yields. "Unclean" in Leviticus is a ceremonial word. That is why the Torah says of camels and rabbits, "They are unclean *for you,* limiting the definition and the discipline to Israel. Chickens and goats, which we can eat, are scarcely cleaner by nature than eagles and lions, but the latter are in the class of the unclean. (Wouk, *This Is My God,* pp. 100—101; italics added.)

Like the Word of Wisdom, the ancient dietary law was first spiritual and only secondarily a health law. This principle has been overlooked in far too many discourses on the Word of Wisdom. Its primary purpose is to keep modern Israel clean— that is, pure, unadulterated, uncontaminated, innocent, and holy —in order that they might have the Holy Ghost as their constant companion. The health benefits are secondary. Of what particular value is it to live to a great age avoiding cancer if we are unworthy to associate with the Spirit of the Lord?

The Mosaic dietary code can only properly be understood when viewed as a symbol of a people consecrated or dedicated to the Lord. Every meal was a reminder to Israel of who they were and what they had covenanted to be. It has been suggested that strength comes from living such a law, vision from understanding it.

THE SABBATH

To such daily ritual as diet was added the commemoration of holy days, the most important and most frequent of which was the Sabbath. Like much of the sacrificial system in the Mosaic code, the Sabbath had existed from the days of Adam. It was given anew in the Decalogue, first as a commemoration of the Creation, and then as part of the lesser law to remind Israel of God's mercy in liberating them from their Egyptian bondage. It was to be a sign between Israel and their God whereby he would know them and they would know that he had consecrated them (Exodus 31:13). Anciently, as today, Sabbath observance was to be one of the solemn and distinctive features of the Lord's people. As renewed to gathering Israel in the last days the revelation states:

> Thou shalt offer a sacrifice unto the Lord thy God in righteousness, even that of a broken heart and a contrite spirit.
> And that thou mayest more fully keep thyself unspotted from the world, thou shalt go to the house of prayer and offer up thy sacraments upon my holy day;
> For verily this is a day appointed unto you to rest from your labors, and to pay thy devotions unto the Most High;
> Nevertheless thy vows shall be offered up in righteousness on all days and at all times;
> But remember that on this, the Lord's day, thou shalt offer thine oblations and thy sacraments unto the Most High, confessing thy sins unto thy brethren, and before the Lord. (D&C 59:8—12.)

Such was the order of the Sabbath anciently. On this day the daily sacrifices were doubled, and the people abstained from all manner of work and attended their holy assemblies, where they were instructed in the doctrines of the gospel.

Symbolism of Birth and Death

The Levitical code was a marvelous teaching device in which every physical defilement had its spiritual counterpart. "But especially was this the case with reference to birth and death, which were so closely connected with sin and the second death, with redemption and the second birth. Hence, all connected with the origin of life and with death, implied defilement, and required Levitical purification." (*The Temple*, pp. 343—44.) A woman who had given birth was ritually unclean for forty days if she had given birth to a male child, eighty days if the child was female. After that period she was to offer for her purification a lamb for a burnt offering and a pigeon or a dove for a sin offering; in case of poverty a dove or pigeon was substituted for the lamb. (Leviticus 12.) This was the offering made by Mary when she presented herself in the temple forty days after the birth of the Christ child. It was at this time that the redemption tax was paid if the child was the firstborn. This ritual of purification connected with the origin of life was not nearly as solemn or important as that necessary for the removal of defilement from contact with death.

So serious was that defilement which came by contact with death, that a very elaborate system of purification was necessary. The defilement lasted seven days and extended not only to those who had touched the dead, but also to the house or tent where the body had lain, and to all open vessels therein. Further, the law stated that "whosoever toucheth one that is slain with a sword in the open fields, or a dead body, or a bone of a man, or a grave, shall be unclean seven days" (Numbers 19:16). Even those touched by one who had been defiled became unclean (Numbers 19:22). For priests and Nazarites the law was even more stringent. The former were not to defile themselves by touching any dead body, except those of their nearest kin; the high priest was not even to approach the body of his own parents.

Purification was obtained in the following manner: An unblemished red heifer, which had never been yoked, was slain by the eldest son of the high priest outside the camp of Israel. A portion of its blood was sprinkled seven times toward the sanctuary; the rest of it, including the entire carcass, was then burned under the direction of the priest, who would cast into the fire cedar wood, hyssop, and scarlet. The ashes were then to be collected by a clean man and deposited in a clean place outside the camp. Then, when needed for the ritual of purification, a clean person would take some of the ashes and place them in a vessel, mix them with spring water, dip hyssop in it, and on the third and seventh days after contraction sprinkle those unclean with it. The tent or house and all the vessels in it were to be similarly purified. The one performing the ritual was also sprinkled and considered unclean until evening.

Although not always clear from our vantage point, every particular of the ritual had symbolic significance. Edersheim notes:

> Its application must have been so frequently necessary in every family and circle of acquaintances that the great truths connected with it were constantly kept in view of the people. In general, it may be stated, that the laws in regard to defilement were primarily intended as symbols of spiritual truths, and not for social, or sanitary purposes; though such results would also flow from them. Sin had rendered fellowship with God impossible; sin was death, and had wrought death, and the dead body as well as the spiritually dead soul were the evidence of its sway. (*The Temple*, p. 348.)

Obviously, the heifer without spot and blemish taken outside the camp of Israel, where its blood was shed, is a type of the atonement of Christ, whose blood was shed outside the city walls. Other details would not be as certain. One scholar suggests the following:

> The sex of the victim (female, and hence life-giving), its red color of blood, (the seat of life), its unimpaired vigor (never having borne the yoke), its youth, and the absence in it of spot or blemish, the cedar and the hyssop (possessing the qualities, the former of incorruption, the latter of purity), and the scarlet (again the color of blood)—all these symbolized life in its fullness and freshness as the antidote of death. At the same time the extreme virulence of the uncleanness is taught by the regulations that the victim should be wholly consumed outside the camp, whereas, generally certain parts were consumed on the altar, and the offal only outside the camp

(comp. Lev. iv. 11, 12); that the blood was sprinkled *towards*, not *before*, the sanctuary; that the officiating minister should be neither the high-priest, nor yet simply a priest but the *presumptive* high-priest, the office being too impure for the first, and too important for the second; that even the priest and the person that burnt the heifer were rendered unclean by reason of their contact with the victim; and, lastly, that the purification should be effected, not simply by the use of water, but of water mixed with ashes which served as a lye, and would therefore have peculiarly cleansing qualities. (Smith, *Dictionary* 3:2644.)

Of this we can be sure, that if death was intended to symbolize the wages of sin, then this purification ritual in all its detail points to the gift of God, which is eternal life, as it comes only through the sacrifice of his Son.

Leprosy a Type for Spiritual Death

The ritual of purification for one cured of leprosy is one of the most impressive and instructive of Levitical laws. Being both loathsome and infectious, leprosy served as the perfect physical counterpart for spiritual infection and spiritual death. As the leper was banished from the camp of Israel, so those whose spirits had been corrupted would be banished from the congregation of Israel, both in this life and in the world to come. In those instances in which the disease was cured it was required that the leper present himself to a priest, who alone was empowered to determine if he was free of the dreaded corruption. Similarly, those who have suffered serious spiritual corruption can only be readmitted to fellowship in the congregation of Israel when they have been judged clean by a bishop or other appropriate ecclesiastical officer. The ritual of fellowship was of two parts, separated from one another by an interval of seven days. The first was that of restoration to fellowship with the covenant nation; the second was that of restoration to fellowship with the Lord and his sanctuary.

In the first of these rituals the leper, now adjudged clean, was to present to the priest two birds "alive and clean," along with

cedar wood, scarlet wool, and hyssop. Under the priest's direction one of the birds was to be killed over a vessel filled with
spring water into which the blood would fall. The living bird,
along with the cedar wood, the scarlet thread, and the hyssop,
were then dipped into the mixture of blood and water. The unclean person was sprinkled seven times with this liquid and then
the bird was permitted to fly away. As with the other cleansing
rituals, the two birds were the vicarious representation of the
person seeking to be made clean; the first, dying by the shedding
of blood, represented the death of the natural or sinful man; the
bird set free represented the newness of life associated with
proper fellowship with Israel. Again, the cedar wood symbolized
the need to avoid that which corrupts or decays, the scarlet wool
typified the atoning blood of Christ, and the hyssop bespoke the
constant necessity of purity. These are among the most essential
elements associated with spiritual life. The mixture of blood and
water symbolized the elements of birth or newness of life, and
announced again the inseparable nature of the blood of atonement and the waters of purification. Once more we are being told
that the blood of atonement does not stand alone but gains the
power of salvation when associated with water, which symbolizes the need to be clean and pure. The candidate was
sprinkled seven times with this mixture of water and blood as a
token of the covenant. The cleansing ritual was concluded by the
candidate's washing his clothes, shaving his hair, and washing
himself. He could then enter the camp of Israel but had to stay
outside his tent for seven days, thus emphasizing that something
was still lacking before he was fully of Israel, though the first
part of the cleansing ritual was now complete.

After the interval of seven days the washing was repeated and
the shaving more rigidly performed to include the eyebrows and
all the hair of his body. The shaving of the hair may have been to
give the likeness of a newborn infant; the washing was clearly the
symbol of cleansing. The following day the one to be cleansed
was presented at the door of the tabernacle by the priest with the
offerings for the Lord. The offerings were to consist of two he-
lambs without blemish, one ewe of the first year without blemish, three-tenths of an ephah of flour mixed with oil for a meat

offering, and one log of oil. One of the he-lambs was offered as a trespass offering together with the log of oil; both were waved as a wave offering before the Lord. In the wave offering, the lamb and oil were symbolically transferred to the Lord as was the life of the one offering them. Thus he was consecrated to the Lord. This was needful to restore the rights belonging to the covenant nation that had been lost in the ban of leprosy. The priest would slay the lamb and apply a portion of its blood to the right ear, the right thumb, and the great toe of the right foot of the candidate; he would next sprinkle a portion of the oil seven times before the Lord, and then apply the oil to the ear, thumb, and foot of the leper as he had done with the blood. The remainder of the oil was poured over the person's head. The blood obviously typified the atoning blood of Christ, the oil the effects of the Spirit or the Holy Ghost. Everything affected by the atonement must in like manner be affected by the spirit: The ear must hear and hearken to the word of the Lord, the hand must labor in the cause of the Lord, the foot must walk or follow paths of righteousness. Thus the one cleansed from leprosy was reconciled to God and reinstated in the covenant privileges. This having been accomplished, the priest could proceed to make expiation for him with the sin offering (for which the ewe had been brought), and then the burnt offering and meat offering were sanctified to the service of the Lord.

Conclusion

As we have seen, the law of Moses was appreciably more than a health code or a system of laws to govern a nation. It was a temporal expression of spiritual reality, an unequalled system of types and shadows. It was a constant reminder to Israel that they were a nation set apart, a people consecrated and dedicated to their God and his service. Its influence reached into every facet of life—be it private, family, or public. If the book of Leviticus be taken as the illustration of the purpose of the law, we note that the first part (chapters 1–16) is for the purpose of instructing Israel in how to approach God and announcing those things that were inconsistent with his presence. In its second part (chapters

17—27) Leviticus instructs Israel in how to maintain the state to which the previous chapters have brought them. It could be said that the forepart of the book exhibits in a symbolical form the doctrine of justification, while the latter part exhibits that of sanctification. As Edersheim put it, the forepart illustrates the "manner of access to God," while the latter illustrates the "holiness which is the result of that access" (Edersheim, OT 2:138). Such was the purpose of the law.

8

A Temple in
the Wilderness

"Let them make me a sanctuary," the Lord instructed Moses as
they stood face to face on Mount Sinai, "that I may dwell
among them" (Exodus 25:8). This sacred sanctuary would be a
portable temple for wandering Israel. Variously called the "tent
of the testimony" (Numbers 9:15), or "the tabernacle of witness"
(Numbers 17:7), all that is associated with this house of learning
and revelation centers in teaching the gospel of Christ and testifying of his role as the Redeemer.

In the Divine Pattern

Every part of this temple in the wilderness was to be built
according to the divine pattern shown Moses on Sinai (Exodus
25:9, 40). Nothing was left to the imagination of man; every
detail of its construction of necessity had to proceed from that
God whose house it was, for in all things it must teach and testify
of him. The tabernacle in the wilderness was to ancient Israel as
one of our modern temples is to us, "a house of prayer, a house of
fasting, a house of faith, a house of learning, a house of glory, a
house of order, a house of God" (D&C 109:8). It was a house
sanctified and consecrated "that the Son of Man might have a
place to manifest himself to his people" (D&C 109:5). It was to be

a place of holiness, a place of his continued presence, and a place in which no unclean thing could be permitted (D&C 109:12, 13, 20).

THE LORD MANIFESTS HIS ACCEPTANCE

That the Lord accepted Israel's efforts in the building of this wilderness sanctuary was evidenced by a fire that came "out from before the Lord, and consumed upon the altar the burnt offering" in the presence of all the people when the system of sacrificing therein was inaugurated (Leviticus 9:23—24). This token of divine acceptance was experienced by Gideon as a confirmation of the Lord's acceptance of his sacrifice and of his call to lead Israel to battle against the Midianites (Judges 6:21); by Manoah and his wife, affirming the angel's promise that they would have a son to be named Samson (Judges 13:20); by David, who sacrificed on the threshing floor of Mount Moriah to stay the plague (1 Chronicles 21:26); by Solomon at the dedication of his temple (2 Chronicles 7:1); and of course by Elijah when he contested with the priests of Baal (1 Kings 18:38).

Modern Israel shared much the same experience when they assembled to dedicate the first temple of this dispensation. In the midst of the dedication service "a noise was heard like the sound of a rushing mighty wind, which filled the Temple, and all the congregation simultaneously arose, being moved upon by an invisible power; many began to speak in tongues and prophesy; others saw glorious visions; and I [said Joseph Smith] beheld the Temple was filled with angels, which fact I declared to the congregation. The people of the neighborhood came running together (hearing an unusual sound within, and seeing a bright light like a pillar of fire resting upon the Temple), and were astonished at what was taking place." (HC 2:428.)

THE TABERNACLE: A LIKENESS OF CHRIST

As true worship centers in Christ, so Israel's worship was to center in the temple as his temporal likeness. A costly and precious structure in the midst of a barren desert, the tabernacle prefigured Christ, who would yet stand similarly contrasted with his environment. In the tabernacle God and man were to meet; here Israel was to find redemption, forgiveness, restoration, and fellowship. So also in Christ were these blessings made available.

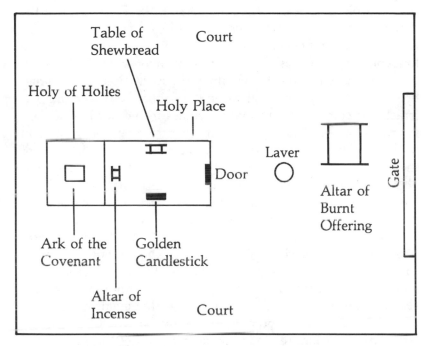

Figure 1. The Tabernacle.

THE WALL AND GATE OF THE TABERNACLE

The court of the tabernacle was surrounded by a wall of fine-twined linen. Its white color, the symbol of righteousness and purity, appropriately identified that which separates the things of the world from the things of God. That righteousness and purity constitute the wall of separation is equally obvious to those standing within and without. There was but one gate to the tabernacle as there is but one gate to the kingdom of heaven. Numerous passages of scripture announce baptism to be that gate (2 Nephi 31:17; D&C 22:2, 4; 43:7). Thus one enters both the earthly and the heavenly kingdom by accepting Christ and taking upon oneself his name. Hence we find Christ calling himself "the door" (John 10:9).

Fine-twined linen like that of the outer wall was also used to screen the gate. Its twenty-cubit length was embroidered with blue, purple, and scarlet (Exodus 27:16—17). This was also the design of the tabernacle. Since the colors were designated by revelation, we anticipate that they will be rich in symbolism. The first color mentioned is blue, the symbolism of which had already been established among the children of Israel. After the man had been stoned for gathering sticks on the Sabbath day, the camp of Israel was commanded to make "fringes in the borders of their garments" and to "put upon the fringe of the borders a ribband [ribbon] of blue" (Numbers 15:38). This ribbon, in the color of the heavens, was to be a constant reminder of their obligation to obey the will of heaven. Blue carries with it the feeling of rest and peace—a rest and peace enjoyed by man only as he places his life in accordance with the principles of heaven.

The next color mentioned was purple. Purple dye, being rare, was therefore expensive and so became known as the color of royalty or of those possessing great wealth. To Israel it was a reminder that they were of the royal or heavenly family. It was also a reminder of the wealth of blessings that awaited righteous heirs. The scarlet or blood red signifies the blood of the Lamb. It served as a constant reminder of the necessity of the atonement. The order of these colors (blue, purple, and scarlet) is repeated at least twenty-four times in the description of the tabernacle. It is assumed that the symbolism associated with them is constant. As related to Christ, might we say that blue presents to us the Heavenly One, the Son of God. The purple reminds us that he is the King of kings, and the scarlet testifies of the blood offering of the suffering servant. The interweaving of the colors suggests the union of obedience, heavenly power, and the blood of sacrifice.

Returning to the gate itself, it should not go unnoticed that the gate was always to be located on the east side of the tabernacle. The first of the sun's rays would always point themselves to it. This heavenly light would thus reveal the beauty of the multicolored gate as the light of heaven reveals Christ as "the way, the truth, and the life" and the only way that men may approach the Father (John 14:6).

THE ALTAR OF BURNT OFFERING

Immediately in front of the gate within the court of the tabernacle stood the brazen altar. The altar was portable and stood only five cubits square and three cubits high. It was made of planks of shittim wood overlaid with brass. The interior was hollow. Each of the corners formed into a projection called a horn, which like the altar itself was made of shittim wood overlaid with brass (Exodus 27:1—8). Everything associated with the altar was symbolic, and as with the entirety of the tabernacle all its symbolism centered in Christ.

Shittim wood is a hard, dark oak that is very durable. In the Septuagint it has appropriately been translated "incorruptible wood." Brass is extremely fire resistant and thus seems an appropriate symbol for one who suffered and was tried in all things. The altar stood on an elevation to foreshadow the atonement of the Lamb of God on the mount Golgotha.

Obviously intended to be the focus of attention upon entering the courtyard of the Lord, this was the altar upon which the offerings were made by which one sought divine acceptance and access into the Lord's presence. The burnt offering being the most perfect type for the atonement of Christ, the placement of the brazen altar dramatized the Atonement and the role of Christ as the focus of all true religious worship.

As none could return to the presence of God save it were for the Atonement of Christ, so none could enter either the Holy Place or the Holy of Holies without having first gained access through the name of Christ and by virtue of his sacrifice—thus the appropriate placing of the altar of burnt offering. The horn is a symbol of power; thus the four horns would represent the universal nature of the Atonement. The blood of the sacrifice was smeared on the horns. By laying hold of these horns a person could find asylum and safety (1 Kings 1:50; 2:28), though not if he was guilty of premeditated murder (Exodus 21:14). The fire, which initially came from heaven (Leviticus 9:24), was never to cease burning (Leviticus 6:13), thus teaching that the Atonement will never lose its power to cleanse man from sin.

The altar, or "table of the Lord," as Malachi called it (Malachi 1:7), was the place of intercession, peacemaking, expiation, and sanctification. That which was consumed by its flames had in a figurative sense been consumed by God and was therefore understood to have been accepted by him.

With the exception of the meal offering, the sacrifices offered on the brazen altar centered in the shedding of blood. They were a portrayal of the guiltless dying for the guilty. The burnt offering of the Mosaic systems differed from that of the patriarchs only in that the blood was shed before the offering was placed upon the altar instead of while on the altar. In all other particulars the ritual appears to have been the same.

Again, the sacrifice was efficacious only as it symbolized the great sacrifice of the Lamb of God. As one of our modern Apostles has explained, the participants in these sacrifices "were in fact making covenants with the Lord to always remember him, to take his name upon them, and to keep his commandments, all in return for his promise to let this Spirit be with them and to give them the eventual inheritance of eternal life" (*Promised Messiah*, p. 386). Of necessity such ritual had to be preceded by baptism. As modern Israel renews covenants through the sacrament, so ancient Israel renewed her covenants through a system of sacrificial rituals (ibid., p. 436).

The Laver of Washing

The other piece of furniture occupying a place in the court of the tabernacle was the brazen laver. It stood behind the altar of sacrifice and before the door of the Holy Place. This vessel or basin contained the water used by the priests to wash their hands and feet before entering the tabernacle or approaching the brazen altar. It taught the absolute necessity of being clean both in approaching the Lord and in rendering service in his name. "They shall wash their hands and their feet," the Lord commanded, "That they die not" (Exodus 30:17—21). Whether in the preparatory gospel of Moses or the fulness of the gospel law, there were no delusions among the ancients about the fact that no unclean thing could enter the presence of the Lord.

The necessity of this washing ritual each time one entered the tabernacle symbolized the constant need to be purified and cleansed from the defilements of the temporal world. To wash the hands was emblematic of the need for works of righteousness. Similarly, the washing of the feet characterized the necessity of walking in paths of righteousness.

THE DOOR OF THE TABERNACLE

As there was only one gate by which one could enter the court of the tabernacle, so there was only one door by which one could enter the tabernacle proper. The curtain forming the door of the tabernacle was made of the same materials as the veil which separated the Holy Place from the Holy of Holies, and the gate admitting people to the court of the tabernacle (Exodus 26:36—37). The colors and arrangement of each were the same. The door of the tabernacle differed from the veil of the Holy of Holies only in that the latter, as we shall see, had the two cherubim on it guarding the most sacred place. Significantly, it was only after having gone through the door that one could see the cherubim. This may suggest that while those who worship in truth may recognize the beauty of the gospel, those who approach the Lord in his service may obtain the more intimate vision of heavenly things.

With regard to the colors of which the curtain-door was made, brief commentary has already been given in our discussion of the gate of the court. Observations have also been made about the symbolism associated with those colors. These are suggestions, not revelations. Scholars and students of the scriptures have differed widely on the matter, some holding that no symbolism was intended. Yet, since the Lord so carefully specifies the colors, it does seem that their purpose was intended to go beyond that of aesthetics. Gold, a dominant feature within the Holy Place and the Holy of Holies, seems to bespeak a glorious and godlike splendor; silver is thought to carry the idea of moral purity (D&C 128:24); white represents purity and holiness; and as we have seen, purple suggested royal majesty, scarlet the color of blood and the necessity of the Atonement.

THE TABLE OF SHEWBREAD

Within the Holy Place were three pieces of furniture—the table of shewbread, the golden candlestick, and the altar of incense. The first mentioned was the table of shewbread, which was to stand on the north or right side as one entered. It faced the candlestick (Exodus 26:35). The table was relatively small—it stood about twenty-seven inches high, three feet in length, and eighteen inches wide. It was made of shittim wood overlaid with pure gold. (Exodus 25:23—25.) Upon the table were to be placed twelve loaves of bread made of fine (unleavened) flour. They were to be placed in two piles of six loaves each, with a container of pure incense placed on the top of both piles. (Leviticus 24:5—7.) Other sacred utensils were also placed on the table; these too were to be made of pure gold. Included were the dishes or flat plates probably used to carry the bread to and from the table; spoons, or perhaps cups, probably for the incense (Leviticus 24:7); and flagons and bowls, believed to have been used for wine (Exodus 25:29). Each Sabbath the bread was to be eaten by the priests "in the holy place" and replaced with twelve new loaves (Leviticus 24:8—9).

Literally translated, the name *shewbread* means "the bread of faces," or "the bread of the presence," signifying that this bread was placed before the face of the Lord or in his presence. That there is a common symbolism between the Sabbath ritual in which the priests were to eat the shewbread and the ordinance of the sacrament as introduced by Christ seems apparent. Of special interest is that at the first sacrament meeting in the New World, a meeting held at the temple in the land Bountiful (3 Nephi 11:1), those assembled were directed by the Savior to eat of the bread and drink of the wine until they were filled (3 Nephi 18:1—9). As the shewbread was to be consumed in full, none being discarded, so it is with the gospel of Jesus Christ—all is to be consumed, there are no principles to be discarded like distasteful crusts. Nor is the gospel something at which we nibble, for like the Nephites we must eat and drink of its marvelous truths until we are filled.

The symbolism of this Mosaic ritual may well have been intended to include the following:

1. The shittim wood setting forth the humanity of Christ, with the pure gold overlay depicting his divinity.

2. Each of the loaves representing one of the tribes of Israel, and the need for all twelve of them to be brought into the divine presence.

3. The nourishment of the bread and wine representing the spiritual food obtained in the holy presence or before the face of God.

4. The unleavened bread suggesting the purity of Christ. Leaven, being the symbol of sin, was not found in this bread as it was not to be found in the life of Christ.

5. As the priests were to partake of this spiritual food (the bread and wine) each Sabbath, so we must be fed that same spiritual food each Sabbath.

6. The placing of the frankincense over the bread typified the holiness of the life of Christ, which was to the Father "a sweet-smelling savour" (Ephesians 5:2).

7. All the symbolism associated with the sacrament naturally associates itself with the table of shewbread and the weekly eating of the bread and drinking of the wine.

THE GOLDEN CANDLESTICK

The second piece of furniture in the Holy Place was the golden candlestick. It was to be the source of light for the Holy Place during the hours of darkness. Called the *menorah* in Hebrew (meaning "place of lights"), its light did not come from candles, but rather from the seven cup-shaped containers resting on the end of each of the seven branches of the candlestick. These were filled with pure olive oil into which a wick was inserted and lit. The menorah, or candlestick, was made of solid gold. (Exodus 25:31—40.)

The light of the menorah betokened the light of the Spirit, or Holy Ghost. Such is the only light that allows us to see in holy places or in the presence of the Lord.

THE ALTAR OF INCENSE

The third piece of furniture in the Holy Place along with the sacred candlestick and the table of shewbread was the altar of incense. It stood directly in front of the veil. Like the ark of the covenant and the table of shewbread, it was made of shittim wood covered with gold and had rings and staves for carrying. Hot coals were placed on the altar, and each morning and evening the high priest would burn incense upon it. The high priest was to "make an atonement upon the horns of it once in a year with the blood of the sin offering" (Exodus 30:1—10).

On the altar of burnt offering we saw Christ as a sacrifice for sin; now, on the altar of incense (the symbol for sweetness and fragrance, perfectly typified in the life of Christ), we see the Savior as our intercessor. His prayers and petitions, carried upon the wings of the perfect goodness and righteousness of his life, allow men to approach God. Through his atonement, which we have already witnessed in the outer court of the tabernacle, we have been brought to the place where our prayers, always offered in his name, can be heard. This ritual seems to signify that only through such prayers can we approach God. The Psalmist wrote, "Let my prayer be set forth before thee as incense; and the lifting up of my hands as the evening sacrifice" (Psalm 141:2).

THE VEIL

A thick curtain separated the Holy Place from the Holy of Holies within the tabernacle (Exodus 26:33). The veil was made of fine linen, as were the gate to the court and the door to the tabernacle, and like them it was beautifully embroidered in blue, purple, and scarlet. It differed from the other entrances because it bore figures of cherubim or the angels of God (Exodus 26:31). Like the dark cloud that rested on the top of Sinai (Exodus 20:19), the veil separated the officiating priest who burned the daily incense and ministered in other ways in the Holy Place from the immediate presence of God (Exodus 40:26; Leviticus 4:6). Aaron was allowed to enter the Holy of Holies only on the Day of Atonement and only with the blood of the atonement in the offering bowl and surrounded by a cloud of incense that arose from the censer. The blood was to be sprinkled on the mercy seat. (Leviticus 16:12—15.) During the migrations of Israel the veil was used to cover the ark of the covenant (Numbers 4:5). At the time of Christ's death the veil of Herod's temple was rent from top to bottom, exposing the Most Holy Place to open view (Matthew 27:51).

Paul identified the veil as a symbol of the flesh of Christ (Hebrews 10:20). It was the rending of the veil, or Christ's death, that enabled all by obedience to the laws and ordinances of the gospel to enter into the divine presence. This symbolized the end of the old covenant of death and announced the new covenant wherein all may receive the "fulness of his glory" (D&C 84:24). The Mosaic dispensation had now ended; the new and everlasting covenant had been reestablished. With the rending of the veil, all exclusive privileges associated with the law of Moses were abolished, distinctions in the flesh were at an end, the carnal law was suspended, and the higher law returned—all was accomplished because of the atoning sacrifice of him of whom the veil was a type. The same hand that rent the beautiful fabric which hitherto had concealed the holiest of all had now opened the graves to a glorious resurrection for that "innumerable company of the spirits of the just, who had been faithful in the testimony of Jesus while they lived in mortality" that they, like the righteous of all future generations, might enter the presence of their divine Father (D&C 138:12).

THE ARK OF THE COVENANT

The Holy of Holies contained the ark of the covenant, so named because it housed the tablets from Sinai upon which God's covenant with Israel was written. The ark was an oblong chest made of acacia or shittim wood overlaid both inside and out with pure gold. It was two and a half cubits long, a cubit and a half wide, and a cubit and a half high. A pure gold lid covered the chest, at each end of which stood a golden cherub. The lid was known as the mercy seat, and was the place of the manifestation of God's glory and his meeting place with his people. (Exodus

25:10—22.) On the Day of Atonement the blood of the sin offering was sprinkled on the mercy seat by the high priest (Leviticus 16:14—15).

The ark was the symbol of the presence of the Lord. It was the place of revelation (Leviticus 16:2; Numbers 7:89). As Israel is always to be led by the Lord and by the word of his mouth, so the ark of the covenant was to go before them as they journeyed to their land of promise. This taught the necessity of Israel in all ages following the path marked by the Lord and giving heed to his voice. The wood from which the ark was made and the gold with which it was overlaid typified, again, the twofold nature of Christ, he being both human and divine.

The Holy Garments of the High Priest

As with all else associated with the wilderness temple, the manner in which the high priest was to be clothed was revealed to Moses in labored detail. By heavenly design the clothing was both practical and richly symbolic. The high priest was to be clothed in "holy garments . . . for glory and for beauty," or as it is rendered in the New English Bible in "dignity and grandeur" (Exodus 28:2). Only craftsmen with divinely given talents, men who were "filled with the spirit of wisdom," were allowed to participate in making these sacred vestments (Exodus 28:3).

Seven special articles of clothing and ornaments composed the official apparel of the high priest: the broidered coat, the robe, the ephod, the girdle, the breastplate, the mitre, and the diadem (Exodus 28:4; 39:30—31). Let us briefly describe each article of clothing, its function, and the symbolism associated with it.

The broidered coat

The innermost garment was the "broidered coat" (as it is rather inappropriately translated in the KJV). It was a pure white garment, woven of fine-twined linen (Exodus 28:39; 39:27). The word *coat* as used here comes from the same root as that of the coat or garment given by God to Adam and Eve in the Garden of

Eden (Genesis 3:21). Apparently the word is derived from a verb meaning "to cover, or hide" (*Tabernacle*, p. 281). Its purpose and symbolism appear to be the same as that associated with the garment given Adam and Eve as discussed elsewhere in this work (see chapter 14, "Rituals of Righteousness.")

The robe

Next in order came the robe, which was worn over the inner garment. It was to be entirely blue. This appears to have been a reference to the heavenly origin, character, and ministry of Christ, the great high priest, of whom Aaron and his successors in the office of high priest were types. Christ came from heaven to minister to his people and returned to heaven as their advocate. The blue robe was to be woven out of one piece of cloth so that it would be without seam (Exodus 28:31—32). Its hem or the robe of the ephod, as it was called, was to be embroidered with pomegranates of blue, purple, and scarlet, between which were to hang golden bells (Exodus 28:33—34). The purpose of the bells was so that the sound of the high priest would be heard when he went "in unto the holy place before the Lord, and when he cometh out, that he die not" (Exodus 28:35). The pomegranates may have represented the fruits of the people being presented to God. Keil and Delitzsch relate the symbolism of the pomegranates to a simile in Proverbs that reads, "A word fitly spoken is like apples of gold in pictures of silver" (Proverbs 25:11). In a like manner, they suggest that "the pomegranates with their pleasant odour, their sweet and refreshing juice, and the richness of their delicious kernel, were symbols of the word and testimony of God as a sweet and pleasant spiritual food, that enlivens the soul and refreshes the heart, and that the bells were symbols of the sounding of his word, or the revelation and proclamation of the word" (*Biblical Commentary*, 2:202—3). The pomegranate, a fruit rich in sweet seeds, seems a natural symbol for a life of fruitfulness.

The seamless robe set forth the idea of perfect wholeness, completeness, and unity. John records for us that Christ was wearing a seamless garment at the time of the crucifixion (see John 19:23).

The ephod

The ephod was an apronlike outer vestment worn over the blue robe. It was to be made of fine linen and embroidered with gold, blue, purple, and scarlet. It was made of two pieces that would be joined at the shoulders and apparently bound around the body by the girdle or belt. These shoulder pieces were joined with an onyx stone, set in gold, upon which were engraved the names of the tribes of Israel, six on one stone and six on the other (Exodus 28:6–12). Symbolically, the high priest carried Israel upon his shoulders and, as we shall see, also upon his heart.

The girdle

The girdle was made of fine-twined linen with blue, purple, and scarlet needlework (Exodus 39:29). The fine linen, always a type for righteousness, found expression in these words describing Christ: "Righteousness shall be the girdle of his loins, and faithfulness the girdle of his reins" (Isaiah 11:5). The object of the girdle was to strengthen the loins for service. It is a natural symbol for the strength obtained by those girded or encircled in truth (Ephesians 6:14) and righteousness.

The breastplate

The breastplate was worn on top of the ephod. It was attached by chains of pure gold. On it were displayed twelve precious stones placed in four rows of three stones each. Each stone was engraved with the name of one of the tribes. Thus Aaron would bear the names of the children of Israel "upon his heart, when he goeth in unto the holy place, for a memorial before the Lord continually" (Exodus 28:15–29).

The bottom of the breastplate was formed into a pocket to carry the Urim and Thummim.

The mitre and the holy diadem

As the crowning feature of the entire vesture, the high priest wore a diadem of fine gold on a white headdress or mitre. On the diadem were written the words: "HOLINESS TO THE LORD" (Exodus 28:36). A diadem or crown is a symbol of kingly power and authority that had been placed upon one's head. The crown of authority, power, and dignity thus placed upon the head of the high priest centered in "HOLINESS TO THE LORD." All power in the heavenly kingdom grows out of such holiness.

Such were the sacred vestments in which the high priest was clothed after he had been washed and just prior to his being anointed. Unlike so much of the symbolism of the scriptures, that of the outer part of his garments is explicitly given. The high priest, in wearing the precious stones on his shoulders and over his heart, was bearing the names of Israel's tribes before the Lord. Israel was the Lord's special treasure; they were his jewels. Prophets ancient and modern have looked to that day of which the Lord said, "I make up my jewels; and I will spare them, as a man spareth his own son that serveth him" (Malachi 3:17; D&C 60:4; 101:3).

The under tunic, however, had no apparent connection with the nation. "It was rather the personal clothing of the high priest; manifesting him, beneath all his official glory as one who could minister before the Lord in a perfect righteousness of his own. A glory and beauty no less costly and precious than was displayed by the other garments, though to the eye of sense not so striking in appearance." Such could not be worn save the high priest could "previously exhibit a spotless purity, diversified in every possible way like the embroidered fine linen coat." (*Tabernacle*, pp. 282–83.)

The vestments of the priests

Aaron's sons and other priests who would minister in the temple were to be clothed like the high priest, in coats, girdles, and bonnets. They did not wear the blue robe of the high priest or the ephod or breastplate (Exodus 28:40). They were arrayed in pure white garments. They wore no ornaments or embroidery — no gold or brilliant colors. The high priest personified the whole nation, and represented it as the Great High Priest, the Messiah himself, yet would do. The role of these lesser priests was limited to that of being a constant reminder of the purity and obedience

necessary in the service of the Lord. They had access to the Holy
Place and could minister at the altar of incense but not beyond
that point. They were also to wear linen breeches to cover their
nakedness (Exodus 28:42). There seems to be no reason for this
beyond that of the appropriate modesty.

The clothing of the tabernacle or temple dramatized the
necessity for purity in every part of worship, the centrality of the
atonement of Christ, the purity and justice of the Savior, and the
absolute necessity of that holiness without which none can see
the Lord. Such is the context of our modern revelation that
states, "For without this no man can see the face of God, even the
Father, and live" (D&C 84:22). Without the application of the
Atonement, personal purity, righteousness, and strict obedience,
all men will die as to the things of the Spirit and thus be separated
from the heavenly presence.

The Holy Anointing

After Aaron and his sons had been washed and clothed in the
garments of the priesthood they were to be anointed. The oil used
in the anointing was prepared according to divine instruction. It
consisted of a blend of four spices with pure olive oil. This oil was
also to be used to anoint all the furniture of the tabernacle and its
court. Not only were they to be thus made holy, but "whatsoever
toucheth them" would thereby become holy. The sacred nature
of the oil was to be carefully guarded. Anyone making it without
proper authority or placing it on unqualified persons would be
excommunicated. (Exodus 30:22–33.)

Subsequent scriptural texts provide both illustration and
explanation of the importance of this action. As we shall see, it is
expressly connected with the communication of the Spirit of
God. As an illustration, when the young Benjamite, Saul, was
anointed Israel's king, Samuel "took a vial of oil, and poured it
upon his head," with the attendant promise that "the Spirit of the
Lord will come upon thee," and that Saul would be "turned into
another man" (1 Samuel 10:1, 6). In the anointing of David we
read: "Samuel took the horn of oil, and anointed him in the midst
of his brethren: and the Spirit of the Lord came upon David from

that day forward" (1 Samuel 16:13). Isaiah wrote, "The Spirit of the Lord God is upon me; because the Lord hath anointed me" (Isaiah 61:1). Remember that it was with this passage that Christ chose to introduce his own ministry (Luke 4:18). That this symbolism was fully understood and remained unchanged in the meridian Church is illustrated in the epistle of John, wherein he took the promise of the Holy Ghost as given by the Savior (John 14:26) and applied it to the anointing: "But the anointing which ye have received of him abideth in you, and ye need not that any man teach you: but as the same anointing teacheth you of all things, and is truth, and is no lie, and even as it hath taught you, ye shall abide in him" (1 John 2:27). In the language of Peter, "God anointed Jesus of Nazareth with the Holy Ghost and with power" (Acts 10:38).

The oil with which the priests were anointed was understood by the ancients to represent the necessity of those on the Lord's errand being filled with his Spirit. More directly, the idea of anointing and the concept of sanctification are consistently associated in the scriptures with the reception of the Holy Ghost (Alma 13:12; 3 Nephi 27:20). The Holy Ghost is the Sanctifier (Mormon Doctrine, p. 675).

One must be consumed by the power of the Holy Ghost to stand in the presence of God (Matthew 17:2; Mark 9:3; 3 Nephi 28:15; Moses 1:5, 11). This is why Moses sought to sanctify Israel that they might enjoy that presence (D&C 84:23). The symbolism is perfect. The priests entering the Holy Place, and the high priest entering the Holy of Holies, must be sanctified and filled with the Spirit, which is symbolized in the anointing.

A Timeless Pattern

We see in the tabernacle, its furniture, and its ritual a temporal representation of heavenly things. Though associated with an ancient law now fulfilled, its representations were of principles that remain everlastingly the same. Twelve chapters of Exodus and the greater part of the book of Leviticus are devoted to the tabernacle and its ritual. Surely, for this to have been preserved for our day, in the economy of God it must contain something of worth and relevance beyond an academic and historical interest. The tabernacle, its wall, the gate, the altar of sacrifice, the laver, the Holy Place, its table, the shewbread, the candlestick, the golden censer, the veil, the ark of the covenant, its lid, the mercy seat, and the cherubim all combine to form a marvelous prophecy. Individually and collectively, they teach and testify of Christ and his atoning sacrifice. They demand obedience, they require faith, they teach purity, and they dramatize our absolute dependence on the Spirit of the Lord. They teach us what has separated us from our God and what we must do to return to his presence.

Though the fulness of the priesthood and its blessings were withheld from Israel generally, the significance of the tabernacle was not lost. We see in the tabernacle three major divisions: the outer court, the Holy Place, and the Holy of Holies. Such is the pattern revealed anew in our day for the building of temples. Therein we find rooms representing the lone and dreary world of our present telestial order, the terrestrial order, and finally the celestial glory. A comparison between the tabernacle in the wilderness and our modern temple is most enlightening. We will discuss the elements of the tabernacle briefly, leaving the reader to work out the various details of comparison at his pleasure.

The first thing encountered upon leaving the outer world and entering the gate of the tabernacle is the altar of sacrifice. Here the various animals and other offerings are slain and offered to the Lord. Here obedience and sacrifice combine as the first step in our symbolic progression toward the presence of God. Only with an acceptable sacrifice can man come near to the living God and enter into his holy presence. All centers in the acceptance of Christ and the exercise of faith in him.

Immediately thereafter comes the laver or basin of water, with its ritual washing. Having progressed to this point, the priest, representing the people, is clothed in the garments of the priesthood and anointed (symbolically clothed in the Spirit) that he might pass as it were from the telestial world to a more holy place—one of a terrestrial order. Doing so, one finds three articles of furniture: the table of shewbread, with symbolism closely associated with the sacrament; the candlestick and its emphasis on the necessity of the spiritual light that comes only from the Holy Ghost; and the altar of incense ever burning, but with increased sweetness in morning and evening, announcing the constant necessity of righteous prayers. Then comes the veil, guarded by the angels of the Lord, through which one must pass before coming into the presence of the Lord. The only article of furniture in this room is the ark of the covenant, which the Lord said was the place where he would manifest himself to his people.

From dispensation to dispensation the symbols may change, yet the principles represented remain constant.

9

The Mountain of the Lord's House

Mountains are the meeting place between heaven and earth. Man's spirit instinctively responds to the solitude and grandeur of these temples of nature. Here it is that prophets and righteous men from time immemorial have gone to meet their God, and here it is that many of earth's most singular events have taken place. So sacred is the mountain summit that our temples have come to be known as the mountain of the Lord's house. As there are sacred moments, so there are sacred places—places, like men, chosen and ordained to stand above the rest and point the way to God.

HOLY PLACES

It was the "mountain of God," according to the scriptural account, that Moses ascended to see the burning bush (Exodus 3:1). Sinai, it would appear, was known as the "mountain of God" long before Moses and the Exodus. Here Moses was instructed to remove his shoes, for the place upon which he stood, he was told, was "holy ground" (Exodus 3:5). Such was the setting in which he was called as prophet and liberator to the nation of Israel, whom he was to bring to Sinai to worship God (Exodus 3:12).

As there are proper forms of worship, so there are proper places of worship. Moses and Israel anciently were required to travel many days in the wilderness that they might make covenants with their God at Sinai. Isaiah prophesied that Israel of the last days would journey from the ends of the earth that they might worship in the mountain of the Lord's house and there be taught in the ways of the God of their fathers (Isaiah 2:2—3). Sinai was a sacred place, a place set apart, a place for the children of Israel to meet their God and make covenants with him. Sinai was Israel's first temple. There Moses taught them about the priesthood and sought to sanctify them that they might enter the presence of the Lord (D&C 84:23—24). Temples, both ancient and modern, are but the "architectural realization" of the Sinai experience. (*Temple Symbolism,* pp. 33—35.)

From the Sinai experience we learn that ascending to the high place or presence of the Lord is a gradual process: First, we see Israel assembled at the base of the holy mountain; then we see the seventy, who were allowed to go up partway; and finally we see Moses, who at the invitation of the Lord passed through the veil of the cloud into the divine presence (see Exodus 24). The same pattern is reflected in the construction of the tabernacle. There we plainly see the pattern of graduated splendor designed to be both instructive and functional. Wood and brass were common to the outer court, whereas the glory of gold was the standard of the inner sanctuary. The sacred furnishings were arranged in such an order that their associated ordinances, performed by the priest, became more and more sacred as he progressed toward the Holy of Holies. The tabernacle itself consisted of three enclosures: the court of the tabernacle, the Holy Place, and the Holy of Holies.

> As an Israelite approached the sanctuary (the Holy Place and the Holy of Holies), he was immediately confronted by the Court of the Tabernacle, which concealed the sacred dwelling place of the Lord by a generous enclosure of one hundred cubits north to south. This court was encompassed by a five-cubit wall of fine-twined linen whose white brilliance typified the cleansing purpose of the sacred ordinances

accomplished therein and served as a symbolic reminder to
the children of Israel of the need for them to enter worthily.
(Garner, p. 93.)

In both pattern and purpose the wilderness tabernacle foreshadowed the temple. The ordinances performed there have been
common to the Saints of all ages. In our own dispensation we
find the Lord commanding Joseph Smith to "build a house to my
name, for the Most High to dwell therein" (D&C 124:27). "How
shall your washings be acceptable unto me," the Lord asked
Joseph Smith, "except ye perform them in a house which you
have built to my name?" Then to emphasize that the ordinances
of salvation and the way to God are always the same, the Lord
explained, "For, for this cause I commanded Moses that he
should build a tabernacle, that they should bear it with them in
the wilderness, and to build a house in the land of promise, that
those ordinances might be revealed which had been hid from
before the world was." (D&C 124:37—38.) The Lord explained to
Joseph Smith that such sacred ordinances as washings, anointings, and baptisms for the dead belonged to his house and were
acceptable when performed outside of such a holy sanctuary
"only in the days of your poverty, wherein ye are not able to
build a house unto me." Thus the Lord's people of all ages have
been commanded to build such holy places unto his name. (See
D&C 124:30, 39.) Further, the place upon which the temple was
to be built was chosen, consecrated, and made holy by the Lord
(D&C 124:42—44). We have every reason to suppose that such
sacred edifices stood in the great city of Adam-ondi-Ahman, in
the city of Enoch, and in Melchizedek's city, Salem.

THE DIVINE MOUNTAIN

Subsequent to his call from the burning bush, yet before the
Exodus, Moses "was caught up into an exceedingly high mountain . . . the name of which shall not be known among the children of men" (Moses 1:1, 42). Here Moses talked with God "face
to face" and "beheld the world and the ends thereof, and all the
children of men which are, and which were created" (Moses 1:2,

8). Others of the prophets were also instructed in world history on this same heavenly campus, not the least of which was Christ himself. Attendant to his wilderness experience, and before he commenced his ministry, he "was in the Spirit, and it taketh him up into an exceeding high mountain, and sheweth him all the kingdoms of the world, and the glory of them" (JST, Matthew 4:8).

Nephi records that as he sat pondering the things that had been revealed to his father he was "caught away in the Spirit of the Lord, yea, into an exceedingly high mountain, which I never had before seen, and upon which I never had before set my foot." Here Nephi was shown the history of his people through the ages, the birth and ministry of Christ, the history of the Gentile nations or the nations of Europe, and the restoration and teaching of the gospel in the last days. Much that he saw he was forbidden to write, for he was told that it was yet to be written by one of the Apostles of the Lamb and that the Apostle's name was to be John (1 Nephi 11:14). Nor was this Nephi's only such experience, for he was later to testify: "Upon the wings of his Spirit hath my body been carried away upon exceedingly high mountains. And mine eyes have beheld great things, yea, even too great for man; therefore I was bidden that I should not write them." (2 Nephi 4:25.)

In harmony with Nephi's revelation of the Apostle John's activities, the Revelator also professed to be among those who had been carried "away in the spirit to a great and high mountain" to entertain the visions of eternity (Revelation 21:10). Ezekiel, who was a prophet of the Babylonian captivity, also spoke of the visions of God in which he was brought to "the land of Israel" and there set "upon a very high mountain" that he might see the vision of the temple (Ezekiel 40:2).

NATURE'S TEMPLES

Sinai was neither the first nor the last instance in which nature provided a place for a prophet and his people to meet their God. Surely Adam worshipped in such places, as did Enoch, the brother of Jared, Abraham, Isaac, Jacob, Nephi, Christ, and

many others. Enoch records the voice of the Lord directing him
to ascend the mount of Simeon. "I turned and went up on the
mount," he said, "and as I stood upon the mount, I beheld the
heavens open, and I was clothed upon with glory; And I saw the
Lord; and he stood before my face, and he talked with me, even
as a man talketh one with another, face to face; and he said unto
me: Look, and I will show unto thee the world for the space of
many generations." (Moses 7:3—4.) Enoch was also shown the
vision of future history.

It will be remembered that the brother of Jared took his six-
teen small stones to the mountaintop, where he sought to have
the Lord touch them with his finger. There the brother of Jared
was privileged to see the Lord and also to obtain a revelation of
the future. Recounting that experience, Moroni said, "The Lord
commanded the brother of Jared to go down out of the mount
from the presence of the Lord, and write the things which he had
seen; and they were forbidden to come unto the children of men
until after that he should be lifted up upon the cross." Further, he
added that "never were greater things made manifest than those
which were made manifest unto the brother of Jared." (Ether 4:1,
4.)

Reference was made in the first chapter of this work to Abraham's journey to mount Moriah, where he and Isaac were to participate in a sacrificial ritual foreshadowing God's sacrifice of his
Son. As with Sinai, Moriah seems already to have been known as
a sacred mountain; in any event, at the conclusion of his experience there Abraham named it Jehovah-jireh. The name conveys
the idea that this is the place where Jehovah "will provide" (that
is, a sacrifice) and also the idea of the place where Jehovah shall
be seen or manifest. (See note to Genesis 22:14 in LDS edition of
the Bible.) After the deliverance of Isaac, Abraham named the
spot Jehovah-jireh, meaning "the Lord will see or provide"
(Genesis 22:14). The name Moriah was revived after the Lord
appeared to David at this same spot (2 Chronicles 3:1).

The idea that certain places have been designated for holy
purposes, and as such are known long in advance, is common to
Latter-day Saints, who look for a day when the New Jerusalem
will be established in Jackson County, Missouri. Along with

Sinai and Moriah, Bethel ("the house of God") appears to be another such place. It will be remembered that as Jacob was traveling from his father's house at Beersheba to seek a wife in Haran, the Lord appeared to him by night in a marvelous dream. Jacob rose up early the following morning and took the stone that had been his pillow and "set it up for a pillar, and poured oil upon the top of it. And he called the name of that place Beth-el: but the name of that city was called Luz at the first." (Genesis 28:10—22.) Years later, upon Jacob's return, God appeared unto him again at the same place and once more we read that "Jacob set up a pillar in the place where he talked with him, even a pillar of stone: and he poured a drink offering thereon, and he poured oil thereon. And Jacob called the name of the place where God spake with him, Beth-el." (Genesis 35:14—15.) Yet, if we accept the precise definition of Genesis 12:8, the name Bethel existed at this spot even before the arrival of Abram in Canaan. In future times it would be to Bethel (or as it is rendered, "the house of God") that Israel would go in times of distress to ask counsel of the Lord (Judges 20:18, 26, 31; 21:2).

In his dream Jacob saw a ladder reaching from earth to heaven, with angels ascending and descending on it. Above the ladder stood the Lord, who (and we must assume that Jacob ascended the ladder) covenanted with Jacob, as he had with Abraham and Isaac, to bless him and his posterity throughout all generations. He was told, as had been his fathers, that through his seed all the families of the earth would be blessed. Joseph Smith tells us that the "three principal rounds of Jacob's ladder" were the same ascended by Paul (2 Corinthians 12:2) and that they represented progression from telestial to terrestrial, and from terrestrial to celestial degrees of glory (HC 5:402). When he awoke Jacob designated the place as "the house of God," and as "the gate of heaven" (Genesis 28:12—17). Describing the second appearance of God to him at Bethel, Jacob mentions the emphasis given to his new name (Israel), the command that he multiply and replenish the earth, and the promises associated with his posterity (Genesis 35:7—12).

The use of mountains as the meeting place between God and men is nowhere better illustrated than in the ministry of the

Savior. In company with Peter, James, and John he went "up into
an high mountain apart" which we have come to know as the
Mount of Transfiguration. That this was a temple experience
there can be little doubt. Christ was transfigured and his "raiment
became shining, exceeding white as snow; so as no fuller on earth
can white them (Mark 9:3). Moses and Elias (Elijah) appeared
and instructed them, causing Peter to say, "It is good for us to be
here: if thou wilt, let us make here three tabernacles; one for thee,
and one for Moses, and one for Elias." Peter's suggestion that
three tabernacles or tents be built brings to mind Moses' tabernacle in the wilderness. That tabernacle or portable temple, with
its three parts, was covered by a veil or cloud which was the
symbol of the divine presence (Numbers 9:15). Such was the
experience of those on the Mount of Transfiguration, for we are
told that as Peter "yet spake, behold, a bright cloud overshadowed them" and they heard a voice saying, "This is my
beloved Son, in whom I am well pleased; hear ye him." (Matthew
17:4—5.)

Describing this experience, Peter said that he and his companions were "eyewitnesses" of Christ's "majesty." "For," he said,
"he received from God the Father honour and glory, when there
came such a voice to him from the excellent glory, This is my
beloved Son, in whom I am well pleased. And this voice which
came from heaven we heard, when we were with him in the holy
mount." (2 Peter 1:16—17.) Then he added, "We have also a
more sure word of prophecy . . ." (v. 18). "The more sure word
of prophecy," Joseph Smith tells us, "means a man's knowing
that he is sealed up unto eternal life, by revelation and the spirit
of prophecy, through the power of the Holy Priesthood" (D&C
131:5). We are also told that Peter, James, and John, while on the
mount, saw, as had so many of the other prophets, the future
history of the earth even to the time when it would be "transfigured" or receive again its paradisiacal glory (D&C 63:21).

Though our account is fragmentary, the high mountain, the
raiment of white, the heavenly messengers, the cloud or veil, the
voice of the Father, and the manifestation of the destiny of the
earth all combine in a harmonious description of a temple expe-

rience. Indeed it has been suggested that Peter, James, and John, while on the mount, received their endowments and were there empowered for all that they would yet be called upon to do (*Mortal Messiah* 3:58; see also *DNTC* 1:400; *Doctrines of Salvation* 2:165). Thus it seems natural that we would read that "as they came down from the mountain, he charged them that they should tell no man what things they had seen, till the Son of man were risen from the dead" (Mark 9:9).

On the night of the Paschal feast, at that event known to us as the Last Supper, Jesus said to his disciples, "But after I am risen again, I will go before you into Galilee" (Matthew 26:32). Lest they forget, at the open tomb the angel of the Lord instructed the two Marys to tell the disciples that Christ would meet them in Galilee (Mark 16:7). The risen Lord himself directed these same women to tell his brethren to go to Galilee with the promise, "there shall they see me" (Matthew 28:10). And so the word went out among those who believed, those of faith and proven devotion. Such was the assembly that gathered in Galilee, "into a mountain where Jesus had appointed them" (Matthew 28:16). Paul tells us that more than five hundred brethren were present (1 Corinthians 15:6), and if we can rightfully assume that their wives and families were with them along with other faithful women, it is an easy matter to suppose that the total congregation was of the same size as the similar meeting held in the New World where "about two thousand and five hundred souls" consisting of "men, women, and children" assembled and met the risen Lord (3 Nephi 17:25). Of this appearance on the mountain in Galilee, Elder Bruce R. McConkie writes, "It is pleasant to suppose it happened at the same site on which he preached the Sermon on the Mount, for that was the ordination sermon of the Twelve, and he now designs to give those same apostolic witnesses their great commission to carry the gospel into all the world. What would be more fitting than to have the great commission to take the gospel to all the world come forth at the same sacred spot whence they received their first apostolic commission, from the mountain which had become to them a holy temple?" (*Mortal Messiah* 4:297.)

The Lord's Mountain

So frequently had mountains served as the meeting place between God and men that Isaiah referred to the temple as "the mountain of the Lord's house" (Isaiah 2:2); Jeremiah used the phrase "mountain of holiness" (Jeremiah 31:23); and the Psalmist wrote of the "hill of the Lord" (Psalm 24:3). Nephi records that when the Lord sought to reveal to him the manner in which he should build the ship that was to bring his family to the Americas, he first heard the voice of the Lord say to him, "Arise, and get thee into the mountain" (1 Nephi 17:7).

It was commonplace among the ancient Near Eastern peoples to view mountains as temples, for they were the meeting place between heaven and earth. Anciently the temple was viewed as the ritual center of the universe. It was believed to be the place where men could establish contact with other worlds. Hugh Nibley writes, "It is now generally recognized that the earliest temples were not, as formerly supposed, dwelling-places of divinity, but rather meeting-places at which men at specific times attempted to make contact with the powers above" (*Temple History*, p. 231). Thus it was natural that the temple be associated with mountains, for as still another scholar observes, "the mountain itself was originally such a place of contact between this and the upper world" (ibid.).

Temple Typology

John M. Lundquist summarized an intensive study of temple worship in the ancient Near East with the observation that there was a universal "ritual language and practice" among the ancients in their systems of temple worship ("Temple Symbolism," p. 34). Despite differences in languages, cultures, and religious beliefs, the centrality of temples and the nature of their rituals suggest a common origin. Bible scholars commonly conclude that Israel borrowed much of its system of worship from its pagan neighbors.

Latter-day revelation enables us to trace these similarities to an earlier common ground. In the book of Abraham we learn of rituals commonly associated with the gospel and which were had by Adam even before the Fall and were known to all the ancients who held the priesthood. Hugh Nibley describes these similarities as "diffusion and usurpation." In fact, it is simply a matter of apostasy. Anciently, as today, the world was full of copies of the original. The problem is that people become so used to bad copies that they fail to recognize the original.

Among those things common to virtually all temples of the ancient Near East as noted by Lundquist in his summary were the following:

1. The temple is the architectural embodiment of the cosmic mountain.

2. The temple is often associated with the waters of life, which will often flow from a spring within the building itself, apparently a symbol of the waters of creation.

3. The place upon which the temple is built is regarded as sacred.

4. The temple is associated with the tree of life.

5. The temple is oriented toward the four world regions or cardinal directions, and toward various celestial bodies such as the polar star.

6. The structural design of the temple expresses the idea of successive ascension toward heaven.

7. The plan and measurements of the temple are given by revelation.

8. The temple is the central, organizing, and unifying institution of the society.

9. The temple is associated with abundance and prosperity.

10. The destruction or loss of the temple foreshadows the death of the community. Such destruction is the result of disobedience to the laws of God.

11. Within the temple, kings, priests, and worshippers are washed, anointed, clothed in temple robes, fed sacramental meals, enthroned and symbolically initiated into the presence of their deity, where they would enjoy eternal life. Annual rites introducing the new year are also held, with the reading of texts and the dramatic portrayal of a pre-earth war in heaven. The forces of good prevail, led by a chief deity. Sacred marriages are also carried out at this time.

12. The temple is associated with the realm of the dead and ancestor worship.

13. Sacral or communal meals are eaten, often as part of covenant ceremonies.

14. God's word is revealed in the temple, usually in the Holy of Holies, to priests, priestesses, or prophets.

15. The building or restoration of a temple is a time of covenant making, a time of renewal, a time to reorder society.

16. The temple is a place of sacrifice.

17. The temple and its rituals are enshrouded in secrecy.

THE TEMPLE AS A SYMBOL

The temple is a symbol of true religion. The Lord's people have always been a temple-building people (D&C 124:39), thus accounting for the endless array of counterfeits in the ancient world. Only among those who deny the principle of revelation and refuse man the right to stand in the presence of his Creator are no temples to be found. As long as some degree of divine favor rested upon the nation of Israel, their temple stood.

When Christ died upon the cross, "the veil of the temple was rent in twain" by the hand of God "from the top to the bottom" (Matthew 27:51), thus symbolizing the end of the old covenant and the fulfillment of its sacrificial types. No longer was man to approach the Lord through its ritual or receive a remission of sins in its performances. The Jewish dispensation had ended, the Messianic had begun, and as the Savior had prophesied, not one stone of that temple would be left standing upon another (Matthew 24:2). The destruction of the temple betokened the destruction of a wicked nation. As its stones were not to be left one upon another, so its people would be scattered among all nations of the earth to await that future day when, in the economy of heaven, a temple would again be built on the sacred hills of Jerusalem. That temple, when built by the proper authority, will stand as a beacon to the scattered remnant of Judah that the days of her distress have passed and that the arm of the Lord now reaches after them. It will signal that the time has come for them to return to their God. Once again "he that hath clean hands, and a pure heart; who hath not lifted up his soul unto vanity, nor sworn deceitfully" will be invited to "ascend into the hill of the Lord" to "stand in his holy place" and to receive "blessing from the Lord" (Psalm 24).

THE SALT LAKE TEMPLE

Contemporary to these events will be the building of another great temple in the Americas. To the Nephite nations, Christ promised that in the last days a New Jerusalem would be built "in this land" for the remnant of Joseph in fulfillment of the promise made to Jacob. "The powers of heaven shall be in the midst of this people," he said, and "I will be in the midst of you" also (3 Nephi 20:22). Isaiah prophesied of a time in the last days "when the mountain of the Lord's house" would "be established in the top of the mountains," and that "all nations" would "flow unto it." "Many people," Isaiah said, "shall go and say, Come ye, and let us go up to the mountain of the Lord, to the house of the God of Jacob; and he will teach us of his ways, and we will walk in his paths; for out of Zion shall go forth the law, and the word of the Lord from Jerusalem." (2 Nephi 12:2—3.) That the Zion from which the law shall go forth, as spoken of by Isaiah, is the New Jerusalem has been plainly stated in revelations given to the Prophet Joseph Smith (D&C 84:2; 133:12 13). The phrase "the mountain of the Lord's house," as we have already seen, has a general application to the hosts of temples that will dot the earth, while having an unusual or special application to the Salt Lake Temple.

Mormon settlers applied for statehood in 1849 under the name *Deseret*—a Book of Mormon name meaning "honeybee" (Ether 2:3). Their bid for statehood was rejected, as were five subsequent attempts. In 1869 they were finally accepted into the Union under the name *Utah*, there being no sentiment among the bodies of Congress to allow the Book of Mormon name. In the meantime, the Saints had completed and dedicated the Salt Lake Temple, which took them forty years to build. Of interest is the fact that *Utah* is a Ute Indian word meaning "tops of the mountains." Thus, the "mountain of the Lord's house" had been built as designated in the "tops of the mountains," or "Utah," if you prefer the language of the Lamanites to whom Christ promised the place of his presence (3 Nephi 20:22).

As with the system anciently, there is considerable symbolism in the structure of our modern temples. The Salt Lake Temple, the design of which was revealed to Brigham Young, serves as an example. Built in the "tops of the mountains," this sacred edifice was designated to stand at the center of the Zion City, as the covenants made therein were to have center place in the hearts and minds of the Saints. Within its granite walls the structure represented the three levels of progression through which one must pass to enter into the presence of the Lord, the symbols of which—the sun, moon, and stars—are represented on the facade of the temple. Also depicted is the Big Dipper, with the pointers directed to the North Star. The stars are so arranged that they are very nearly in line with the North Star itself. As the North Star is a fixed point from which landlubber and mariner alike could find their way, so those who follow the path marked by the priesthood will be able to return to their heavenly home.

The most distinctive feature of the temple is its towers. Three towers rise on the western end and three on the eastern. The three pillars at the western end represent the presiding bishopric; the three towers on the eastern end, standing six feet taller than those on the west, represent the three presiding high priests of the Church, or the First Presidency. Upon the main tower is the inscription "Holiness to the Lord," designating the temple as a place set apart from the world.

The keystones of the lower windows of the east and west center towers have inscribed on them the words "I am Alpha and Omega." Below the keystones has been carved the emblem of clasped hands, and on the stones at the top of the upper windows in the same towers is depicted the symbol of the all-searching eye. At the top of the buttresses of the east center tower are carved representations of rays of light breaking through clouds. These rays of light represent the light of the gospel as it dispels the clouds of darkness that have so long covered the earth, shadowing the knowledge obtained only in the mountain of the Lord's house.

10

Robes of Righteousness

One of the most sacred symbols to the Saints of all ages is that of "robes of righteousnes" or "garments of salvation." Common to a host of scriptural settings, and richly endowed with layer upon layer of meaning, this marvelous similitude may best be introduced here as it was by the Savior—in the form of a parable. Teaching in the temple during the final week of his mortal ministry, with priest and scribe, Sadducee and Pharisee among his listeners, he delivered what has come to be known as the parable of the king's son. For our purposes we shall call it the parable of the garment.

The Parable of the Garment

The kingdom of heaven, Christ said, was like unto a king who, having prepared a feast for his son's wedding, sent his servants to summon the guests he had invited, but they would not come. Other servants were sent to tell of all the good and rich things that had been prepared for those that had been invited. Still those invited had no interest in coming, being variously involved in their own affairs. Some of their number attacked the servants of the king and killed them. In anger, the king sent an army to destroy the murderers and burn their city. Then he said to his servants that the wedding feast was ready but that they which were bidden were not worthy. The servants were sent to the highways to invite all that would come to attend the feast. Many were gathered together, "both bad and good: and the wedding was furnished with guests." When the king made his appearance he saw among his guests a man who was not clothed in a wedding garment. When asked why he was not properly dressed the man was speechless. The king then directed his servants to "bind him hand and foot, and take him away," casting him into outer darkness, the place of weeping and gnashing of teeth. The parable is concluded with the announcement that "Many are called, but few are chosen." (See Matthew 22:1–14.)

The interpretation of much of the parable is obvious. The king is God; the son is Christ; the place of the wedding feast is the kingdom of heaven; those bidden to the feast are those to whom the message of the gospel is taken; the servants are obviously the prophets who had been rejected and killed by those of their own nation; the army, it appears, was that of Rome; and the city, Jerusalem. After their rejection by Israel, the servants went to the gentile nations, preaching to all, the righteous and unrighteous alike. What is not immediately evident is why a particular dress is so necessary for the wedding feast and why the punishment (the endless woe of outer darkness) is appropriate for one not properly dressed.

It was well known to the Savior's audience that one had to be suitably dressed to appear before a king. The apparel of the guest was a reflection of respect for the host. It was also a matter of common knowledge that the appropriate dress for such an occasion was that of white robes (Clarke 3:210). It appears evident that people brought in from the highways of the earth would have neither time nor means to procure wedding garments. The king had obviously supplied his guests from his own wardrobe. All had been invited to clothe themselves in the garments of royalty. The man cast out had chosen to trust in his own dress rather than that provided by the king. By interpretation, he had chosen to join the true worshipers, that is the church or kingdom of God, yet he had not chosen to dress as the others had dressed. He was not one with them. He desired the full blessings of the kingdom, but on his own terms, not those of the king. He had spurned the ritual garment and the righteousness associated with it. This is emphasized in the JST, which adds to the statement that many are called but few chosen the explanation that "all do not have on the wedding garment" (JST, Matthew 22:14).

All who are to feast in the heavenly kingdom must be properly clothed. They must be wearing the garments of purity and holiness, garments made white through "the blood of the Lamb" (Revelation 7:14). Christ's audience had a rich background of scripture and tradition that gave depth of meaning to this parable. Isaiah had spoken (in the context of imagery about a wedding feast) of those who were clothed in the "garments of salvation" and "covered . . . with the robe of righteousness"; such, he said, were those who would yet rejoice (Isaiah 61:10). Zephaniah wrote of the Lord preparing a sacrifice and bidding his guests and then punishing all who were "clothed with strange apparel" (Zephaniah 1:7–8). And Joshua, the high priest at the time of Zerubbabel, is said, in the book of Zechariah, to have been taken and tried before a heavenly court. "Clothed with filthy garments," Joshua was apparently accused of being unworthy to minister in the temple, having been made unclean by his sojourn in Babylon. He was, however, acquitted and the command was given, "Take away the filthy garments from him." Purified, he was then clothed "with change of raiment," and a mitre placed upon his head. He was charged to walk in the path of righteousness and continue the building of the temple, and told that he was empowered to return to the heavenly court. (See Zechariah 3:1–7.)

In addition to these passages, we have many traditions which reflect the understanding of those to whom Christ spoke. Our understanding will be enhanced by a review of them.

PARALLEL TRADITIONS

That one must be properly clothed to enter the heavenly courts is perhaps best illustrated by the necessity of proper dress to enter their earthly counterpart. On the Day of Atonement when the high priest entered the Holy of Holies he was, as we have seen, to be clothed entirely in white linen garments. The necessity of proper dress is a constant theme in the accounts of prophets being taken into the presence of the Lord. In 2 Esdras, one of the intertestamental books, we are told of a heavenly feast to be attended by those who have been "sealed." Here they are to "receive glorious garments from the Lord." Ezra, who is seeing the vision, is told that these now "clothed in white" are those who "fulfilled the law of the Lord," and that they were "called from the beginning" to be "made holy." (2 Esdras 2:38—41.) The angel attending him explained, "These are they who have put off mortal clothing and have put on the immortal, and they have confessed the name of God; now they are being crowned, and receive palms" (2 Esdras 2:45).

Similarly, in the Secrets of Enoch we have an account of Enoch being taken unto the presence of the Lord. In this instance the Lord instructs Michael, "Go and take Enoch from out his earthly garments, and anoint him with my sweet ointment, and put him into the garments of My glory." This having been done, Enoch records, "I looked at myself, and was like one of his glorious ones." (2 Enoch 22:8—9.) In another Enoch manuscript, an account is given of Enoch being taken again into the heavenly court, clothed with the garments of glory, and invited to sit upon the heavenly throne. He had a crown placed upon his head, and was called the "Lesser YHWH" (Jehovah) in the presence of the heavenly household. (3 Enoch 12:2—5.)

Describing the manner of his dress when he was taken to the heavenly court, Levi said he "put on the robe of the priesthood, and the crown of righteousness, and the breastplate of understanding, and the garment of truth, and the plate of faith, and the turban of the head, and the ephod of prophecy." In so doing he was assisted by seven angels.

> The first anointed me with holy oil, and gave to me the staff of judgment. The second washed me with pure water, and fed me with bread and wine (even) the most holy things, and clad me with a holy and glorious robe. The third clothed me with a linen vestment like an ephod. The fourth put round me a girdle like unto purple. The fifth gave me a branch or rich olive. The sixth placed a crown on my head. The seventh

placed on my head a diadem of priesthood, and filled my hands with incense, that I might serve as priest to the Lord God. (Testament of Levi 8:2—11.)

We also have an account of Isaiah ascending to heaven, where he sees the manner in which the angels are clothed. He is told that when he is so clothed he will be equal to them. He also records, "I saw Enoch and all who were with him, stript of the garment of flesh, and I saw them in their garments of the upper world, and they were like angels, standing there in great glory." (Ascension of Isaiah 8:14—15; 9:9.)

From an ancient Syrian source we find the plan of salvation depicted in an allegory. It is a story of a king's son who is required to leave his father's kingdom, where he enjoyed great wealth, to obtain a pearl. The pearl, it becomes quite apparent, is his own soul. His parents see that he is properly provisioned for his journey, though before leaving their presence he must surrender his splendid robe. This robe, or garment of light, we are told, had been woven to the measure of his stature. Before he leaves his parents' presence he enters into a covenant with them to obtain the pearl and return, that he might once again enjoy their presence and wear his splendid robe. The covenant is written upon his heart.

Though the way is dangerous and difficult, an intimate friend, referred to as "an (anointed one)," warns him of the dangers that beset him. Notwithstanding all this he soon forgets that he is a king's son and forgets his mission to obtain the pearl. At this point a council is held, attended by his father, mother, brother (the crown prince), and many other great and mighty ones. They determine to send him a letter imploring him to awake and remember who he is and what king he serves. He is encouraged to remember his splendid robe and to so conduct himself that his name might be written in the book of the heroes and that he with his brother might be an heir in his father's kingdom.

Thus reminded, he commences again his efforts to obtain the pearl, which he must wrestle from a terrible serpent. This he is able to do only by naming his father's name, that of his brother, and that of his mother. Having obtained the pearl he flees Egypt, sheds his dirty and unclean garments, and is further guided by the letter. At this point he is greeted by messengers from his parents who clothe him once more in his royal robe, and he returns as an heir to his father's kingdom. (*NT Apocrypha* 2:498—504.)

The two threads binding our scriptural and apocryphal accounts together are: first, the necessity of putting on the raiment of glory to enter the heavenly court; and second, that one must have a celestial or holy nature to be so clothed. According to our Enoch text, when the Lord comes in glory to take vengeance on the wicked, "the righteous and elect shall be saved," they will be those "clothed with garments of glory" (Enoch 62:13, 15).[1]

FIGURATIVE OR LITERAL

Let us now return to the parable of the garment where we began, asking whether we are to understand the garment in this parable to be a cloak of cloth or a mantle of deeds. None would question that the garment is a symbol, but is it more than a symbol? Water symbolizes purity because it purifies. To symbolize the constant need for spiritual nourishment we speak of the "bread of life." We do so because bread is, in fact, the staff of life. A shield or coat of armor is used to symbolize protection because it provides protection. Modesty and dignity in dress are both symbol and source of that same modesty and dignity. Sometimes we get so captivated with symbolic meanings that we overlook the importance of the object being symbolized, such as the Savior's warning to "beware of false prophets, which come to you in sheep's clothing." None have missed the point that not all those who profess to be prophets are prophets, but how many have recognized that sheep's clothing was indeed the dress or uniform of the true prophet?

The traditional attire of the prophets was a "rough garment" (Zechariah 13:4) made of goats' hair, coarse wool, or the coarse pile of the camel. It will be remembered that John the Baptist came so attired (Matthew 3:4), and that Paul indicated that the common lot of the prophets was a wardrobe of "sheepskins and goatskins" (Hebrews 11:37). (See Clarke 1:484.) Even Elijah's mantle is described in the Septuagint as a "sheep skin" (LXX 2 Kings 2:8). The origin of the tradition is thought to trace itself to the skins with which Adam and Eve were clothed when they were expelled from the Garden of Eden. In any event, what the Savior is telling his hearers is that the mockery of false prophets would extend to wearing the robes of the priesthood. It was those wearing the robes of the priesthood who condemned him to death.

That earthly powers associated certain clothing with positions of honor was evidenced by the "gorgeous robe" with which Christ was dressed by Herod when mocked in his court, and again the purple or scarlet robe placed on him by Pilot's soldiers when they taunted and abused him. Luke recounts the attempt of Herod Agrippa to appear as a god in his "royal apparel" and of the angel of the Lord smiting him for his efforts (Acts 12:20–23). Josephus describes how Agrippa dressed himself in a garment made of silver and then timed his entry into the outdoor theater at Caesarea so as to catch and reflect the rays of the rising sun. "So resplendent" was his appearance, Josephus said, "as to spread a horror over those that looked intently upon him: and presently his flatterers cried out, one from one place, and another from another (though not for his good), he was a god" (Josephus, p. 412). Similarly, Constantine came clad in gold and precious stones to preside over the Council of Nicaea (*Catholic Encyclopedia* 11:44).

As there are no copies without originals, no reflections without images to reflect, no shadows without bodies to block the rays of light, so there can be no allegories without the clay of reality from which they are fashioned. The former is the creation of the latter. Surely there can be no "second" without there having been a "first." Where the scriptures freely use an image or shadow, we can hardly err in the assumption that the image reflects its original, or that something cast the shadow.

THE GARMENT OF POWER AND AUTHORITY

The idea that power and authority were associated with certain clothing is also sustained by both scripture and tradition. In Facsimile 2 in the book of Abraham we find a depiction of God "sitting upon his throne, *clothed with power and authority*; with a crown of eternal light upon his head. (Explanation to figure 3; italics added.)

The idea that Adam and the Old Testament patriarchs and prophets were clothed with garments that granted them power and authority is common among the ancient traditions. Jewish tradition holds that Adam received a "garment of light" from God while in the Garden of Eden before the Fall (*Legends* 5:97, 103—4). The Abraham quotation just cited clearly states that the authority and power with which Adam was clothed were given him "in the Garden of Eden." It will be remembered that it was in the Garden that Adam was given dominion over all things on the earth (Genesis 1:28). Here he received the priesthood and was married in an eternal union to Eve, all at the hands of God. The tradition holds that when Adam fell "he lost his celestial clothing—God stripped it off him" (ibid 1:79). Adam was then clothed in "garments of skins." The celestial garment forfeited by Adam was believed to have been the same as the garment worn by Enoch, Abraham, Isaiah, and others in their heavenly ascents as previously mentioned. Yet the tradition also holds that the garments Adam and Eve received after the Fall "were of a superior and unusual kind." These garments, it is held, were worn by Adam and his descendants "at the time of the offering of the sacrifice." They are described as having "extraordinary brilliance," and as possessing "supernatural qualities." (Ibid. 5:103—4.)

The tradition associated with the supernatural qualities of Adam's garment weaves its way through much of the Old Testament. The garment is said to have descended from Adam to Enoch, and from him to Methuselah, who gave it to Noah, who took it with him on the ark. Ham is accused of stealing it and giving it to his firstborn sun, Cush. (This is offered as the explanation for the difficult story in Genesis 9 where Ham finds Noah drunk and tells his brothers that he has seen his father's nakedness, for which Ham's son is cursed. It is suggested that the story is an allegorical expression for a priesthood garment and birthright struggle.) From Cush the garment is said to have gone to Nimrod, to whom it gave great strength and who by the power of it became a great hunter. From Nimrod, Esau, another hunter, is said to have inherited the garment, only to lose it to Jacob, from whom it passed down to Moses (ibid. 1:177; Jasher 7:23–32).

Such traditions are of no doctrinal worth, yet they do illustrate that it was commonly thought that the patriarchs and prophets wore certain robes or garments with which was associated the idea of power and authority. This accords with our understanding obtained through the Restoration that the ancients had the same gospel rites and ceremonies as we enjoy today.

Perhaps the best known and least understood of the Bible garment stories is that of Joseph and his coat of many colors. Joseph, it will be recalled, was favored above his brothers by his father with a coat of many colors (or at least so we have been told). The coat and Joseph's dreams, in which his brothers paid obeisance to him, combined to kindle within his brothers a murderous hatred. It ought to be obvious, even to the casual reader, that there is something more involved in the story. The self-aggrandizing dreams of a young boy and a gaudy coat given by a doting father do not justify such bitterness. When, however, it is realized that the coat was a symbol, one that announced to Joseph's brothers that Jacob had chosen him to rule over them and had given the birthright to him, their actions become plausible. People murder for birthrights. As indicated in chapter 3, the "coat" given by Jacob to Joseph appears to have been the garment of the priesthood.

It will be recalled that the first thing that Joseph's brothers did upon taking him captive was to strip him of his coat (Genesis 37:23). Though they had not as yet determined what they would do with him, it is clear that he was not to have the coat. The coat was then dipped in the blood of a kid and returned to Jacob for identification. At this point the Book of Mormon picks up the story. Joseph's brothers had rent his coat into many pieces so that it would appear that he had been ravaged by a wild beast. Jacob kept the various pieces of the garment, apparently viewing them as sacred. Years later he announced to his family that some of the pieces of the garment had decayed while others had been preserved. From this Jacob prophesied, "Even as this remnant of garment of my son hath been preserved, so shall a remnant of the seed of my son be preserved by the hand of God, and be taken unto himself, while the remainder of the seed of Joseph shall perish, even as the remnant of his garment." (Alma 46:23—24).

There is no shortage of traditions in the Old World about this garment of Joseph. Ginzberg recounts various stories about appearances of Gabriel to Joseph. One of these appearances was while Joseph was imprisoned in the pit before his brothers sold him into slavery. Here it is said that Gabriel placed upon him a special garment of protection which he wore throughout all his Egyptian experiences (*Legends*, 2:17). Ginzberg also records that after Joseph was reunited with his family in Egypt his father gave him two gifts, the first being the city of Shechem and "the second gift was the garments made by God for Adam and passed from hand to hand, until they came into the possession of Jacob" (ibid. 2:139). He also notes that "according to the view of later authors, Joseph's coat was the holy tunic of the priest" (ibid. 5:326).

These traditions also include Joseph's wife, Asenath, the daughter of the priest of On. According to such, she renounces the luxury, splendor, and rank of an Egyptian princess and "is washed and clothed in white by an angel" who then records her name in the book of life, with the declaration, "From this day forward thou art newly created and formed and given a new life, eating the bread of life and receiving the anointing with the oil of immortality." She is then given a new name and married to Joseph by the Pharaoh himself, "who after giving the couple his blessing, crowns them with gold crowns, and then laying his hands on their heads pronounces the operative blessing: 'May the Lord, the Most high God, bless you, and multiply and exalt and glorify you throughout all Eternity.' " (*Egypt*, p. 216.)

Biblical references to the robes or garments of righteousness begin as the Bible story begins with Adam and Eve in the Garden of Eden. There they were clothed in robes of protection, robes given them by God himself before they left his presence. The protection afforded them by those "coats of skin" was associated with the blood of an innocent and vicarious sacrifice, one which Adam would yet understand to be a type for that sacrifice which would atone for the effects of his fall (Moses 5:7) and allow those worthy to return to the divine presence. Eden, it would appear, was a symbol of the presence of God or the house of God, it being the place where Adam and Eve walked and talked with him, the place of their marriage, the place where they were taught the law of sacrifice and "clothed with power and authority." Here Adam received the priesthood and its keys, and it was the place from which, of necessity, they were driven when they assumed the nature of fallen man, for the natural man cannot abide the presence of God.

JERUSALEM AND HER BEAUTIFUL GARMENTS

Among the most often-quoted passages dealing with the redemption of Israel is Isaiah's call for Israel to "Awake, awake; put on thy strength, O Zion; put on thy beautiful garments, O Jerusalem, the holy city: for henceforth there shall no more come into thee the uncircumcised and the unclean. Shake thyself from the dust; arise, and sit down, O Jerusalem: loose thyself from the bands of thy neck, O captive daughter of Zion." (Isaiah 52:1—2; see also 2 Nephi 8:24—25; 3 Nephi 20:36—37; D&C 82:14.)

In this passage Isaiah directs himself to the seed of Abraham —the rightful heirs to the promises made to the fathers. Spiritually speaking, Israel has worn rags and eaten dust long enough. Now is the time for her to come forth and assume the dignity and power that were once hers. In a revealed commentary on this passage given through the Prophet Joseph Smith, the Lord affirmed that Isaiah had reference to those of the last days who would be called to hold the priesthood, establish Zion, and bring about the redemption of Israel. "To put on her strength," Joseph was told, meant that Israel would again be clothed in the "authority of the priesthood" which she had a "right to by lineage." The loosing herself from the bands of her neck would be the breaking of the "curses of God upon her" in her scattered and apostate condition as she returned to the Lord from whence she had fallen. (D&C 113:7—10.)

It was a paraphrase of these verses that Moroni chose as a conclusion to the Book of Mormon. Speaking to scattered Israel of the last days, Moroni said, "Awake, and arise from the dust,

O Jerusalem; yea, and put on thy beautiful garments, O daughter of Zion; and strengthen thy stakes and enlarge thy borders forever, that thou mayest no more be confounded, that the covenants of the Eternal Father which he hath made unto thee, O house of Israel, may be fulfilled" (Moroni 10:31).

As the nation of Israel is to put on her beautiful garments, so is her citizenry. Describing the millennial Jerusalem of both the Old and the New worlds, Ether said that their inhabitants will have their garments made white through the blood of the Lamb (Ether 13:10—11). In so doing he was echoing Nephi's description of the righteous generations in the Americas following the visit of Christ (1 Nephi 12:10—11). Jacob testified that the righteous will come forth in the resurrection "clothed with purity, yea, even with the robe of righteousness" (2 Nephi 9:14). Surely no other dress is acceptable in heaven. To the Nephites, Christ declared, "No unclean thing can enter into his kingdom; therefore nothing entereth into his rest save it be those who have washed their garments in my blood, because of their faith, and the repentance of all their sins, and their faithfulness unto the end" (3 Nephi 27:19). Teaching the same principle, Alma said that no man can

> be saved except his garments are washed white; yea, his garments must be purified until they are cleansed from all stain, through the blood of him of whom it has been spoken by our fathers, who should come to redeem his people from their sins.
>
> And now I ask of you, my brethren, how will any of you feel, if ye shall stand before the bar of God, having your garments stained with blood and all manner of filthiness? Behold, what will these things testify against you?
>
> Behold will they not testify that ye are murderers, yea, and also that ye are guilty of all manner of wickedness?
>
> Behold, my brethren, do ye suppose that such an one can have a place to sit down in the kingdom of God, with Abraham, with Isaac, and with Jacob, and also all the holy prophets, whose garments are cleansed and are spotless, pure and white? (Alma 5:21—24.)

These teachings of the Book of Mormon prophets are in perfect accord with the vision of John in the book of Revelation.

It will be remembered that John saw 144,000 high priests, twelve thousand representing each of the twelve tribes of Israel, plus "a great multitude, which no man could number," standing before the throne of God "clothed with white robes, and palms in their hands." In response to his question, Who are these "arrayed in white robes? and whence came they?" John was told, "These are they which came out of great tribulation, and have washed their robes, and made them white in the blood of the Lamb." (Revelation 7:9—14.)

THE GARMENTS OF THE RIGHTEOUS

Of the Saints of his day who had not "defiled their garments" the Revelator was told, "they shall walk with me in white: for they are worthy." Then, extending the promise to those of all dispensations, he was assured, "He that overcometh, the same shall be clothed in white raiment." (Revelation 3:4—5.) In the same spirit we find Nephi imploring the heavens, "O Lord, wilt thou encircle me around in the robe of thy righteousness" (2 Nephi 4:33). Such was the appeal of Moroni, who was assured by the Lord that even though many would reject his testimony and the record he had written, he need not lament, for he had been faithful and his garments would be made clean (Ether 12:35—37).

On that June morning when Hyrum Smith left Nauvoo with his brother Joseph for Carthage and a sure death, he read and marked this same passage of Moroni's:

> And it came to pass that I prayed unto the Lord that he would give unto the Gentiles grace, that they might have charity. And it came to pass that the Lord said unto me: If they have not charity it mattereth not unto thee, thou hast been faithful; wherefore thy garments shall be made clean. And because thou hast seen thy weakness, thou shalt be made strong, even unto the sitting down in the place which I have prepared in the mansions of my Father. And now I . . . bid farewell unto the Gentiles; yea, and also unto my brethren whom I love, until we shall meet before the judgment-seat of Christ, where all men shall know that my garments are not spotted with your blood (D&C 135:5.)

Such has been the prayer of the righteous of all ages. Alma told those of his day to have faith, hope, and charity and to "abound in good works," promising that the Lord would bless them that keep their "garments spotless," that they might "sit down with Abraham, Isaac, and Jacob, and the holy prophets who have been ever since the world began, having . . . garments spotless even as their garments are spotless, in the kingdom of heaven to go no more out" (Alma 7:24—25).

The Marriage of the Lamb

Isaiah spoke of a day in which the Lord of hosts would celebrate a "feast of fat things" in Mount Zion with those of all nations. The feast was to come at a time when the veil would be lifted from their eyes and death swallowed up in victory. (Isaiah 25:6—10.) Such a feast, Joseph Smith was told, was to take place in the Mount Zion of the New Jerusalem. To Joseph Smith's revelation, which draws on the language of Isaiah, is added the announcement that this feast will be "a supper of the house of the Lord." To this feast the rich and the learned, the wise and the noble will all be invited; then is to come the day of the Lord's power, when "the poor, the lame, and the blind, and the deaf, come in unto the marriage of the Lamb, and partake of the supper of the Lord." (D&C 58:8—12.)

In dedicating the Kirtland Temple, Joseph Smith prayed that the Lord would remember the sick and afflicted along with the poor and the meek of the earth, that the kingdom that had been restored might fill the whole earth, and that it might be "adorned as a bride" for that day when the Lord would unveil the heavens, and the trump sound, and the righteous be caught up in the cloud to meet him. In preparation for such a day the Prophet prayed "that our garments may be pure, that we may be clothed upon with robes of righteousness, with palms in our hands, and crowns of glory upon our heads, and reap eternal joy for all our sufferings" (D&C 109:72—76).

Describing these same events, John the Revelator wrote: "Let us be glad and rejoice, and give honour to him: for the marriage of the Lamb is come, and his wife hath made herself ready. And to her was granted that she should be arrayed in fine linen, clean and white: for the fine linen is the righteousness of saints. And he saith unto me, Write, Blessed are they which are called unto the marriage supper of the Lamb." (Revelation 19:7—9.)

NOTES

1. This theme is well illustrated in the Odes of Solomon. Having forsaken the vanity of the world and turned to God, the ancient writer declared, "I stripped it off and cast it from me: And the Lord renewed me in His raiment, and possessed me by His light, and from above He gave me rest in incorruption" (Odes of Solomon 11:9—10; as found in *The Lost Books of the Bible and the Forgotten Books of Eden*, reprinted by Collins World). Again he writes, "I was clothed with the covering of thy Spirit, and thou didst remove from me my raiment of skin; For thy right hand lifted me up and removed sickness from me: And I became mighty in the truth, and holy by thy righteousness; and all my adversaries were afraid of me" (ibid. 26:10). And still again, "I put off darkness and clothed myself with light, And my soul acquired a body free from sorrow or affliction or pain" (ibid. 21:2—3).

2. Cf. Hugh Nibley, *Lehi in the Desert* (Salt Lake City: Bookcraft Publishing Co., 1952); also Hugh Nibley, *The Timely and the Timeless* (Provo: Religious Study Center, Brigham Young University, 1978), pp. 160—64.

11

Like Unto Me

Not only did the prophets of Old Testament times believe in Christ and worship the Father in his name but they also lived in such a way that each could say of the promised Messiah, as did Moses, he shall be "like unto me" (Deuteronomy 18:15). From Adam to Malachi, their lives constituted marvelous prophetic types of the life of Christ.

ADAM AND HIS SONS

Appropriately, Adam is the first earthly type for Christ. Both were the firstborn of the Father—Adam the first created in the flesh, Christ the first of his spirit children. Paul described Adam as the "figure of him that was to come" (Romans 5:14). Physically and spiritually both were in the image and likeness of their Father. Both were called and ordained before the foundations of the earth—Adam to be the father of mortality, Christ to be the father of immortality. Paul succinctly captures the roles of these two firstborn of the Father in his often-quoted statement to the Corinthian Saints, "For as in Adam all die, even so in Christ shall all be made alive" (1 Corinthians 15:22). To further emphasize this likeness Paul describes Christ as the "last Adam" (1 Corinthians 15:45).

As Adam ruled in a paradisiacal kingdom and was granted dominion over all things, so his elder brother Christ will yet rule the earth in its paradisiacal splendor, having dominion over all. Adam was earth's first prophet, priest, and king. He obtained the promise of the Lord that he would reign over his posterity forever (D&C 107:55). In our pre-earth home he bore the name of Michael, meaning "who is like God," and now holds the "keys of salvation" for all God's children (D&C 78:16). Similarly, Christ, known as one "like unto God" (Abraham 3:24), became the "author of eternal salvation" (Hebrews 5:9). Surely Adam was earth's first living prophecy of what the Messiah would be.

Nor is Adam a type of Christ alone, for to be like the Son is to be like the Father. All men have both Adam and God as their father. Each had a son renowned for righteousness and obedience (Christ and Abel), and each had a son who became Perdition (Lucifer and Cain). Both righteous sons were martyred by the shedding of blood at the hands of one called Perdition (Moses 5:24, 32; John 17:12).

Adam's son Seth was to him as Christ was to the Father. Of Seth the scriptures say he "was a perfect man, and his likeness was the express likeness of his father, insomuch that he seemed to be like unto his father in all things, and could be distinguished from him only by his age" (D&C 107:43). Paul described Christ as being in the "express image" of his father (Hebrews 1:3). Joseph Smith, to whom both the Father and the Son appeared, said they "exactly resembled each other in features and likeness" (HC 4:536).

Abel, who Joseph Smith tells us held the keys of his dispensation, was also an obvious type for Christ (HC 4:208). Abel was "a keeper of sheep" (i.e., a good shepherd) who offered an acceptable offering to the Lord, an offering made in faith, one which involved the shedding of blood and was in all things a similitude of the manner in which the Lamb of God would yet be offered. In so doing he was opposed by his brother, whose offering did not involve the atoning blood and was therefore rejected. All of this was but the earthly shadow of the events of a heavenly council in which the Father accepted the offering of him who chose to do His will and make the proper sacrifice, and rejected the offering of the son of the morning who sought not to be obedient nor to do the will of the Father in making the necessary sacrifice.

ENOCH AND NOAH

So much did Enoch resemble Christ that with perfect propriety the Church was called after his name, or the "church of Enoch" (D&C 76:67). Enoch's name means "the dedicated," or "dedicated to Jehovah," and as such constitutes an apt description of Enoch and the church over which he presided (*Names*, p. 73). In the Epistle of Jude, Enoch is described as "the seventh from Adam" (Jude 1:14). Symbolically this takes on an added significance, seven being the number that conveys the idea of divine completion and rest. Thus Enoch and the seventh generation from Adam were thought to typify the millennial dispensation, or the seventh thousand years, when the earth will be sanctified and will enter into its rest. As Enoch and the host of his city were caught into heaven, to return during the millennial Zion, so Christ, the firstfruits, and those that were caught up with him, along with all the righteous dead, will return to usher in that great millennial kingdom (Moses 7:63; JST, Genesis 9:21).

Noah had many experiences like those of Enoch. Both were great preachers of righteousness who taught the doctrines of faith, repentance, and baptism. Both were hated by unbelievers, who sought their lives, yet both were preserved by the power of God. Both were great missionaries, standing at the heads of their dispensations; both conversed and "walked with God." Noah, like Enoch, bore a name with spiritual significance. It means "rest," "consolation," and "comfort" (*Names*, p. 126; Moses 8:9). Thus even his name was to serve as a reminder of the rest and comfort found only in Christ and obedience to the laws and ordinances of his gospel. Further, Noah was described as a "just" and "perfect" man, as obviously Enoch was also (Moses 8:27). Noah was required, by the authority of his priesthood, to baptize the earth that it might be cleansed from sin (*Answers* 4:20; see also JST Genesis 14:30–31). This was but the foreshadowing of the baptism of the earth by fire in its final cleansing at the hands of the returning Christ. Surely both Noah and Enoch were types of him who was and is to come.

Melchizedek: King of Righteousness

No Bible character is more of an enigma to Jew and Christian alike (unless it is Christ himself) than Melchizedek. Without introduction in the scriptural text he appears on the scene to bless Abraham and receive tithes from him. He bears the title that Jews recognize as designating their Messiah (*Melchizedek* means "king of righteousness"), while at the same time bearing gifts that recall to Christians the Lord's Supper (Genesis 14:18—20). He then disappears from the Bible as mysteriously as he appeared. He goes unmentioned for a thousand years, and is then referred to in the Psalms (110:4) as a type for the coming Lord of David. Again the Bible falls silent, another thousand years pass, until we find Paul announcing him to the Hebrew Christians as a proof that salvation is not to be found in the law of Moses and that the Levitical Priesthood is subservient to that of Melchizedek (Hebrews 7). So scanty are the texts that the world has supposed him to be a Canaanite priest who, it has been argued, was "an angel (Origen), the Holy Spirit (Epiphanius), Christ (Ambrose), Enoch (Calmet), Shem, (Targums, Jerome, Luther), et al" (*Wycliffe BD* 2:1099). All manner of theological mischief has grown out of the mistranslation in Hebrews 7:3 which announces Melchizedek to be "without father, without mother, without descent, having neither beginning of days, nor end of life. . . ." As the passage now reads it is at least true of the many tales woven into various theological explanations of Melchizedek, for they seem to be without beginning or end.

For Latter-day Saints, there is no mystery surrounding Salem's king. We know him to have been a great high priest after whom "the church in ancient days" named the priesthood in order to avoid the too frequent use of the name of the Supreme Being. "Before his day it was called the Holy Priesthood, after the Order of the Son of God" (D&C 107:3—4). Melchizedek received his priesthood through the fathers from Noah and in turn conferred that same priesthood upon Abraham (D&C 84:14). It is the priesthood, not Melchizedek, that is without father and mother, without beginning of days or end of years (JST, Hebrews 7:3; D&C 84:17).

In a great discourse on the priesthood, Alma described Melchizedek as the perfect type and shadow for Christ. "Melchizedek," he stated, "was a king over the land of Salem; and his people had waxed strong in iniquity and abomination; yea, they had all gone astray; they were full of all manner of wickedness; But Melchizedek having exercised mighty faith, and received the office of the high priesthood according to the holy order of God, did preach repentance unto his people. And behold, they did repent; and Melchizedek did establish peace in the land in his days; therefore he was called the prince of peace, for he was the king of Salem; and he did reign under his father." (Alma 13:17—18.) Alma's profile is of a great preacher of righteousness, a teacher of repentance, whose message, once it was accepted by his people, established peace throughout the land. This prince of peace then ruled Salem (meaning "peace") as prophet, priest, and king, "under his father." The likeness to Christ is made even more perfect by adding the description from the JST, from which we learn that Melchizedek "was called the king of heaven by his people, or, in other words, the King of peace," and that his people "wrought righteousness, and obtained heaven," seeking for the city of Enoch (JST, Genesis 14:34—36).

Abraham's meeting with Melchizedek in the king's dale (one of the valleys surrounding Jerusalem, possibly the Kidron Valley) is of considerable typological significance. The JST describes it thus: "Melchizedek, king of Salem, brought forth bread and wine: and he brake bread and blest it; and he blest the wine, he being the priest of the most high God. And he gave to Abram, and he blessed him, and said, Blessed Abram, thou art a man of the most high God, possessor of heaven and of earth; And blessed is the name of the most high God, which hath delivered thine enemies into thine hand. And Abram gave him tithes of all he had taken." (JST, Genesis 14:17—20.) The ritual was apparently a foreshadowing of a future day when another King of Righteousness would introduce such a ritual in the blessing of his servants (Matthew 26:26–28).

ABRAHAM AND ISAAC

Abraham, who was promised that he would be the father of nations or multitudes, is venerated as such today by Jews, Christians, and Mohammedans alike. Among Christians no Old Testament figure is more universally recognized as a type for Christ. Known also as the father of the faithful (which title, like that of father of multitudes, is a likeness of Christ), Abraham and Isaac were understood to be "a similitude of God and his Only Begotten Son," even in Old Testament times (Jacob 4:5). The Abraham narrative begins with his obedient response to the command of God in leaving Ur of the Chaldees. To Abraham the Lord said, "Get thee out of thy country, and from thy kindred, and from thy father's house, unto a land that I will show thee" (Abraham 2:3). So Abraham departed his country, his kindred, and the honors of his father's house, "not knowing whither he went," yet willing that God be his guide (Hebrews 11:8). Ultimately this and the sacrifices yet to follow would be rewarded with a greater country, a faithful posterity, and the fulness of the honors of his divine Father's house. Yet the journey would be long, the trials plentiful, and for the moment of mortality he would be but a stranger and pilgrim on the earth.

Abram and Sarai first went to Haran, where they won many souls to the Lord (Abraham 2:15) and proved their willingness to separate themselves from the world. At the direction of the Lord they continued their journey into the land of Canaan, building altars at Jershon, at Shechem, and between Bethel and Ai. Whether we are to see significance in each of these places is not certain. *Shechem* signifies "shoulder," suggesting the place of strength; it was situated in the plains of Moreh, which means "instruction." Perhaps this is to suggest that as we separate ourselves from the world, and depend on the Lord to direct our paths, we come to the place of strength from which we are entitled to receive instruction at his hand. From Shechem they journeyed to a mountain on the east of Bethel (house of God) and west of Ai (heap of ruin), where again they built an altar and from thence journeyed to Egypt, where Sarai was tested and they were rewarded with great wealth before returning to Canaan.

When the Lord established his covenant with Abraham in the land of Canaan he promised him a son, to be born of Sarah in her old age. Accordingly, when Abraham was a hundred years of age and his wife but ten years less, the promise of the Lord was fulfilled as their only son, Isaac, was born to them. That the events of his birth were symbolic there can be no doubt. He was the long-awaited son, the son of promise, the son of whom more had been spoken before his birth than any other save only He of whom he was a type. He was known by name before his birth, a name designated in the heavens (Genesis 17:19). He was the child of God's miracle upon his mother, the child born at the "set time of which God had spoken" (Genesis 21:2), the child destined to receive all that his father had (Genesis 24:36).

As Isaac grew, his older brother, Ishmael, turned on him to mock, and thus Ishmael and his mother were cast out by Abraham and Sarah. Paul saw this as a type. He likened Ishmael, the child of the flesh or the child of bondage (he being the son of the bondwoman), to the Mosaic law; Isaac, the child of promise and son of the freewoman, he likened to the fulness of the gospel. Those seeking to embrace the higher law were persecuted in like manner by those born of the carnal law. Yet they are heirs to the promise, while their persecutors are destined to wander in the wilderness. (Galatians 4:22—31.)

In all scriptural writ there is no more perfect similitude of events yet future nor any more detailed Messianic prophecy than the command of God to Abraham that he offer his son as a sacrifice. "Take now thy son, thine only son Isaac, whom thou lovest, and get thee into the land of Moriah; and offer him there for a burnt offering upon one of the mountains which I will tell thee of" (Genesis 22:2). Father and son immediately commenced the three-day journey from Beersheba to the appointed place— Moriah. The Genesis account refers to Isaac as "the lad"; Josephus gives his age as twenty-five, while the rabbis held that he was thirty-six or thirty-seven. Reasoning from the perfection of the rest of the type, we would conclude that he was thirty-three years of age, that being the age at which Christ, like Isaac, offered himself as a willing sacrifice. Such being the case, Abraham would have been 133 years of age, again emphasizing that Isaac was fully willing to yield himself to the will of his father.

The place of the offering we have already identified. Mount Moriah was the sacred spot where the temple of the Lord was yet to be built and where both typological and actual sacrifice would yet be wrought out. As they ascended the hill, "Abraham took the wood of the burnt offering, and laid it upon Isaac" to carry as the Christ would yet carry his own cross. When Isaac inquired, "Where is the lamb for a burnt offering?" Abraham responded, "God will provide himself a lamb," for in very deed only God could provide a sacrificial lamb that would redeem all mankind. (Genesis 22:6—8.) And thus the Lord did, for the ram in the thicket was a double type, representing the substitute for Isaac as Christ is the substitute for all, and of course representing Christ himself as the great and last offering.

Abraham's life personified faith and typified the blessings that flow from obedience. Through Isaiah the Lord said: "Hearken to me, ye that follow after righteousness, ye that seek the Lord: look unto the rock whence ye are hewn, and to the hole of the pit whence ye are digged. Look unto Abraham your father, and unto Sarah that bare you: for I called him alone [when he was but one], and blessed him, and increased him." (Isaiah 51:1—2.) To Joseph Smith the Lord said: "Abraham received all things, whatsoever he received, by revelation and commandment, by my word, saith the Lord, and hath entered into his exaltation and sitteth upon his throne. . . . Go ye, therefore, and do the works of Abraham." (D&C 132:29, 32.)

JACOB

Jacob was instructed by the messenger of God that his name was to be changed to Israel, "for as a prince" he was to have "power with God and with men," and was to prevail (Genesis 32:28). In the receipt of this promise he became a type for the

promised Messiah. Both were loved of God before their birth
(Romans 9:10—13), both would be prince and servant, both
would have power with God, both would bless Israel, and both
would ultimately triumph.

In blessing his sons (Genesis 49) Jacob used events of their
lives to foreshadow the future of their tribes. Similarly, his life
was a prefiguring of the history of Israel. As he left the house of
God (Bethel) (Genesis 28:19) for the land of exile, so would the
nation that descended from him. As God would yet say, "Return
unto the land of thy fathers, and to thy kindred; and I will be
with thee" (Genesis 31:3), and again, "Arise, go up to Beth-el"
(Genesis 35:1), the place of divine manifestation and covenant, so
Israel of the last days is to be invited to return to the land of their
fathers and to the house of the Lord. As the immediate effect of
God's call upon Jacob was to get him to purge his family from
idolatry, saying to "all that were with him, Put away the strange
gods that are among you, and be clean, and change your garments" (Genesis 35:2), so the righteous of Israel in the last days
will leave their "strange gods," change their ways, and be clothed
with robes of righteousness. As God responded to Jacob in the
day of his distress, so he will answer Jacob's children as they
gather (Genesis 35:3). As the "terror of God was upon the cities
that were round about them" (Genesis 35:5), so it is prophesied of
the New Jerusalem that "the terror of the Lord also shall be there,
insomuch that the wicked will not come unto it" (D&C 45:67).
And as Jacob returned to Bethel to build another altar (Genesis
35:7), so Israel of the last days will again build a house of God
where they might kneel at its altars. As ancient Israel testified of a
God who appeared to them (Genesis 35:7), so Israel of the last
days will testify.

Moses: A Type for Christ

When God called Moses to represent him as his servant he
said to him, "Thou art in the similitude of mine Only Begotten;
and mine Only Begotten is and shall be the Savior, for he is full of
grace and truth" (Moses 1:6). True it is that all men are created in
the image and likeness of God their Father, for as the Psalmist

declared, all are "children of the most High" (Psalm 82:6). Yet of Moses it appears that there is a special likeness, perhaps even a physical likeness, but of greater importance a likeness in works and experiences. Indeed, in one of the greatest of the Old Testament prophecies Moses described Christ for his people, saying, "The Lord thy God will raise up unto thee a Prophet from the midst of thee, of thy brethren, like unto me; unto him ye shall hearken" (Deuteronomy 18:15). Moses, his life, and his ministry were plainly to serve Israel as an introduction to and likeness of the Savior himself. The reader is invited to consider the following likenesses:

1. Both were numbered among the noble and great ones of the premortal life.

2. Both were foreordained to their earthly ministries having proven themselves through the exercise of "exceeding great faith" and "good works" in the first estate.

3. Both were known by name generations before their birth, and of both there were detailed prophecies of the works they would do (JST, Genesis 50:29—35; Mosiah 3:5—10).

4. At birth both of their lives were in peril as Satan, who knew their destinies, sought to destroy them. In both instances the first attempt to take their lives came at the hand of a king who saw them as a threat to his kingdom.

5. Both were rejected when they first came to Israel. Moses fled into the wilderness, where he was to remain for forty years. Christ was also rejected by Israel, and his church was forced into the wilderness (Revelation 12:6).

6. Both went into the wilderness to be with God and both were administered to by angels. Moses was "ordained by the hand of angels" (JST, Galatians 3:19); Christ was also administered to by angels (Mark 1:13).

7. Both fasted for forty days and forty nights (Deuteronomy 9:18; Matthew 4:2).

8. Both were confronted by Satan, who sought to have them worship him (Moses 1:12—23; Matthew 4:1—10).

9. Both had the experience of being carried by the Spirit to a high mountain, where they were transfigured and shown the destiny of the earth (Moses 1:1, 8, 11; JST, Matthew 4:8).

10. Both introduced their ministries with great miracles.

11. Both controlled the elements. Moses turned the rivers of Egypt to blood and commanded the Red Sea to part; Christ turned water to wine and walked upon the Sea of Galilee.

12. Both miraculously fed their followers, Moses with manna from heaven, and Christ in the miracles of the loaves and the fishes.

13. Both left Egypt to fulfill prophecy (JST, Genesis 50:29; Matthew 2:15; Hosea 11:1).

14. Both were known as the shepherds of the Lord's flock (Isaiah 63:11; John 10). Moses tended the flock of Jethro, his father-in-law, for forty years as a preparation for the last forty years of his life, when he was to shepherd the flock of God. He took his flock to the "backside of the desert, and came to the mountain of God," where he received the instruction that he was to bring his Egyptian flock to that same place (Exodus 3:1, 12).

15. Each was known as a prophet, a priest, and a king. That Moses personified what a prophet ought to be is illustrated by Christ's reference to "Moses and the prophets" (Luke 16:29). He received the priesthood at the hands of Jethro (D&C 84:6) and was referred to as the king of Israel (Deuteronomy 33:5; *Jeshurun* is a symbolic name for Israel). Christ, of course, is the great Prophet, Priest, and King.

16. Each was to Israel a Redeemer, Deliverer, or Liberator. Moses freed them from the oppression and bondage of Egypt, while Christ frees from the oppression and bondage of sin all who will follow him, leading them through the wilderness of life to an eternal inheritance according to the heavenly promise.

17. Both were mediators of a covenant—Moses the old and Christ the new. In his day we see Moses pleading, interceding, reconciling, standing between the Lord and his people, even offering to have his own name stricken from the book of life if the Lord will not forgive his people (Exodus 32:32). Christ's role is everlastingly that of a mediator, intervening between God and man so that all who believe and obey may be reconciled with the Father.

18. Both were lawgivers, Moses giving that law which came to bear his name, as Christ restored anew the fulness of the gospel law which in turn bore his name.

19. Both were revelators; both received by revelation that which they taught, and both taught that all true religion must be a revealed religion.

20. Both were teachers and both taught as one having authority. Christ taught the gospel in its fulness, Moses taught it in part, yet the principles that they taught were one and the same.

21. Both were and are judges. As Moses was a judge in Israel, so Christ will yet render judgment upon the wicked. As there were those destroyed in the camp of Israel for wickedness and rebellion, so the wicked and rebellious will be destroyed in the last days.

22. Both were meek. The scriptural account tells us that Moses was "very meek, above all the men which were upon the face of the earth" (Numbers 12:3). Of himself Jesus said, "I am meek and lowly in heart" (Matthew 11:29). In all attributes Moses would have been like unto Christ, differing from him only in degree of perfection.

23. Both restored the Church in their day, both presided over it, both chose, called, and set apart others to lead. Both had their Twelve and both had their Seventy, and if we had the full scriptural account it is assumed we would know that in both dispensations these officers had like powers and ministered in like manner. (*Mortal Messiah* 3:100.)

24. Both prophesied concerning the destiny of Israel. Moses gave as it were a patriarchal blessing to each of the tribes of Israel in which he foreshadowed their future (Deuteronomy 33). In his discourse on the Mount of Olives, Christ detailed the destruction of the nation of Israel and their scattering and eventual gathering (Matthew 24).

25. Both ascended into heaven in a cloud. Moses, contrary to the Bible record, did not die (Deuteronomy 34:5–6) but rather, as the Book of Mormon tells us, was translated (Alma 45:19). Old World traditions confirm this. Josephus writes, "A cloud stood over him on the sudden, and he disappeared in a certain valley, although he wrote in the holy books that he died" (Josephus, p. 103).

26. Moses obtained acceptance by Israel when he came the second time in power to redeem them and free them from their enemies. Similarly, Christ will be accepted at his Second Coming.

DAVID THE BELOVED

Excluding Moses, there is no character more prominent to the story of the Old Testament than David, the son of Jesse. Virtually every recorded event to the time of his great sin seems fraught with symbolic meaning pointing to Christ. He was the child of Bethlehem, the faithful shepherd; he bore a name meaning "beloved," or "my beloved." He was anointed Israel's king long before he received the kingship.

Clothed only with the armor of faith, David defeated Goliath and put the enemies of Israel to flight. Without justification or provocation he was opposed by Saul, thus providing a type for Christ (the Anointed One) and his servants, who have ever been opposed by those whose allegiance is to another kingdom. Foreshadowing events of the last days, David conquered the Jebusites and gave Israel the city of Jerusalem and the holy mount where the temple would be built. He then brought the ark of the covenant to Jerusalem, it being the symbol of the presence of the Lord. It was David who unified the tribes of Israel, brought safety to the nation, and subjugated their enemies within and those at her borders. He extended the kingdom of Israel to the borders that had long before been promised to Abraham. His kingdom was a type of the glory and power that will attend the Son of David during the time of the millennial reign. Such phrases as "the city of David," "the house of David," "the throne of David," "the seed of David," "the oath sworn unto David" carry both a memory of what once was and the announcement of what is yet to be.

THE SUFFERING SERVANT

Much of the Old Testament temple ritual was a prophetic dramatization of the suffering of Christ. For instance, the gold for the mercy seat and the candlestick was not only to be pure gold but beaten gold. The spices for the holy ointment, the incense, and the frankincense were to be crushed—otherwise they could not give off their fragrance—and the perfume which was thus made was also to be beaten very small (Exodus 30:36). The oil with which the ointment was compounded, and the oil for the meal offering, was beaten oil, and for the candlestick "pure oil olive beaten for the light" (Exodus 27:20). The corn for the meal offering was to be beaten out of full ears; the flour for the same offering, symbolically representing Christ's spotless life, was fine flour, as was the flour used for the shewbread.

The Old Testament is also replete with what are called suffering servant passages. These passages foretell the rejection, abuse, and martyrdom of the Messiah. Because, as we have seen, the lives of his faithful servants are so much like his own, these passages are often appropriately applied to them also. Christ himself took such verses (Isaiah 52:13—15), which were obviously fulfilled in him, and applied them anew to the Prophet Joseph Smith (3 Nephi 20:43—45; 21:10). Isaiah 53, which is the most sublime of Messianic prophecies, has been applied by various scholars to Hezekiah, Uzziah, Jehoiachin, and Zerubbabel, all kings of Israel. It has even been applied to the Persian king Cyrus. Of prophets, it has been applied to both Isaiah and Jeremiah (IB 4:293). Such applications are inappropriate only when they seek to deny the primary purpose of the passage, which is to testify of Christ.

THE MESSENGER OF THE LORD

Though the Old Testament contains only a fragmentary account of the lives and teachings of its prophets, all who are sensitive to the voice of the Spirit will see it as a messenger to prepare the way for the coming of the Messiah. All its prophets, in the events of their lives, their teachings, prophecies, and their testimonies, were in greater or lesser degree prophetic types of what the Christ would be. Appropriately, Malachi, the concluding book of the Old Testament, has as its central theme the coming of the Lord and the messengers who would prepare the way before him (Malachi 3:1; 4:5). Nor should it be lost on the reader that *Malachi* is a Hebrew name meaning "my messenger." It is believed to be a contraction of the name *Malachijah*, which means "messenger of Jehovah." The apocryphal work 2 Esdras interprets *Malachi* to mean "the messenger of the Lord" (2 Esdras 1:40).

John the Baptist was one such messenger in both the meridian dispensation and our own, as was Elijah. The gospel is always such a messenger (D&C 45:9), as are the mortal instruments through whom it is taught. The great fulfillment of Malachi's prophecy of the messenger who will precede the sudden appearance of the Lord to his temple is the Prophet Joseph Smith, through whom the knowledge and testimony of the ancients was restored. As Adam and the prophets of the Old Testament were types of what Christ would be, so the apostles and prophets of the New Testament were types of what he was. Similarly, in our day, Joseph Smith and his successors are types of what the Christ is. In like manner, all who go forward as messengers of the Lord are obligated to so live that they too are types of Him whom they serve, for all should be able to say, as did Moses, he shall be "like unto me" (Deuteronomy 18:15).

12

Prophets
and Pageants

The Old Testament is rich in stories in which the prophets used the "it is like this" principle to teach and prophecy. As Christ did, they used the whole of their nation as a synagogue for preaching and as a stage for dramatizing those teachings. Their lives became symbols; they were living types and shadows of the very things of which they testified. Props, costumes, marriages, births, and deaths all were used as part of the prophetic drama. The world has known few such teachers. They taught a people who did not want to understand with a plainness that they could not misunderstand. Consider the following acted parables of inspired teachers.

SAMUEL

Saul, the first king of Israel, was commanded to destroy the Amalekites and all that they had. Disregarding this command, he spared Agag, the Amalekite king, and the best of their oxen and sheep, the latter for sacrifices. When the prophet Samuel discovered this he told Saul that because he had rejected the word of the Lord, the Lord had rejected him as king. "As Samuel turned to go away, Saul caught at the hem of his garment and it tore" (JB, 1 Samuel 15:27). Samuel, capturing a great teaching moment, said, "The Lord hath rent the kingdom of Israel from thee this day, and hath given it to a neighbour of thine, that is better than thou" (1 Samuel 15:28). That is, "As you have rent the garment of the prophet [i.e., the priesthood], so the kingdom of Israel shall be rent from thee and given to another."

Ahijah

We see a somewhat similar story taking place during the reign of Solomon. The prophet Ahijah accosted Jeroboam, the Ephrathite, as he left Jerusalem. Ahijah was wearing a new garment, which he took and rent into twelve pieces. He told Jeroboam to take ten pieces, saying, "Thus saith the Lord, the God of Israel, Behold, I will rend the kingdom out of the hand of Solomon, and will give ten tribes to thee" (1 Kings 11:29–31). The prophecy was filled at Solomon's death when his stubborn and foolish son Rehoboam split the kingdom and ten of the tribes chose to follow Jeroboam.

Elijah

In extending the call to the prophetic office to Elisha, Elijah merely walked into the field where Elisha was plowing and placed his mantle on his shoulders (1 Kings 19:19). Though Elisha was subsequently anointed, no other explanation was needed to announce his call than this simple ceremony or action on the part of Elijah. Implicit within the story is the idea that there is something peculiar to the garb of a prophet. Zechariah makes reference to "a rough garment" (Zechariah 13:4) worn by prophets. Such dress was one of the distinctive features of John the Baptist (Matthew 3:4).

This mantle figured prominently in the parting scene between these two prophets. With it Elijah smote the waters of the Jordan that they might cross to the east side, from whence Elijah was taken into heaven. Then Elisha "took up also the mantle of Elijah that fell from him" and smote the waters of the Jordan in like manner, and again they parted, causing the sons of the prophets who witnessed it to say, " 'The spirit of Elijah doth rest on Elisha.' " (2 Kings 2:8–15.)

ISAIAH

To dramatize to Israel that their hopes of safety were falsely placed in their anticipation that Egypt and Ethiopia would shield them from Assyria, the Lord instructed Isaiah: "Go and loose the sackcloth from off thy loins, and put off thy shoe from thy foot. And he did so, walking naked and barefoot. And the Lord said, Like as my servant Isaiah hath walked naked and barefoot three years for a sign and wonder upon Egypt and upon Ethiopia; So shall the king of Assyria lead away the Egyptians prisoners, and the Ethiopians captives, young and old, naked and barefoot, even with their buttocks uncovered, to the shame of Egypt." (Isaiah 20:2—4.)

It is generally agreed that Isaiah did not go entirely naked. He was, however, to take off his shoes, a sign of distress and humiliation, and to remove his shirt of "sackcloth" which he obviously wore to dramatize the need for repentance. The "sackcloth" or "hairy mantle," as already mentioned, was apparently the customary garb of prophets. "Now he was to strip off shirt and sandals and go about clad only in the apron or loincloth of a prisoner or slave," illustrating the fate that awaited Egypt and Ethiopia. Perhaps he was only required to do this periodically during the three years, but in any case it was a dramatic way to call attention to his message.

MICAH

Nor was Isaiah alone in such an experience. Micah, a contemporary, also went "stripped and naked" to impress on the inhabitants of Samaria and Jerusalem that they too would soon be as destitute as himself because of their immorality and idolatrous worship (Micah 1:7—8).

JEREMIAH

Jeremiah, in an attempt to dissuade Zedekiah, king of Judah, and the kings of the surrounding nations from rebelling against Babylon, was instructed of the Lord, "make thee bonds and yokes, and put them upon thy neck" (Jeremiah 27:2), that they might know of the greater bondage that would be theirs should they rebel against Nebuchadnezzar. Hananiah proved himself a false prophet by taking the yoke from Jeremiah's neck and breaking it, promising freedom from Nebuchadnezzar within two years. Jeremiah's prophetic response was, "Thou hast broken the yokes of wood; but thou shalt make for them yokes of iron" (Jeremiah 28:10—13).

One of the most difficult of these stories for scholars and Bible students alike is that of Jeremiah and his linen girdle. In this instance he was instructed to gird a linen girdle about his loins which was not to be washed. After having worn it for some time he was directed to take it to the Euphrates and hide it there in a hole in a rock. This he did. Later he was instructed to go back and get it. When he did so he found it in a decayed and worthless condition.

Interpreting the parable, the Lord explained that the girdle represented both Judah and Jerusalem, who through wickedness and the worship of false gods were as the rotted garment. "For as the girdle cleaveth to the loins of a man," the Lord said, "so have I caused to cleave unto me the whole house of Israel and the whole house of Judah, saith the Lord; that they might be unto me for a people, and for a name, and for a praise, and for a glory: but they would not hear" (Jeremiah 13:11).

The difficulty in this story is the some three hundred miles, much of it desert country, that separates the Euphrates from Jerusalem. For the story to be interpreted literally Jeremiah would have had to traverse that distance four times. That seems highly impractical for this single teaching device. We are left to wonder why a more convenient hiding place would not have served as well. It has been suggested that the corruption of the garment on the banks of the Euphrates typified the corruption of Israel in her Babylonian captivity, but this does not seem to be Jeremiah's message. His emphasis is the corruption that causes captivity, not the corruption of captivity. The fact that no really satisfying answers have been given to these questions seems to sustain the idea that in this instance we may be dealing with a graphic illustration rather than an actual experience of the prophet.

Before we leave Jeremiah, one other instance merits mention. While he was a prisoner because of his prophecies against the state, and while the city was under siege, he purchased property to dramatize to the people that there would be a return from Babylon, and that each family would possess again their former inheritances. Actions, especially when they involve money, speak louder than words. (See Jeremiah 32.)

EZEKIEL

With the exception of the Savior with his miracles, no prophet used more dramatic or unusual teaching devices than Ezekiel. A prophet of the Babylonian captivity, he by revelation kept his people informed as to the status and destiny of those still in Jerusalem.

To illustrate the siege and fall of Jerusalem he took what was apparently a large building brick and made a portrait of the city. He then laid his model city siege with trenches, mounds of dirt, miniature battering rams, and so forth. (Ezekiel 4:1—3.) To illustrate the length of the siege he was to lie on his left side one day for each year that the Northern Kingdom would be under siege, and on his right side one day for each year the Southern Kingdom would be under siege. In so doing the Lord said that he would lay bands on him so that he could not turn from one side to the other, thus depicting the restraint that would be experienced by each nation. (Ezekiel 4:4—8.)

The years given are 390 for the Northern Kingdom and 40 for the Southern Kingdom. It would be approximately forty years before the Southern Kingdom would return from their Babylonian captivity. No satisfactory explanation has been given for the 390 years the Northern Kingdom would be in seige. It is difficult to suppose that the Lord required Ezekiel to be imprisoned for over fourteen months just to make this point. Thus it is supposed that he was so bound only at night.

To illustrate the scarcity of food and the humility to which those of the beleaguered city would be subjected, Ezekiel was given a diet by the Lord that consisted of a half pound of bread and a pint and a half of water per day for the 390 days that he lay on his side. His bread loaf was to be made of wheat, barley, beans, lentils, millet, and fitches—this being a system of stretching the finer grain by mixing it with coarser ones. The bread was to be cooked over a fire made from human dung to further manifest the wretched conditions to which those of Jerusalem would be exposed. (Ezekiel 4:9—17.)

Finally this fourteen-month stage play was to end by Ezekiel cutting the hair from his head and beard and dividing it with the use of scales into three parts. He was to burn one third of it in the midst of the city, take another third and cut it up with a knife, and then take the final third and scatter it with the wind. A few hairs were to be spared, some of which he was to bind in his robe. The others he was to cast into a fire. (Ezekiel 5:1—4.)

The meaning associated with this strange ritual was explained as follows: "A third part of thee [Israel] shall die with the pestilence, and with famine shall they be consumed in the midst of thee: and a third part shall fall by the sword round about thee; and I will scatter a third part into all the winds, and I will draw out a sword after them" (Ezekiel 5:12). The scales obviously represented divine justice and the exactness with which it is rendered. The few hairs bound in his robe represented those who would be left; the throwing of the last of these into the fire was intended to show the miseries that even they would suffer.

Such exaggerated teaching devices were necessitated by the rebelliousness and hardheartedness of Israel. On another occasion Ezekiel was instructed to pack as if he were going into exile. He was to do so by the light of day, that all might see. At dusk he was to dig a hole in the wall, then put his pack on his shoulders, place a covering on his head so that he could not see the ground, and make his exit through the hole in the wall. (Ezekiel 12:1—7.)

The next day when his people asked him why he had done this he was to tell them that it was a prophecy concerning the prince of Judah and his people. Ezekiel was to explain: "I am your sign: like as I have done, so shall it be done unto them: they shall remove and go into captivity. And the prince that is among them shall bear upon his shoulder in the twilight, and shall go forth: they shall dig through the wall to carry out thereby: he shall cover his face, that he see not the ground with his eyes." (Ezekiel 12:11—12.)

The prophecy was fulfilled when Zedekiah, the prince of Judah, fled Jerusalem by night by way of the gate between the two walls but was overtaken on the plains of Jericho. His eyes were put out by his captors and he was carried in chains to Babylon. (2 Kings 25:1—7.)

A dramatic illustration of an event in the life of a prophet being a type foreshadowing the future is recorded in Ezekiel 24. To Ezekiel the Lord said, "I take away from thee the desire of thine eyes with a stroke: yet neither shalt thou mourn nor weep, neither shall thy tears run down" (Ezekiel 24:16). When this happened he was to do none of the things associated with an expression of mourning. He was not to remove his shoes, a sign of grief; he was not to cover his mouth, a practice among mourners; nor was he to eat of the funeral meal. "So I spake unto the people in the morning," the text reads, "and at even my wife died; and I did in the morning as I was commanded" (Ezekiel 24:18).

In response to the queries as to his strange behavior, Ezekiel prophesied that the temple would be profaned, it being the desire of their eyes, and that their sons and daughters in Jerusalem would fall by the sword, and yet they would not mourn. "Thus Ezekiel is unto you a sign," his people were told, "according to all that he hath done shall ye do," and when this happened they would know that the Lord was God (Ezekiel 24:24). As an additional sign Ezekiel was to be struck dumb until his prophecy was fulfilled (Ezekiel 24:27; 33:22).

These experiences of Ezekiel serve to give understanding to one of the greatest of his prophecies and certainly the best known prophecy of Ezekiel among Latter-day Saints. Reference, of course, is made to the story of the two sticks in Ezekiel 37. In this instance Ezekiel was instructed to take two wooden writing tablets, the equivalent of two books in his day, and write these words on one of them: "For Judah, and for the children of Israel his companions." That is, this book was to be written primarily as a blessing to Judah and his companions. Then on the other book or wooden tablet he was to write, "For Joseph, the stick of Ephraim, and for all the house of Israel his companions." That is, this book was to be written as a special blessing to the tribes of Joseph, meaning Ephraim and Manasseh, yet it was also to be a blessing "for all the house of Israel." It was also to be known as "the stick of Ephraim," by which title it is referred to in modern revelation (D&C 27:5). Then Ezekiel was to take his two books and join them together as one book, that he might hold them together as one in his hand.

When his people came to ask why he was standing there with these sticks or books in his hand they knew by long experience that his strange behavior was intended to teach some great lesson and that it would be prophetic. Nor is it without significance that he had established his credibility as a prophet at this point because they had seen his prophecies come true. By way of explanation, he said that the stick or book of Joseph which would come from Ephraim and his fellows was to be put with the stick or book of Judah, and they were to be one book. Then Ezekiel gave his people a synopsis of what these books would contain. He told them they would tell the story of the gathering of Israel, their restoration to their own land, their becoming one nation once again when they had one king, the Messiah, the son of David, to rule over them. He spoke of their being cleansed, of the building once again of the temple of the Lord, and of the making of an everlasting covenant with them. (Ezekiel 37:15—28.)

Jonah

The experiences of Jeremiah and Ezekiel are sufficient to assure us that sorrow, pain, and humiliation are chief among the teachers in the school of prophets. From the context of their experience and that of so many other prophets and righteous men, the "three days and three nights" (Jonah 1:17) Jonah spent in the fish's belly seems appreciably less peculiar. Still, an experience so unusual seems destined in the providence of the Lord to speak of greater things, and in such an anticipation we are not disappointed. It was the Savior who gave the meaning to this story beyond that of disciplining a wayward prophet. "For as Jonas was three days and three nights in the whale's belly," he said, "so shall the Son of man be three days and three nights in the heart of the earth" (Matthew 12:40). Jonah's experience was a prophetic sign of the resurrection, and to those who would doubt the reality of this Old Testament story it might be observed that

Jonah's experience was considerably less of a miracle than the resurrection which it represents. If one believes in the resurrection, it is a small matter to accept as true the experiences of Jonah.

HOSEA

Among our prophetic allegories none is more provocative, or appalling, and yet more depictive of ancient Israel and her sins than that of the marriage of Hosea to the adultress Gomer. Needless to say, this saga has called forth a veritable ocean of commentator's ink in a hapless effort to explain God's strange meddling in his prophet's domestic affairs. The story begins with God commanding Hosea to take "a wife of whoredoms" and father children by her (Hosea 1:2). This Hosea does, though not unpredictably she forsakes him and runs off to live lasciviously with other lovers. Hosea divorces her but still continues to love her. Eventually he purchases her freedom, apparently from a house of ill fame to which she was in bondage, and after a period of probation accepts her back as his beloved wife. (Hosea 1—3.)

The allegorical part of the story is obvious and simple. Hosea represents the Lord; his marriage symbolizes the covenant God made with Israel; and faithless Gomer typifies the religious harlotry of the nation of Israel. Their divorce is the broken covenant, and their reconciliation the latter-day gathering and return of Israel to God and his statutes, of which we as Latter-day Saints are the literal fulfillment. The allegory would represent historical fact more perfectly if Gomer had not been a harlot at the time of the first marriage. If the Bible text is in error in that part of the story, and the command of God to Hosea to take "a wife of whoredoms" can be viewed as language used in telling the story after the event, and not as a command requiring the event, the great difficulty in the story is resolved and the allegory becomes more nearly perfect.

In any event, three children were born into the union of Hosea and Gomer. Each was named by God. The first, a son, was named Jezreel, meaning "God will disperse," with the appended prophecy that the nation would be destroyed (Hosea 1:4—5). The second child was a daughter named Lo-ruhamah, meaning "not having obtained mercy," for the Lord said he would have no mercy upon Israel because of their wickedness (Hosea 1:6—7). And finally, another son was named Loammi, meaning "not my people," for the Lord said, "Ye are not my people, and I will not be your God" (Hosea 1:9).

Still, notwithstanding these prophecies of doom, the Lord told Hosea that the children of Israel would yet be as the sand of the sea, so great would be their number, and that they would return to the place where it had been said to them, "Ye are not my people," and there it would be said to them, "Ye are the sons of the living God," and Israel and Judah would be united once again (Hosea 1:10—11).

Lehi

It was Alma who showed us that the journey of Lehi and his family to the New World was more than just the story of the origin of the American Indian. A brief rehearsal of the story is sufficient to illustrate how it mirrors the struggle and the necessity of faith in the lives of all who have hopes of obtaining the inheritance promised them by the Lord. Lehi lived in or near Jerusalem, the great city that professed to be the spiritual capital of the world. Yet the Lord told him that if he and his family were to avoid bondage they must flee the city. They did so, leaving wealth and worldly comfort behind. They were then given a strange instrument called a Liahona, which was to guide them in their arduous journey to a new land. Things went well for a while, but then because of the quiet and rather natural manner in which they were being blessed they became spiritually lazy and slothful, whereupon the Liahona ceased to work for them. After a period of wandering in the wilderness and experiencing hunger and thirst they humbled themselves and turned again to Christ. When they did so the Liahona began again to work for them.

The story is a mirror reflecting experiences that are universal. We live in our own Jerusalems or worlds, feeling secure in our earthly passions and spiritual knowledge. Yet it is a false God that is worshipped in such a world, and we must accept the Lord's invitation to leave it or we too will find ourselves in bondage. As with Lehi and his family, we too have received promises of a better land, but as with our ancient prototype the journey is long and arduous and requires our leaving behind the riches and comfort of Jerusalem. We too will be dependent on the Lord for direction in our journey, direction that will come, at least for the most part, in quiet and unobtrusive ways. If we also become spiritually negligent our heavenly direction will cease and, until we repent, we will wander in the wilderness. Only faith, repentance, and diligence in following the prescribed course can bring us to the land of our destiny.

ABINADI

The most dramatic type of the Old Testament era was the prophet Abinadi. He it was who told wicked King Noah and his priests that what they did to him would be the type of what would befall them (Mosiah 13:10; 17:13—19). Noah had Abinadi burned to death and in so doing sealed his own doom. He too died by burning (Mosiah 19:20).

MORONI

Responding to a rebellion in his own land, Moroni, the chief commander of the Nephite armies, "rent his coat; and he took a piece thereof, and wrote upon it—In memory of our God, our religion, and freedom, and our peace, our wives, and our children—and he fastened it upon the end of a pole" (Alma 46:12). This symbol of all that was precious and dear to the Nephites was called the "title of liberty" by Moroni. This giant of the Lord went forth waving his rent garment in the air that all might see it. "Whosoever will maintain this title upon the land," he cried, "let them come forth in the strength of the Lord, and enter into a covenant that they will maintain their rights, and their religion, that the Lord God may bless them" (Alma 46:20). His people, in turn, rent their own garments as a token or covenant that they would not forsake their God, their religion, or their families, saying that the "Lord should rend them even as they had rent their garments," if they were not true to their covenant. They cast their garments at Moroni's feet, saying, "We have cast our garments at thy feet to be trodden under foot, if we shall fall into transgression." (Alma 46:21—22.)

Moroni reminded them that they were a remnant of the seed of Jacob and of Joseph and linked the symbolism of their rent garments to an incident in the life of Joseph of Egypt which has been lost to the Bible record. He told them that as Joseph's coat had been rent into many pieces by his brothers in their bitterness, so his people would be rent by their dissenting brothers if they were not true to their covenant. Moroni then said that Jacob had prophesied before his death using the remnants of Joseph's coat as a type. Jacob noted that part of what had been brought him had decayed, while part of it had been preserved, and he prophesied that part of the seed or remnant of Joseph would like-wise be destroyed, while part would be preserved. (Alma 46:22—24.)

CHRIST AS A SIMILITUDE

Christ is the most perfect example of a prophet whose life was intended as a teaching device. He was both a living representation of his Father and the illustration of what those desiring salvation must become. To have seen him was to have seen the Father (John 14:9), for as Joseph Smith said, they "exactly resembled each other in features and likeness" (HC 4:536). Christ was the perfect representation of the Father; to know what he did in a given instance was to know what the Father would have done in the same situation. To love and obey the Son was to love and obey the Father, and, conversely, to reject him was to reject his Father. Our entire system of gospel teaching and the performance of gospel ordinances is an extension of this principle. We teach his gospel, in his name, with his authority, and in doing so are similitudes or likenesses of him. Of the Nephite Twelve Christ asked, "What manner of men ought ye to be?" and answering for them said, "Verily I say unto you, even as I am" (3 Nephi 27:27). All who represent him are to both do and teach as he did and taught.

13

Names: A Story Within the Story

Names play a significant part in the scriptural story. This is true of both place-names and personal names, and is illustrated by the countless instances in which the Bible pauses in its narrative to explain the meaning of names. Place-names are often a form of verbal archaeology, describing an area or setting. Personal names were considered of such importance that on occasion they were announced by heavenly messengers or some other form of revelation. It was so important that the name and the person match that in other instances names were changed by divine decree. Personal names served as miniature biographies, descriptions of character, testimonies or expressions of praise to God, reminders of significant events, and divine warnings. In short, Bible names served as memorials, symbols, and prophecies.

DESCRIPTIVE PLACE-NAMES

From *Eden* ("delight," "pleasantness") to *Armageddon* (the great battlefield of the Old Testament and symbol of the final great battle), from *Genesis* ("the beginning") to *Apocalypse* (the revelation of the ultimate triumph of the Lord), Bible names are rich with symbolism and descriptive meaning. For instance, *Sharon* means "plain"; *Gibeah*, "hill"; *Pisgah*, "height"; *Mizpah*, "watchtower"; *Beer*, "well"; and *Beth*, "house." A suffix may be added to such descriptive place names to memorialize significant events. Thus *Beer-sheba*, meaning "well of the oath," designates the place where Abraham and Abimelech entered into covenant (Genesis 21:27—32), and *Bethel*, meaning "house of God," identifies the place where Jacob saw God (Genesis 28:13, 17—19).

The name *Babel*, from the story of the tower of Babel, comes from an Akkadian word meaning "gate of God." It has no Hebrew equivalent, though by drawing on a word with similar sound it has by tradition been given the meaning "confusion." Jacob named the place where he wrestled all night with an angel of God *Peniel* ("the face of God"), for he said, "I have seen God face to face, and my life is preserved" (Genesis 32:30). *Horeb*, the great mountain range of the Sinai Desert, appropriately means "desolate" or "parched." In contrast, *Carmel*, the beautiful green mountain jutting out on the upper coast of Palestine, means the "garden," "orchard," or "well-wooded place." *Hermon*, the majestic, snow-capped peak of the northeastern border of Palestine, carries the meaning "consecrated place" or "sanctuary." This seems most appropriate if in fact this is the Mount of Transfiguration. Its melting snow is carried in the River *Jordan*, meaning "to descend" or "carry down." These waters find their final resting place in the Dead Sea, properly named, for there is no life in this salt sea.

The name *Zion* also has an intriguing etymology. It may be related to the Hebrew *sayon*, meaning "dry" or "solitary place," "a desert" (Isaiah 25:5; 32:2). Some hold that its roots are found in the Arabic *sahweh*, which is interpreted as a "mountainous ridge," "safe place," "refuge," "citadel," or "stronghold." Any or all of these possibilities make it most appropriate to apply the name *Zion* to the desert refuge and mountain home of the Latter-day Saints.

The names given by Moses and wandering Israel to the places where they camped in the wilderness were to be everlasting reminders of the events that transpired there. After wandering for three days in a waterless waste they found water that was undrinkable because of its bitterness. The place was called *Marah*, meaning "bitterness." Here the people murmured against Moses, who, in response to his prayer, was shown a particular tree which when cast into the water made it sweet. Following this experience Israel entered into a covenant to obey the Lord, who in turn promised to free them from the diseases of Egypt. (Exodus 15:23—26.) When again the children of Israel found themselves without water, they murmured once more against Moses, who sought the Lord and was instructed to smite a rock and bring water from it. Moses called the name of the place *Massah* ("testing," "proving"), and *Meribah* ("strife," "complaint"), because of the contention in the camp of Israel and because the people questioned whether the Lord was among them. (Exodus 17:1—7.)

Then came the battle with the Amalekites, in which Israel was victorious because of the intervention of God, In memory of which Moses built an altar which he named *Jehovah-nissi* ("the Lord is my banner") (Exodus 17:15—16). After leaving Sinai, Israel commenced their craving for flesh. The Lord responded by sending innumerable quail, in which they overindulged. As a result an epidemic broke out and many died. Their graves gave the place its name, *Kibroth-hattaavah* ("the graves of lust" or "craving"), "because there they buried the people that lusted." (Numbers 11:31—34.)

Jerusalem, which is felt to be the heart of Bible geography, is a classic example of the descriptive nature of Bible names. It is a city built upon a hill; indeed, it is built upon a rock. It was, as we have already seen, known as "the mountain of the Lord's house" (Isaiah 2:2). When Bible peoples journeyed to Jerusalem, their expression was, "we go up" (Mark 10:33). The name *Jerusalem* is formed by the addition of *Jeru* to *Salem*, the name of Melchizedek's city which stood on the same spot. *Salem* is a form of *shalom*, or "peace." Scholars are uncertain as to what additional meaning is attached to Salem by adding *Jeru* to it. What is certain is that it was a sacred place long before David captured the city. Salem is identified in a Psalm as the place of God's dwelling (Psalm 76:2), and Josephus tells us that Melchizedek had a temple there (Josephus, p. 588).

Reference was made earlier to Mount Moriah or the Temple Mount; let us now briefly identify the topographical features that surround it. To the east of the Temple Mount is the Mount of

Olives, upon which was found the Garden of Gethsemane. The two mounts are separated by a valley called Kidron or, in some texts, the Valley of Jehoshaphat. At the southern end of the Temple Mount is the Hinnom or Gehenna Valley. To the west of the Mount is the Tyropoeon Valley. Each of these names contains a story within the story.

From the Kidron, literally the "dark" valley, Christ ascended the Mount of Olives to enter the Garden of Gethsemane, meaning the "oil press," where he was to take upon himself the sins of the world and bleed at every pore (Luke 22:44; Mosiah 3:7; D&C 19:18). This valley of "darkness" or "mourning" is also known as the Valley of Jehoshaphat, meaning "Jehovah judges" (Joel 3:2). It is the symbolic representation of the place of judgment and is so accepted by Jew, Christian, and Moslem alike. It is joined at the southern end of Mount Ophel by the notorious Valley of Hinnom, called by Jeremiah the "valley of slaughter" (Jeremiah 7:32), it being the place where some among Israel offered their own sons and daughters as burnt offerings to Molech. In New Testament times it was called Gehenna and became the receptacle of the city's refuse. Because of the continuous burning of fires it became a symbol for hell.

The Name of God

Names identify and describe. In biblical thought a name was an expression of the nature of its bearer. The Hebrew word for name is *shem*, meaning "memorial." To declare one's name was to reveal one's self. Nowhere is the importance of properly descriptive names more evident than in the names of Deity. When the Lord called Moses from the burning bush and commissioned him to bring his people out of Egypt, Moses' question was, "When I come unto the children of Israel, and shall say unto them, The God of your fathers hath sent me unto you; and they shall say to me, What is his name? what shall I say unto them?" Knowing the importance of names, Moses could fully anticipate that his people would inquire by what name and in what authority he came. In response the Lord said, "I AM THAT I AM," that is, that Moses was to say that "I AM" had sent him.

Moses was further instructed that he was to say, "The Lord God of your fathers, the God of Abraham, the God of Isaac, and the God of Jacob, hath sent me unto you: this is my name for ever, and this is my memorial unto all generations." (Exodus 3:13–15.) This instruction is clarified in JST, Exodus 6:2–3, which reads, "God spake unto Moses, and said unto him, I am the Lord: And I appeared unto Abraham, unto Isaac, and unto Jacob, I am the Lord God Almighty, the Lord JEHOVAH. And was not my name known unto them?"

Within the two passages just quoted, the personality of Moses' God is distinctly expressed. *Jehovah* is the English rendering of the Hebrew tetragram *YHWH*. It is derived from the verb "to be," which implies his eternal nature. *I AM* is the first person singular form of the verb "to be." In the name Jehovah, or I AM, God manifests himself as a personal living being who labors in behalf of Israel and who will fulfill the promises made to the fathers. All of this conveys the idea of an unchanging, ever-living God, who through all generations is true to his word. "God's personal existence, the continuity of His dealings with man, the unchangeableness of His promises, and the whole revelation of His redeeming mercy, gather round the name Jehovah" (Girdlestone, p. 38).

Thus, to declare the name of the Lord was to testify of the Lord, a concept lost to both Jews and Christians alike by false traditions and faulty Bible translations. "For this cause," the Lord told Moses, "have I raised thee up, for to shew in thee my power; and that my name may be declared throughout all the earth" (Exodus 9:16).

The Lord had identified himself to those of our dispensation by the same name, doing so for the same purpose. A revelation addressed to a conference of the Church in January of 1831 begins, "Thus saith the Lord your God, even Jesus Christ, the Great I AM, Alpha and Omega, the beginning and the end, the same which looked upon the wide expanse of eternity, and all the seraphic hosts of heaven, before the world was made; The same which knoweth all things, for all things are present before mine eyes; I am the same which spake, and the world was made, and all things came by me" (D&C 38:1–3; see also D&C 39:1).

All who properly represent the God of heaven must profess to come in the name and authority of the Great I Am. This is as essential today as it was in the days of Moses. "Whoso taketh upon him my name, and endureth to the end, the same shall be saved at the last day. Therefore, whatsoever ye shall do, ye shall do it in my name," he has said. (3 Nephi 27:6—7.)

Conversely, it must be remembered that the Lord has vowed that those taking his name in vain shall not be held guiltless (Exodus 20:7). Such was the course of ancient Israel who transgressed his laws, changed his ordinances, broke his everlasting covenants (Isaiah 24:5), and went a-whoring after false gods. They had desecrated the sacred name and were to feel the chastening hand of the Eternal God as they lost their land of promise and were scattered among every kindred, tongue, nation, and people. Yet, foreshadowing a time of future hope by the pen of Ezekiel, the Lord said:

> But I had pity for mine holy name, which the house of Israel had profaned among the heathen, whither they went.
> . . . I do not this for your sakes, O house of Israel, but for mine holy name's sake, which ye have profaned among the heathen, whither ye went.
> And I will sanctify my great name, which was profaned among the heathen, which ye have profaned in the midst of them; and the heathen shall know that I am the Lord, saith the Lord God, when I shall be sanctified in you before their eyes.
> For I will take you from among the heathen, and gather you out of all countries, and will bring you into your own land. (Ezekiel 36:21—24.)

The Lord then promised to cleanse them and to give them a "new heart" and a "new spirit," for he said: "I will put my spirit within you, and cause you to walk in my statutes, and ye shall keep my judgments, and do them. And ye shall dwell in the land that I gave to your fathers; and ye shall be my people, and I will be your God." (Ezekiel 36:25—28.)

We add to this the prophecy of Jeremiah, who foretold a time when Gentiles would come from the ends of the earth, saying: "Surely our fathers have inherited lies, vanity, and things wherein there is no profit. Shall a man make gods unto himself, and they are no gods? Therefore, behold, I will this once cause them to know, I will cause them to know mine hand and my might; and they shall know that my name is The Lord." (Jeremiah 16:19—21.)

Adam's Family

To give continuity to our study of proper names we will consider them chronologically as they appear in the Bible record, beginning with the immediate family of Adam, that is, Adam, Eve, Cain, Abel, and Seth.

Adam

The Hebrew root for the name *Adam* is a generic term meaning "man" or "mankind" and so appears over five hundred times in the Old Testament. Its usage there as a proper name is unusual. Scholars are uncertain as to its etymology. The statement that God formed "man" from the dust of the earth and breathed into him the breath of life and thus "man became a living soul" (Genesis 2:7) represents a popular etymology in the form of a word play. Other suggestions have included "red soil," "to show blood," "be like," "likeness," and "to make or produce." Given what we know about Adam, any or all of these suggestions seem reasonable. He was, the scriptures tell us, the first man, the first of God's creatures to possess the corruptible element of blood, and he was of course created in the image and likeness of God. The book of Abraham suggests to us the possibility that his name means "first father," as in our corrected versions it refers to "Adam, or first father" (Abraham 1:3). The book of Moses suggests the interpretation "many" (Moses 1:34).

Through modern revelation we know that Adam is Michael, the archangel described in the book of Revelation, and that he is the Ancient of days spoken of in Daniel (D&C 27:11; 29:26; Revelation 12:7; Daniel 7:9). His pre-earth name, Michael, means "who is like unto God?"

Eve

The meaning of the name of Eve, like that of her husband, Adam, is subject to endless scholarly debate. If the simplicity of the scriptural story is accepted, Eve was "called Woman, because she was taken out of man" (Genesis 2:23; Moses 3:23), and Eve "because she was the mother of all living" (Genesis 3:20; Moses 4:26). As the name *Adam* carries the meaning "first man," so the name *Eve* carries the meaning "first woman" (Moses 4:26), and as such their names testify of their role in introducing both mortality and birth whereby they became the parents of all living (2 Nephi 2:15—25).

Cain

Without the book of Moses, which comes to us from the Joseph Smith Translation, the meaning of the name *Cain* would appear as strange and confusing to us as it does to Bible scholars. Its Hebrew root means to "possess" or "acquire." The name in no way relates to the Bible text. From the book of Moses we learn that Adam and Eve had given birth to many sons and daughters before the birth of Cain and Abel. Yet, greatly to the disappointment of our first parents, these offspring had not chosen to walk in paths of righteousness. Adam and Eve longed for a righteous posterity, and it was with the greatest anticipation and expectation that they welcomed this new infant into the world. In hopeful longing Eve rejoiced over the birth of her new son, saying, "I have gotten a man from the Lord; wherefore he may not reject his words" (Moses 5:16). Such was the hope of Eve in her new heaven-sent "possession," and hence the name Cain. The Moses account continues, "But behold, Cain hearkened not, saying: Who is the Lord that I should know him?"

Abel

Abel's name is associated with a root meaning "vanity," "breath," or "vapor." Figuratively it seems to carry the connotation of transitoriness, which is apt, his having been murdered by Cain. "Adam," the scriptural accounts continues, "knew his wife again, and she bare a son, and he called his name Seth. And Adam glorified the name of God; for he said [the Bible mistakenly had Eve making this statement]: God hath appointed me another seed, instead of Abel, whom Cain slew." (Moses 6:2; Genesis 4:25.) *Seth* means "the appointed" or "substitute," he being effectually the second Abel. As such he becomes a natural type for Christ, who like Abel was first a martyr, and then like the second Abel, Seth, ruled in glory with his father (Moses 6:3—4).

NOAH'S FAMILY

We turn now to the story of Noah and his family. *Noah* means "rest" or "comfort." Lamech's anticipation was that this son would give rest or comfort from the toil incurred by the curse brought by the Fall (Moses 8:9). As one who would deliver those of faith from the effects of the curse, Noah was an obvious type for Christ. Noah in turn was the father of three sons: Shem, Japheth, and Ham. *Shem* as we have seen means "name," more directly in this instance, "distinguished." *Ham* is thought to mean "hot," "heat," or "black." *Japheth* means "let him [God] enlarge." Ham we are told married a Canaanite woman by the name of Egypt and also had a daughter by the same name. *Egypt*, the record of Abraham tells us, comes from the Chaldean and "signifies that which is forbidden" (Abraham 1:23). Thus through Ham and Egyptus came the race which "preserved the curse" placed on Cain's posterity (Abraham 1:24).

Other names closely related with the story of the Flood are Methuselah, Noah's grandfather, with whom Noah did missionary work up until Methuselah's death in the year of the Flood. Cruden renders his name as "when he is dead it shall be sent," meaning the Flood (Cruden, p. 799). *Methuselah* is most generally rendered "man of the javelin." Should Cruden prove to be right it would be a most appropriate name, for this greatly witnesses of the impending doom. It will also be remembered that it was after the Flood in the days of Peleg that the earth was divided (Genesis 10:25). The name *Peleg* means "division." The name of Noah's rebellious great-grandson, Nimrod, in Hebrew means "to rebel."

ABRAHAM'S FAMILY

Abraham and Sarah

In the Old Testament the significance of names becomes most conspicuous in the story of Abraham and his family. Abram ("exalted father") was instructed by the Lord that his name was to be changed to Abraham ("father of a multitude") in the context of the Abrahamic covenant, in which the Lord promised him an endless seed (Genesis 17:5). At the same time his wife Sarai (possibly meaning "contentions," though probably another form of Sarah) was directed to change her name to Sarah ("princess"). The same promise given to Abraham and Sarah in their eternal union is renewed with each couple who are married for time and eternity (D&C 132:30—31). Thus, through the covenant of eternal marriage, each man becomes a "father of multitudes" and each woman a "princess."

Ishmael and Isaac

Hagar, who fled the wrath of Sarai, was instructed by an angel of the Lord that she would bear a son, and was further told that she was to name him Ishmael, "because the Lord hath heard thy affliction" (Genesis 16:11). The name *Ishmael* means "God hears." Similarly, God told Abraham that Sarah would bear him a son, "and thou shalt call his name Isaac: and I will establish my covenant with him for an everlasting covenant, and with his seed after him" (Genesis 17:19). The name *Isaac* means "to laugh," meaning to "rejoice" (JST, Genesis 17:23), for both Abraham and Sarah rejoiced when the promise of the Lord was given them. The KJV conveys the idea that they doubted the promise of the Lord because of their great age. The JST corrects this impression.

Esau and Jacob

Isaac in turn became the father of Esau and Jacob. Esau was ruddy or reddish in color at birth and "like an hairy garment," hence his name, which carries the same meaning (Genesis 25:25). Jacob, the second born, took hold of his brother's heel at birth, hence his name, meaning "supplanter." Later, when Jacob would steal his older brother's blessing, Esau would affirm that his brother was rightly named Jacob, "for he hath supplanted me these two times: he took away my birthright; and, behold, now he hath taken away my blessing" (Genesis 27:35—36).

Yet, as with his grandfather Abraham, Jacob was to have his name changed by the Lord. "Thy name," Jacob was told, "shall be called no more Jacob, but Israel: for as a prince hast thou power with God and with men, and hast prevailed" (Genesis 32:28). Jacob's new name, the name by which his descendants and eventually the righteous of all future ages would be known, was Israel, announcing that they too had prevailed with God.

Jacob's Family

Jacob became the father of twelve sons, the name of each of which was something of a battle marker in the struggle between Leah and Rachel for the affections of their husband. Leah gave birth first and named her son Reuben ("Look, a son"), saying, "Surely the Lord hath looked upon my affliction; now therefore my husband will love me." She conceived again, and bore a son whom she named Simeon ("hearing"), saying, "the Lord hath heard that I was hated, he hath therefore given me this son also." She conceived a third time and bore a son, whom she named Levi ("joined" or "pledged"), saying, "Now this time will my husband be joined unto me, because I have born him three sons." She conceived a fourth time and bore a son, whom she named Judah ("praise"), saying, "Now will I praise the Lord" (Genesis 29:31—35).

Rachel, unable to bear children and ready to die of shame, gave Jacob her maidservant Bilhah as wife that she might have seed through her. Bilhah conceived and bore a son, whom Rachel named. The name given was Dan ("judge"). Rachel said, "God hath judged me, and hath also heard my voice, and hath given me a son." Bilhah conceived and bore a second son; again Rachel named the child. The name given was Naphtali ("to twist" or "wrestle"). Rachel said, "With great wrestlings have I wrestled with my sister, and I have prevailed." (Genesis 30:4—8.)

When it became apparent to Leah that she might not have any more children, she gave her handmaid to Jacob as wife that she might have seed by her. And Zilpah, Leah's maid, gave birth to a son, whom Leah named. The name was Gad (the name combines the idea of a "troop" and "fortune"). Leah said, "A troop cometh." Again Zilpah bore a son. Leah named the son Asher ("happy" or "blessed"). She said, "Happy am I, for the daughters will call me blessed." (Genesis 30:9—13.)

At this point in the story Leah's oldest son, Reuben, found some mandrakes, believed to be something of a fertility potion. He brought them to his mother. Rachel, learning of it, asked Leah for this precious herb. A hard bargain was struck. Leah would give Rachel the mandrakes; Rachel would give Leah Jacob for the night. Leah, it appears, dealt most wisely, for she conceived and gave birth to another son. Rachel remained barren. Leah named her son Issachar ("recompense"), saying, "God hath given me my hire, because I have given my maiden to my husband." Leah conceived again and bore Jacob a sixth son whom she named Zebulun ("exalted abode"). At the birth of this son she said, "God hath endued me with a good dowry; now will my husband dwell with me, because I have born him six sons." Thereafter she bore a daughter, whom she named Dinah ("judged" or "avenged," from the same root as Dan). In this instance no speech is recorded. (Genesis 30:14—21.)

And finally we read, "And God remembered Rachel, and God hearkened to her, and opened her womb," and she gave birth to a son. "God hath taken away my reproach," she said, and named him Joseph (meaning in part "to add"), and prophesied, "The Lord shall add to me another son." Though she died in childbirth, Rachel gave birth to another son, whom she named Ben-oni, meaning "son of my sorrow." After her death Jacob called him Benjamin, meaning "son at the right hand" (Genesis 35:18).

Moses' Family

We turn now to Moses, the great deliverer and lawgiver. Moses was named by the daughter of Pharaoh, who found him in a basket made of bulrushes in the Nile. She called him Moses because she "drew him out of the water" (Exodus 2:10). In Hebrew the name means "to draw out." It signified that he was saved from death by being drawn out of the water, and it foreshadowed his destiny as the one who would save Israel by leading them through the waters of the Red Sea. His name can also be seen as suggesting baptism, the waters from which all men are freed from the bondage of sin.

Aaron, destined to become the high priest and as such a type for Christ, bore a name that carried with it such meanings as "kindred of the Highest," "mountain of strength," and "light" or "enlightened."

Generations before their births, Moses and Aaron were identified by name by Joseph of Egypt in his great prophecy. It was in that same prophecy that he spoke of the prophet of the last days and said that he would bear the name Joseph (JST, Genesis 50:29,33,35). Surely we are justified in the anticipation that these names, chosen in heaven, would prophetically reflect the destinies of the prophets who would bear them.

Under the hand of his father-in-law, Jethro ("excellent"), Moses received both the priesthood and much wise counsel (D&C 84:6, Exodus 18). Moses was the father of two sons; the first he named Gershom ("sojourner there"), for he said, "I have been an alien in a strange land." The second he named Eliezer ("God of help"), "for the God of my father," said he "was mine help, and delivered me from the sword of Pharaoh" (Exodus 18:3-4).

Message Names

Many Bible names were formed by taking a divine name, usually El ("God") or Jah ("Jehovah") and combining it with a noun or verb to create a sentence that praises God or testifies of him. As examples let us take Old Testament books that bear the names of prophets.

Samuel

The name means "heard of God" and is a testimony that the Lord heard the prayers of his mother Hannah, who had been barren (1 Samuel 1:20).

Nehemiah

The name means "God has consoled" and is borne by one of Judah's great leaders, who tirelessly pushed dispirited Jews to return from exile in Babylon to rebuild the walls of Jerusalem.

Isaiah

The name means "the Lord or Jehovah is salvation." This is a most appropriate name for the author of our greatest Messianic prophecies.

Jeremiah

Various explanations are given of the name, including, "exalted of God," "appointed of the Lord," and "God will elevate." His record begins with the Lord saying of Jeremiah, "Before I formed thee in the belly I knew thee; and before thou camest forth out of the womb I sanctified thee, and I ordained thee a prophet unto the nations" (Jeremiah 1:5).

Ezekiel

This name, which means "God strengthens," was borne by the great priest and prophet of exile who encouraged his people with his visions of the future redemption of Zion.

Daniel

His name means "God is judge." His prophecies dealt with the judgment of God on the great nations of the earth, his judgment on Nebuchadnezzar, his condemnation of Nebuchadnezzar's son Belshazzar, and the opening of the books of judgment in the valley of Adam-ondi-Ahman (D&C 116; Daniel 7:10).

Joel

The name, which means "Jehovah is God," was borne by the author of the often-quoted prophecies of the war and destruction that are to immediately precede the triumphant return of Christ and his millennial reign.

Obadiah

This name, which means "servant of God," was borne by the author of the shortest book of the Bible. His one-chapter book contains the prophecy of saviors who will stand on mount Zion.

Micah

His name means "who is like God," which he uses as an interesting word play, asking, "Who is a God like unto thee, that pardoneth iniquity, and passeth by the transgression of the remnant of his heritage? he retaineth not his anger for ever, because he delighteth in mercy" (Micah 7:18).

Zephaniah

Apparently the name means "the Lord has hidden" or "hid of the Lord." Other suggestions are "sheltered" or "treasured" by the Lord. He was a contemporary of Jeremiah and like Jeremiah wrote of events of the last days.

Zechariah

His name means "Jehovah remembers" or "remembered of God." His prophecies center in both the first and the second comings of the Messiah.

Malachi

His name means "messenger of the Lord" and is in such perfect harmony with his prophecy about the messenger that will come to prepare the way for the Lord (Malachi 3:1) that scholars have argued that the book was named for its message and that there was no such person as Malachi. Speaking to the Nephites, Christ refers to the revelation "given unto Malachi," and thereby affirms that there was indeed a prophet by that name who wrote this record (3 Nephi 24,25).

ANCIENT KINGS

Melchizedek

Of the Old Testament kings none was greater than Melchizedek. An earlier chapter considered him as a type for Christ; here we refer briefly to the significance of his name. The root for the forepart of his name, *Melch* (Melek), means "king" or "royal." *Zedek*, the latter part of the name, means "just" or "righteousness." Thus the name *Melchizedek* carries the meaning "king of righteousness." No more appropriate name could be used to substitute for the name of Deity in referring to his priesthood (D&C 107:3—4). It is through the Melchizedek Priesthood that we become priests and kings unto God. Christ is our king and Righteous is one of his names (Moses 7:45), and it is only through him and the powers of righteousness that anyone can lay claim to the blessings of the priesthood.

David and Solomon

David ("beloved" or "my beloved") as a type for Christ has also already been discussed. Let us add to the list of great Old Testament kings the name Solomon. Solomon, too, at least to the extent that he was righteous, was a type for Christ. His was the great reign of peace; his name meant "peaceful." By revelation the Lord had told David that "a son shall be born to thee, who shall be a man of rest; and I will give him rest from all his enemies

round about: for his name shall be Solomon, and I will give peace
and quietness unto Israel in his days" (1 Chronicles 22:9). When
David asked Nathan to bless the child he gave Solomon the name
Jedidiah ("beloved of the Lord"), "because," the text says, "of the
Lord" (2 Samuel 12:25), meaning obviously the love of the Lord.

Josiah and Cyrus

Among those known by name long before their births were
two Old Testament kings. The first was Josiah, named in
prophecy more than four hundred years before his birth, as was
the great work he would do as a reformer (1 Kings 13:2). His
name seems to carry the meaning "given of the Lord," "founded
of the Lord," or "Jehovah heals or saves."
    The other king named before his birth was not a king of Israel
but of Persia. This was Cyrus, who, though not of the covenant,
was referred to by the Lord as "my shepherd," and as the
"anointed" (Isaiah 44:28; 45:1).

Zerubbabel

Of interest in our list of kings is a descendant of David who
was the governor of Jerusalem at the close of the Exile,
Zerubbabel. Be it remembered that the temple of that era bore his
name, which meant "born in Babylon" and thus aptly described a
people scared by their own history.

THE NATIVITY STORY

In no story in the Bible do names assume greater importance
than they do in that of the birth of Christ. The story opens with
our being introduced to the priest Zacharias and his wife,
Elisabeth. Both are righteous and have walked blameless before
the Lord, yet they are childless, a matter over which they have
grieved for many years. Now in their old age that blessing seems
lost to them. In the drama that follows, the meaning of their
names seems relevant. Zacharias, as we have already learned,

means, "remembered of God." Elisabeth means "God of the oath," or "consecrated to God."

John

On the occasion of being selected to enter the holy place within the temple Zacharias is greeted by the angel Gabriel ("man of God"), who tells him that he and his wife will bear a son and that they are to name him John (Luke 1:13), meaning "Jehovah is gracious." This son is to be the earthly forerunner of the Christ.

Mary and Jesus

Shortly thereafter, this same angel appears to a young virgin by the name of Mary in Nazareth of Galilee. Her name is also important, for it has been spoken by prophets as they foresaw this marvelous event for hundreds of years (Mosiah 3:8; Alma 7:10). *Mary* is the Greek form of her name, *Mariam* the Hebrew. Many etymologies are suggested; the most appropriate are "exalted of the Lord" and "bitter tears." Both would be prophetically true. The virgin girl was told that she was to give birth to a son and that the son was to be named Jesus (Luke 1:31). The same instruction was given to Joseph, who would be the guardian of the child (Matthew 1:21). *Jesus* is the Greek form of the Hebrew *Joshua*. It means "Jehovah saves." As to the reason for his name, Joseph was given this explanation, "For he shall save his people from their sins."

In his account of the nativity, Matthew tells us that he would be called "Emmanuel, which being interpreted is, God with us" (Matthew 1:23). And so in fulfillment of an ancient prophecy (Micah 5:2), Joseph and Mary traveled to Bethlehem ("the house of bread") that he who would be the bread of life might be born there.

Peter the Rock

Upon their first meeting Christ said to Peter, "Thou art Simon the son of Jona," then by way of prophecy he added, "thou shalt be called Cephas," to which our Bible writer adds, "which is by interpretation, a stone" (John 1:42). *Cephas* and *Peter* are identical in meaning; both mean "Rock." The JST makes a significant addition to our commentary on the name and its purpose. It reads, "Thou shall be called Cephas, which is, by interpretation, a seer, or a stone" (JST, John 1:42). Thus Christ announced that Peter's destiny was to be a seer.

The subject of Peter's name and the destiny ascribed to him by Christ has fueled theological debates by which countless tempers have been warmed for nearly two thousand years. The debate centers in the Savior's statement to Peter, "Thou art Peter, and upon this rock I will build my church; and the gates of hell shall not prevail against it" (Matthew 16:18).

The text of this argument is important to our study of names. Jesus had asked his disciples whom men said that he the "Son of man" was. The proper understanding of his question has been lost to scholars and divines alike. The "m" in "son of man" should have been capitalized (see JST, Matthew 16:14) to identify it as a proper name. Jesus was revealing himself in that name title to be the Son of Man of Holiness, or literally the Son of God. Man of Holiness is a name by which God the Father is known to his people (Moses 7:35). As with all names of Deity, it reveals his character and being. In this instance it teaches that he is an exalted, glorified man, in whose image his children have been literally created.

A variety of answers were given when Christ asked his disciples whom others thought him to be. Peter, acting as spokesman, said, "Thou art the Christ, the Son of the living God." That is, "thou art the Messiah, the son of Elohim." His answer and understanding were perfect and elicited praise from the Savior, who said, "Blessed art thou, Simon Bar-jona (that is Simon, son of mortal man): for flesh and blood hath not revealed it unto thee, but my Father which is in heaven." That is, Simon Peter knew that Jesus was the long-sought Messiah and Son of the Eternal Father, for the Father himself had revealed it to him. After that dialogue the Savior used his word play on Peter's name to emphasize the importance of the principle of revelation, saying, "Thou art Peter [Greek *petros*, meaning small rock but, as we have seen, also seer stone], and upon this rock [Greek *petra*, meaning bedrock] I will build my church; and the gates of hell shall not prevail against it." (Matthew 16:18.)

Opponents of Christ

Even our study of those opposed to Christ is enriched by an appreciation of the meaning of names. The name *Satan* means "adversary." John refers to him as the "accuser of our brethren" in the context of the war in heaven from whence Satan was cast down (Revelation 12:10). Every Old Testament reference to Satan is in the context of an adversary bringing an accusation (see Job 2; Zechariah 3). The rest of the standard works use the name more generally. *Perdition* means "destruction," carrying the connotation of being eternally lost. Lucifer is the name borne by the adversary in the premortal existence. It refers to one of renown, a morning star, literally the "shining one." Before his fall, Lucifer was "a son of the morning" (Isaiah 14:12; D&C 76:26). A devil is a demonic being, the name meaning "slanderer."

During Christ's ministry much of the opposition to him came from religious associations, tightly formed communities at odds with each other on virtually every issue. The only thing that could unite them was their opposition to Jesus of Nazareth. Chief among them were the Sadducees, "followers of Zadok." These were the lay nobility, the patrician families who claimed some tie to the priest of Solomon's Temple. Also prominent were the Pharisees, meaning "the separate ones," or the " holy ones," who by their devotion and obeisance to the Mosaic law claimed great righteousness.

The Day of Restoration

Ours is the day and dispensation of restoration. It seems appropriate that if names and their meanings were of such importance to the ancient Saints, they ought to carry that same richness of meaning for us. Our theology ought to embrace the idea, as did that of the ancients, that there are occasions, very sacred in nature, when in the context of making sacred covenants and receiving blessings we too would be found receiving new names. Indeed, Joseph Smith spoke of a white stone to be given to "each of those who come into the celestial kingdom, whereon is a new name written, which no man knoweth save he that receiveth it." This "new name," Joseph Smith said, "is the key word" (D&C 130:11).

Nor should it be without significance to those of this dispensation that we too have a prophet who was known by name many hundreds of years before his birth. It was Joseph of Egypt who prophesied of the great latter-day seer who would do a work such as he had done in gathering his family, and a work such as Moses had done in freeing Israel from the bondage of wickedness and falsehood masquerading as religious truths in Egypt. "And his name shall be called Joseph, and it shall be after the name of his father," the ancient Joseph prophesied (JST, Genesis 50:33, 2 Nephi 3:15).

The etymology of the name *Joseph* is usually given as "the Lord addeth" or "increaser." Though appropriate, such renderings have veiled a richer meaning associated with it. At the point at which our ancient progenitor Rachel named her son Joseph, the Hebrew text reads *Asaph*, meaning "he who gathers," "he who causes to return," or perhaps most appropriately "God gathereth" (Genesis 30:24). Thus the great prophet of the Restoration bears the name that most appropriately testifies of his divine calling. Nor is it without significance that it is the tribes of Joseph, Ephraim and Manasseh, that Moses prophesied would do the work of the gathering, pushing Israel together from the ends of the earth (Deuteronomy 33:17).

This story also has an interesting sequel. Joseph's brother Hyrum, the man who jointly held with him all the keys of the restored kingdom, the man who went to Carthage with him to die at his side, that they together might seal their testimony with their blood, also had a good Hebrew name. His name means "my brother is exalted."

In a patriarchal blessing given by his father, Joseph Smith, Sr., he was told, "Behold thou art Hyrum, the Lord hath called thee by that name, and by that name He has blessed thee" (Joseph

Fielding Smith, *Origins of the Reorganized Church*, 4th ed. [Independence, Missouri: Zion's Printing and Publishing Co., 1945], p. 60; see also *Joseph*, p. 158.)

NOTES

Scholarly sources freely disagree with each other over the etymology of names. There is also the debate as whether the story gives rise to the name or the name to the story. This is the chicken-or-the-egg argument all over again. Does the name *Job* mean an "enemy," "foe," one "persecuted" and "afflicted" because of Satan's enmity and animosity against the man Job, or was he so named as a prophetic foreshadowing of the experiences and trials that would be his? Of a certainty the story fixes the meaning of the name as one "persecuted" and "patient."

The method employed in the writing of this chapter can be illustrated with the name of the Savior's mother, Mary. Scholarly etymologies give the following range of meanings: "obstinacy" (*Who's Who*, p. 281), "the corpulent one" (IBD 3:288), "bitterness," or "rebellion" (*Concordance* [*Dictionary of the Hebrew Bible*], p. 72), "Bitter tears; bitter water," (*Names*, p. 302), and "exalted of the Lord." The reasoning here is that the name is a derivation of Mara, "to lift up oneself, and Yah, the abbreviated form of the name of Jehovah." (Cruden, p. 798.)

Given such choices, by what standard does one choose? Rather than attempt to outscholar the scholars, one need simply be reminded that King Benjamin (Mosiah 3:8) and Alma (Alma 7:10) both announced by revelation that the mother of the Son of God would be named Mary. With the knowledge that her name was determined in the heavens, we proceed with the confidence that it carries a proper and an appropriate meaning. "Obstinacy" hardly fits her perfect example of submission to the will of the Lord. Mary's response to Gabriel's announcement that she was to be the mother of the son of God, "Be it unto me according to thy word" (Luke 1:38), is quoted as the classical illustration of faithful submission. The suggestion that the name means "corpulent" or obese seems quite out of harmony with Nephi's description of "a virgin, most beautiful and fair above all other virgins" (1 Nephi 11:15). Surely even Nephi with all his piety would not so describe an obese woman. On the other hand, the scriptures assure us that she was to weep bitter tears (see Simeon's prophecy to her, Luke 2:34—35) and that she was exalted of the Lord (see Gabriel's salutation to her, Luke 1:28). If one prefers prophets over uninspired scholars the choice is both natural and obvious.

14

Rituals and Righteousness

Nowhere is the importance of symbolism more important than in the gospel rituals that mark the way by which we return to God. All ordinances of salvation involve rites or ceremonies rich in symbolism—divinely chosen—to emphasize the sacred covenants being made. These rituals and the symbols in which they are clothed are of such importance that they were decreed in heaven before the foundations of the earth were laid (see D&C 132:11). Their importance is further emphasized by Christ's perfect compliance with them during his mortal ministry. Taking the ordinance of baptism as an example, Nephi taught that Christ showed all men "the straitness of the path, and the narrowness of the gate, by which they should enter" the kingdom of heaven, "he having set the example before them" (2 Nephi 31:9). Joseph Smith added, "If a man gets a fullness of the priesthood of God he has to get it in the same way that Jesus Christ obtained it, and that was by keeping all the commandments and obeying all the ordinances of the house of the Lord" (*Teachings*, p. 308).

These sacred rituals emphasize to those entering into them, and remind those witnessing them, of the absolute necessity of steadfastness in keeping covenants or promises made with heaven. The changeless nature of these ordinances illustrates the universal character of the language of symbolism. These symbols span all cultures and all ages of earth's history, speaking with the same eloquence today as they did to father Adam and the faithful of all past dispensations.

Baptism of Water

Paul described baptism as a similitude of the death, burial, and resurrection of Christ. "We are buried with him by baptism into death," he stated in his epistle to the Romans, and we come forth out of the water "in the likeness of his resurrection." Our body of sin having been crucified with him, we too come forth through baptism into a newness of life. (Romans 6:3—6.) Christ referred to baptism as being born again (John 3:5), as had Enoch generations before. Noting the elements associated with birth as water, blood, and spirit, in a revelation given to Adam we are told that by the water we keep the commandment, by the Spirit we are justified, and by the blood we are sanctified (Moses 6:59—60). Each element of this imagery (water, blood, and spirit) was also present in the atoning sacrifice of Christ, which granted immortality and the possibility of eternal life to all men. Thus, because of the atonement, each of us through the waters of baptism is born into the family of Christ, and we take upon ourselves his name (2 Nephi 31:13) and become his sons and daughters (Mosiah 5:7).

Many so-called Christians have argued that baptism is only an outward ordinance, a symbol of inner conviction, and as such it is not essential to salvation. In such reasoning we are tempted to agree with them. We would reason then that the lack of an outward manifestation represents the lack of an inward conviction. It would also follow that a baptism of sprinkling represents a sprinkling of conviction, and that one by immersion represents complete commitment to or immersion in the cause of Christ.

Baptism of Fire

Baptism of water is not sufficient in itself to bring one into the presence of the Lord. Joseph Smith explained: "You might as well baptize a bag of sand as a man, if not done in view of the remission of sins and getting of the Holy Ghost. Baptism by water is but half a baptism, and is good for nothing without the other half—that is, the baptism of the Holy Ghost." (*Teachings*, p. 314.) The Holy Ghost is a sanctifier. "To be sanctified is to become clean, pure, and spotless; to be free from the blood and sins of the world; to become a new creature of the Holy Ghost, one whose body has been renewed by the rebirth of the Spirit" (*Mormon Doctrine*, p. 675). Alma described those who have been sanctified as not being able to "look upon sin save it were with abhorrence" (Alma 13:12). The scriptural expression "baptism of fire and of the Holy Ghost" (2 Nephi 31:13–14) emphasizes that the Holy Ghost is both a purifier and a revelator. The figure of fire represents both cleansing and enlightenment.

The symbolism of receiving the gift of the Holy Ghost is that of lighting a perpetual flame within the soul, one which provides light and warmth while constantly purging that which is unclean from it. This is very different from the notion in the sectarian world that some supposed spiritual experience brings the assurance of salvation. That is more like being struck with lightning than the scriptural imagery of a flame that was to perpetually burn within the temple, fueled with works of righteousness.

The Laying On of Hands

The "baptism of fire, and the Holy Ghost" comes only by the laying on of hands (D&C 20:41). The ordinance must be performed by one holding the higher or Melchizedek Priesthood (D&C 49:14). The symbolism associated with the laying on of hands is that of having been touched by the hand of God. This was illustrated when the Lord said to Edward Partridge "I will lay my hand upon you by the hand of my servant Sidney Rigdon, and you shall receive my Spirit, the Holy Ghost, even the Comforter, which shall teach you the peaceable things of the kingdom" (D&C 36:2).

The laying on of hands always accompanies the conferral of authority, an office, or the right to preside. It is a visual and documentable event that enables us to avoid the sectarian heresy that one can be called to the Lord's service by a "feeling in his heart." This prevents impostors from claiming an office or position on the strength of a private or secret commission. "Ye have not chosen me, but I have chosen you, and ordained you," the Savior said—that is, I confirm your ordination by the "laying on of hands" (John 15:16).

The laying on of hands is also the system whereby special blessings and promises are given. All such occasions are sacred, and the recipient of such a blessing should have the sense and feel that he has been touched by the hand of God. Illustrations include ordinations to the priesthood, patriarchal blessings, fathers' blessings, and administrations to the sick.

The Sacrament

As with baptism, the ordinance of sacrament is of two parts, partaking of bread and wine. As the sacrificial ritual of the Old Testament was designed to point the attention of the faithful forward to the great and last sacrifice, so the partaking of the sacrament is to return our attention to Christ's atonement. The bread, consecrated by the blessing of a priest, who stands as the representation of Christ, is broken in remembrance of the broken body of Christ. The wine or water is consecrated by a priest and partaken of in remembrance of the blood of Christ which he shed for us. (D&C 20:77—79.)

Through partaking of the sacrament we are accorded the privilege of renewing the covenant made in baptism (Mosiah 18:8—10), obtaining a remission of sins (JST, Matthew 26:24), and placing ourselves in harmony with the Lord (3 Nephi 18). The substance used in partaking of the sacrament is of no particular importance; the symbolism is. When Joseph Smith went to purchase wine for the sacrament he was met by a heavenly messenger who told him not to purchase wine from his enemies. The angel explained that "it mattereth not what ye shall eat or what ye shall drink when ye partake of the sacrament, if it so be that ye do it with an eye single to my glory—remembering unto the Father my body which was laid down for you, and my blood which was shed for the remission of your sins" (D&C 27:2).

The Sabbath

The Sabbath has always been a sign by which the Lord's people could be identified. From Adam to the Exodus it commemorated God's resting on the seventh day after his labor of the six days to create man and the earth (Exodus 20:8—11). From the Exodus to the resurrection of Christ the Sabbath commemorated the deliverance of the children of Israel from their Egyptian bondage (Deuteronomy 5:12—15). From the days of the early Apostles to the present it has commemorated the day upon which Christ came forth from the tomb and made resurrection a reality for all (Acts 20:7).

Though that which it commemorates has changed, the Sabbath has in all dispensations been a time to rest from temporal labors while devoting oneself to matters of the Spirit. If Christ be the example of proper Sabbath observance, then we note with some interest that his Sabbaths were spent preaching in the synagogues, teaching in the temple, and healing the sick.

Edersheim observes that "the Sabbath was symbolic of the millennial kingdom at the end of the six thousand years' dispensation, when the Lord would reign over all, and His glory and service fill the earth with thanksgiving" (*The Temple*, p. 173). Because in creating the earth the Lord labored for six periods and rested during the seventh and designated the seventh thousand-year period of the earth's temporal existence (D&C 77:6) as the time when the earth will again rest (Moses 7:64), the number seven has become the symbol of "completeness," "fullness," or "perfection" (*Customs*, p. 239; Smith, *Dictionary*, 4:2935). During the earth's second Sabbath, the millennial era, it will rest and enjoy peace and righteousness and a perfect system of worship.

Temple Ordinances

The temple, or house of the Lord, is the most sacred place on earth, and as such is the place where the most sacred rites of salvation are performed. It is also in the temple that the system of teaching through rituals reaches its fullest expression. To enter the temple is symbolically to enter the presence of the Lord. Since no unclean thing can enter his presence, those entering the temple must first be judged worthy to do so. This typifies the eternal ver-

ity that all men will be judged by their works and that only those
who have kept their "garments spotless" will sit down with
Abraham, Isaac, and Jacob, and the holy prophets (Alma 7:25).
The judgment for temple worthiness can be made only by those
who have been granted the stewardship for such by the "laying
on of hands." The procedure complies with the law of witnesses,
for two interviews are necessary; normally those conducting the
interviews will be the bishop and then a member of the stake
presidency.

To enter the temple is to leave the world, an act symbolized
by exchanging daily dress—clothing in the style and fashion of
the world—for white clothes bespeaking the purity required to
enter the presence of the Lord. The ritual most basic to the temple
is called an endowment, because through the faithful observance
of the covenants associated with it one is "endowed" or granted
"power from on high" (D&C 38:32). To be endowed, according
to Brigham Young, was "to receive all those ordinances in the
House of the Lord, which are necessary for you, after you have
departed this life, to enable you to walk back to the presence of
the Father, passing the angels who stand as sentinels . . . and
gain your eternal exaltation in spite of earth and hell" (JD 2:31).

The best commentary on the endowment, its ordinances, and
its symbolism is the scriptures. All the standard works contain
imagery and symbolism associated with the endowment that can
be fully appreciated only by those who have experienced its
blessing. Much of that imagery and symbolism has already been
considered in this work, thus only a brief summary and
application will be made at this point.

Washings

Water, the most common medium of cleansing in daily life, is
an obvious and natural symbol for the necessity of cleanliness
and purity in spiritual things. It is clear from both the Bible and
the Book of Mormon that the ancients by revelation understood
the necessity of ritual observances in obtaining a state of purity.
It is equally plain that they clearly understood that no unclean
thing could enter the presence of God. Symbolically, in ancient

ritual, uncleanness was either washed or burned away. In fact, ritual washings were universal to the religions of the ancient Near East. One scholar notes, "In the minds of the ancients there was a close connection between the notion of purity or cleanness and the notion of being consecrated to God" (*Wycliffe BD* 1:7). Various forms of washings were the primary scriptural metaphors for cleansing from sin. For instance, the priests would wash their hands and feet before entering the sanctuary of the temple or performing any of the temple rituals. The high priest was washed at the time of his appointment and again each year on the Day of Atonement before he performed any of the rites of propitiation.

The restoration of the temple ritual did not take place all at once, rather it was restored "line upon line," rite upon rite, over a period of time. A partial endowment was administered in the Kirtland Temple, and even before that the ritual of washing and anointing found some expression. In relation to the school of the prophets, Joseph Smith was instructed, "Ye shall not receive any among you into this school save he is clean from the blood of this generation; And he shall be received by the ordinance of the washing of feet, for unto this end was the ordinance of the washing of feet instituted" (D&C 88:138–39).

Anointings

In the Old Testament, anointing was the divinely appointed rite for the inauguration of prophets, priests, and kings—all of whom were types of Christ, the great Prophet, Priest, and King. The Book of Mormon also speaks of the "consecration" of prophets and priests and the "anointing" of kings. The principle was obviously the same on both hemispheres. The ritual of consecrating or anointing followed that of washing. Symbolically it represented the conferring of divine authority. So great was the respect had for those thus endowed that David refused to raise his hand against Saul, even when Saul repeatedly sought his life, because Saul was the "Lord's anointed" (1 Samuel 26:9).

The anointing was also a symbol of the outpouring of the Holy Spirit or Holy Ghost. Significantly, in the ordinance of

baptism one is first ritually washed and then given the gift of the
Holy Ghost or the promise of the outpouring of the Spirit.
Anointing with oil is also associated with administering to the
sick and afflicted, an ordinance through which a remission of sins
is also granted (James 5:14—15; Mark 2:9—12).

Garments

Before Adam and Eve left the Garden of Eden, the Lord
taught them the law of sacrifice and placed them under covenant
to live that law and all other principles necessary to return to his
presence. A sacrificial offering was made, symbolizing the
necessity of sacrifice by the shedding of blood. From the skin of
that sacrifice, robes or garments were made for Adam and Eve,
thus symbolizing the protection necessary in the world they
would now enter, and that the only protection that could assure
them the privilege of returning to the presence of their Father was
that which would be found through the great sacrifice to be made
by the Son of God. Only such a sacrifice could answer the ends
of the Fall. Thus our first parents were "clothed with power and
authority" and given promises of protection through righteousness, of which this sacred clothing, made by God himself, would
be a constant reminder.

This endowment and its blessings of power, authority, and
protection were, we are told, also enjoyed by "Seth, Noah,
Melchizedek, Abraham [they being representatives of the princi-
ple], and all to whom the Priesthood was [has been] revealed"
(Abraham, Facsimile 2, figure 3). As the gospel is everlasting, so
are its ordinances, and as we have previously seen, those who
stand in the presence of the Lord (symbolically the temple) must
be properly clothed, and hence have put upon them the garment
of the priesthood and the robes of righteousness. This is as much
a part of the endowment and temple ritual today as it ever was in
ages past. Alma testified that none could enter the kingdom of
heaven except they be so clothed and their garments be washed
white through the blood of Christ. Of the wicked whose
garments would be stained with sin he asked, "Do ye suppose
that such an one can have a place to sit down in the kingdom of

God, with Abraham, with Isaac, and with Jacob, and also all the holy prophets, whose garments are cleansed and are spotless, pure and white?" (Alma 5:21—24.)

Similar testimony has been borne by many of the prophets. Moroni described those who would live in the New Jerusalem of the last days as those "whose garments are white through the blood of the Lamb" (Ether 13:10-11). Joseph Smith in his dedicatory prayer for the Kirtland Temple prayed that "our garments may be pure, that we may be clothed upon with robes of righteousness, with palms in our hands, and crowns of glory upon our heads, and reap eternal joy for all our sufferings" (D&C 109:76).

Kings and priests

The revelation on the degrees of glory describes those who obtain the highest heaven as having received the promise of "all things." These, it states, are "priests and kings" who have received the fulness of the glory of God. (D&C 76:55—56.) Later Joseph Smith explained that to have the fulness of the priesthood one "must be a king and priest," yet he assured us that "a person may be anointed king and priest long before he receives his kingdom" (HC 5:527). Such was also the doctrine of John the Revelator, who testified of Christ as he who had "washed us from our sins in his own blood, And hath made us kings and priests unto God and his Father; to him be glory and dominion for ever and ever. Amen." (Revelation 1:5—6.)

In these passages and the endowment ceremony we learn that the Old Testament and Book of Mormon anointing of prophets, priests, and kings was not only a type and shadow of Christ but a representation of the blessings to be enjoyed by the faithful Saints of all ages.

Marriage

Celestial marriage can properly be thought of as the crowning ordinance of the temple. The sacred union created by the sealing of a man and a woman in the temple by the authority of the priesthood cannot be dissolved by death, for it is intended to span the endless eternities. Such a union constitutes the earthly type of heavenly things. Marriage and families are the order of heaven. Joseph Smith illustrated the nature of eternity with the use of a ring, for it is without beginning or end.

15

Figurative or Literal?

If the cloud of darkness created by confusing that which is literal with that which is figurative and vice versa in the scriptures were to be blown away, it would disrobe the devil himself. Turning things inside out is high fashion among the legions of hell and has provided many a devil with a clever disguise. Plain and precious truths, from the greatest to the least, have been dressed in costumes of myth and allegory, their glory hidden, and their purpose lost, while the threads of metaphors have been stretched to cover the most ridiculous of religious garb worn in the name of piety. From Christ's claim to Divine Sonship to the reality of his resurrection (from Genesis to Revelation) the letter has been used to kill the Spirit and the Spirit to kill the letter.

Idols of Sophistry

The idols of our day have not been cast in molds or hewn from wood or stone; rather they have been shaped in sophistry and gilded with false traditions. As with our ancient counterparts, we too have been fed on meat offered to idols and have dressed ourselves in robes of heresy that we might be fashionable in a world "ever learning" yet "never able to come to the knowledge of the truth" (2 Timothy 3:7).

The greatest heresies stand opposite the greatest truths. Their ploy is to feign acceptance of principles while cleverly redefining them in such a way that their true purpose and significance have been lost. One need not deny the existence of God if he can by definition describe Him as uncreated, invisible, incorporeal, and incomprehensible. The whole thing works out rather nicely. Truth is slain with the dagger of definition while the schemer sits in church piously saying his amens. No saving doctrines have escaped the purge. God, the Creation, the Fall, the Atonement, baptism, marriage, priesthood, temples—all have felt the blade of the assassin as the literal is said to be figurative and the figurative is said to be literal.

The Nature of God

Every Christian religion that ascribes to a creed has described God as an immaterial being. The God of these creeds is an invisible spirit who has neither body, parts, nor passions. The creeds are united in stipulating that the Father, the Son, and the Holy Ghost are one in essence or substance. Joseph Smith stood in sharp contrast to such views when he said, "The Father has a body of flesh and bones as tangible as man's; the Son also; but the Holy Ghost has not a body of flesh and bones, but is a personage of Spirit" (D&C 130:22). So we have the Prophet Joseph on one side of the fence and the Christian world on the other. Since both profess a belief in the Bible, a review of its testimony of the nature of God is in order.

In describing God the Bible speaks of his head, face, eyes, ears, nostrils, mouth, voice, arm, back, hand, palm, fingers, foot, heart, bosom, and bowels. The Bible describes God with such titles as king, judge, father, and master. It testifies that "we are the offspring of God" (Acts 17:29), that we were created in his "image" (Genesis 1:27), in his "likeness" (Genesis 5:1,3), and in his "similitude" (James 3:9). Christ affirmed this truth, saying, "He that hath seen me hath seen the Father" (John 14:9). We are told that Enoch "walked" with God (Genesis 5:24), that Jacob saw him "face to face" (Genesis 32:30), as did Moses (Exodus 33:11).

Others of the Bible prophets who saw the Lord include the seventy elders of Israel, Micaiah, Isaiah, Jeremiah, Daniel, and Ezekiel from the Old Testament, and Stephen, Paul, and John the Revelator from the New Testament. Moses, Aaron, Nadab, Abihu, and seventy elders of Israel saw God and partook of a sacral or covenant meal with him (Exodus 24:11; *IB* 1:1016; *Ezekiel 1*, p. 240). Micaiah testified, "I saw the Lord sitting on his throne, and all the host of heaven standing by him on his right hand and on his left" (1 Kings 22:19). Isaiah said, "Mine eyes have seen the King, the Lord of hosts" (Isaiah 6:5). Jeremiah left us with no description but announced that any professing to be prophets must have stood before him in the heavenly assembly where they are to receive their message (Jeremiah 23:18, 22; modern translations are necessary to clarify the KJV here). Daniel's description was of "one like the Son of man" (Daniel 7:13). Ezekiel described God's "likeness as the appearance of a man" (Ezekiel 1:26). In the New Testament Stephen before his death testified, "Behold, I see the heavens opened, and the Son of man standing on the right hand of God" (Acts 7:56). Paul wrote that he had seen the risen Lord and was instructed as Christ "stood" before him (Acts 22:18; 23:11; 1 Corinthians 15:8). The Revelator records seeing "one like unto the Son of man, clothed with a garment down to the foot, and girt about the paps with a golden girdle. His head and his hairs were white like wool, as white as snow; and his eyes were as a flame of fire; And his feet like unto fine brass, as if they burned in a furnace; and his voice as the sound of many waters." (Revelation 1:13–15.)

With such passages so common to the Bible we are left to ask why there is such confusion about the nature of God. The response is that such references are "merely figurative," and we are reminded that "No man hath seen God at any time" (John 1:18). It was the symbol of his presence that the prophets saw, we are told, but certainly not God himself. Such references, it is argued, are merely metaphorical and are no different than such expressions as the "eye of a needle," the "shoulder of the road," or the "foot of the mountain." Further, it is pointed out that the scriptures use such imagery as "the Lord God is a sun and shield" (Psalm 84:11), a "Rock" (Deuteronomy 32:15), a "fountain of

living waters" (Jeremiah 2:13), and "a consuming fire" (Deuteronomy 4:24). Starting with the premise that God is an
incomprehensible mystery, all references to him are held to be
metaphorical. References to God as the sun, a rock, a spring, and
a fire, are used in the Bible, it is held, for the very purpose of
providing "a useful corrective" to balance the anthropomorphic
metaphors which tend to "domesticate the remote, the mysterious and the uncontrollable," all of which are necessary attributes of the sectarian God (*Imagery*, p. 174).

A favorite text used by a leading anti-Mormon spokesman in
attacking missionaries for teaching that God is a personal being is
the Psalm which states that God will protect his people with "his
feathers, and under his wings." In a mocking tone the question is
asked, "Is God a chicken, or some other kind of a bird that he
would have feathers and wings?" The line brings a good laugh,
and young missionaries are not always prepared to respond,
though a reading of the text would be more than adequate.
Dramatizing the protection one finds in the Lord and by
obedience to gospel principles, the Psalmist referred to God as a
refuge and fortress. Then to further illustrate his point he wrote:
"Surely he shall deliver thee from the snare of the fowler, and
from the noisome pestilence. He shall cover thee with his
feathers, and under his wings shalt thou trust: his truth shall be
thy shield and buckler." (Psalm 91:3—4.) The expression is an
obvious metaphor.

A thousand additional Bible texts describing God as having
body, parts, and passions, along with the testimony of prophets
and righteous Saints to whom he had appeared, would be of no
avail. As long as there is a single text that is figurative, it will be
argued that all other texts are figurative also. Nor can the matter
be resolved by an independent revelation, for those preferring to
worship a God of mystery have sealed the heavens to such a possibility. Like the honor rendered to dead prophets, their
allegience to the Bible is unbounded. Having silenced God they
interpret his word according to their pleasure. From such a
comfortable pew there is little difficulty in singing praises to the
sacred book. They have made their position unassailable with the
dagger of definition. They have the carcass, the dead word, but

the spirit of revelation, that spirit which gave it life, they deny. To praise dead prophets is one thing, to accept living prophets quite another. All the lip service in the world isn't worth a single revelation. They worship in museums rather than temples.

THE CREATION, FALL, ATONEMENT, AND RESURRECTION

It is a common practice for books dealing with the Bible to begin with the story of Abraham, skipping the first twelve chapters of Genesis. This is done on the premise that the events described in these early chapters, from the account of the Creation through the Flood, are myth or legend. Since they cannot be harmonized with science, it has become popular with those who still desire to profess a belief in the Bible to liken them to fables or parables. As such, their value is not in their factual reality but rather in their ability to preserve culture, tradition, and meaning. This approach has been attractive to many within the Church. Unable, for instance, to harmonize the statement in the Doctrine and Covenants that the earth is to have seven thousand years of temporal history—that is, seven thousand years in which there can be death—with the millions of years necessary in scientific theory, they simply resolve the matter by suggesting that the Doctrine and Covenants reference was not intended to be interpreted literally.

The great difficulty with making the creation story allegorical is the chain reaction that it causes. If we have tampered with the reality of the creative account, we have tampered with the reality of Adam and Eve. If we have made myth of Adam and Eve, we have made myth of the Fall, and if the Fall is not a reality neither is the Atonement, and if there is no need for an atonement, then we have no need for a Savior, and if we have no Savior and no atonement we have no resurrection, and without the resurrection we have no judgment by works or degrees of glory, and so on.

Illustrating this position I was scolded by a rabbi in a gospel discussion for using the phrase "plan of salvation." He explained that he had nothing to be saved from and thus eschewed such words as "saved," or "salvation." Having rejected Christ as the

Savior, he was consistent in rejecting the doctrine of the Fall and any need for a plan whereby men needed to be redeemed.

"A corrupt tree bringeth forth evil fruit," Christ said (Matthew 7:17), and the "corrupt tree" that makes a myth of Adam and the Fall, with the attendant "evil fruit" of no Atonement, no Christ, and no resurrection, is the perfect example. One bad doctrine can have progeny without number.

THE LITERAL MADE FIGURATIVE

This confusion is reminiscent of the thick darkness with which Moses cursed the Egyptians while among the children of Israel there was light (Exodus 10:21-23). The meaning of such titles as Father in Heaven, Son of God, Son of Man, and sons of God have been lost to the world. The world has lost the knowledge that God is literally the father of our spirits, that he fathered Christ "after the manner of the flesh" (1 Nephi 11:18), and that Son of Man means Son of Man of Holiness (Moses 6:57). Nor have they ever supposed that when the scriptures declare Adam to be the son of God, they mean precisely what they say (Luke 3:38).

Nephi described our day as one in which the reality of the devil and hell would be spiritualized away (2 Nephi 28:21—22). In fulfillment of that prophecy, even within the Church we find those who suppose that hell is merely a state of mind and not an actual gathering place for the wicked. Similarly, it has been with something of a sense of pride that the churches of the world have announced that they have outgrown the idea of a literal hell. One prominent Christian publication responded to the question as to whether hell is an actual, literal place, by suggesting that "The idea of hell is going to hell." "The question is not pertinent," the article held, for the value of hell is in the sense of eventual justice it gives us when we see wickedness that goes unpunished. (Stranberg, "A Hell for Our Time," p. 1104.)

An article in *U.S. Catholic* announced, "That charming place of everlasting fire, pitchfork-bearing demons, and constant gnashing of teeth is going out of style for many contemporary believers, partly because they cannot reconcile a merciful God with a damning divinity, partly because hell seems like such a childish belief, and partly because they don't really understand what hell is supposed to be. Threat? Punishment? Myth? Reality? Just what is hell?" A major conclusion of this article was that "Hell may be paved with good intentions, priests' skulls, and spike helmets; it may be full of worms and fire like Gehenna; it may be everlasting underarm odor or an eternal cocktail party. Whatever it is, hell has lost the power to terrify people." (Brieg, pp. 6—10.)

A sophisticated statistical study of religious commitment in America conducted by the University of California published in 1968 found that only 38 percent of Protestants and 66 percent of Catholics surveyed believe that the devil actually exists (Stark, *Commitment*). In 1977, *U.S. Catholic* reported that only one out of three Catholics believed in a literal hell (Brieg, p. 7).

THE FIGURATIVE MADE LITERAL

As marvelous truths have been lost by making that which is real into a figure, so they have also been lost by making the figurative literal. No example better illustrates the darkness of apostasy than that by which the symbolic bread and wine of the sacrament is declared to be literally the flesh and blood of Christ. According to this dogma, known as transubstantiation, the priest in administering the mass brings Christ back to life that he might be sacrificed again, thereby literally making his flesh and blood available for repeated consumption. Scriptural justification is found in texts that have introduced the ordinance of the sacrament by saying: "Take, eat; this is my body"; and, "Drink ye all of it; For this is my blood" (Matthew 26:26—28). What Christ would actually have said has been restored for us in the Joseph Smith Translation of the Bible. It reads: "Take, eat; this is in remembrance of my body which I give a ransom for you"; and, "Drink ye all of it. For this is in remembrance of my blood" (JST, Matthew 26:22—24).

Another of the prominent illustrations of a symbol being made literal is the reference in the creative account to the creation of Adam from the dust of the earth and Eve from the rib of Adam (Genesis 2:7, 21). Some have sought to sustain this idea by making literal the statement of John the Baptist to the Sadducees and Pharisees "that God is able of these stones to raise up children unto Abraham" (Matthew 3:9).

The Book of Moses tells us that all men were created from the dust of the earth (Moses 6:59). It seems obvious that the Bible account of the creation of Adam and Eve is figurative. Brigham Young called the idea that Adam was "fashioned the same as we make adobies" a "baby story" and that if he had been made in such a manner he would be nothing but a brick in the resurrection (JD 2:6). "He was made," Brigham Young said, "as you and I are made, and no person was ever made upon any other principle" (JD 3:319).

The scriptures provide no better illustrations of the cult of excess and extremism in which the symbolic and figurative are made into a physical burden than in the traditions of the Pharisees. In their preoccupation with the letter of the Mosaic law they lost the spirit which gave it life and meaning. The public display of righteousness became the end and purpose of righteousness. Christ, who honored in both letter and spirit the law given on Sinai, ignored rabbinic traditions that required a ceremonial cleansing of pots and vessels, the ritual washing of the hands before eating, and the rabbinic injunction against the husking of grain on the Sabbath day.

The commandment that Israel write the word of God on their hand and on their head (Deuteronomy 6:8) was given a literal interpretation. Passages from the Torah were written on tiny pieces of parchment and placed in small cubical boxes made of the skins of clean animals. These boxes, called phylacteries, were fastened to the arm and head with leather straps. "The common people wore them only during prayers, but the Pharisees wore them continually" (*Customs*, p. 368). To call attention to their righteousness, Pharisees also made their phylacteries larger than those used by others. And since Moses had commanded the children of Israel to put fringes on the borders of their garments as a reminder of their duty to God (Numbers 15:38), the Pharisees also enlarged these fringes on their clothes (Matthew 23:5).

How much better it would have been had their "eyes been single" and the labor of their hands consecrated to works of righteousness, that they might have accepted their Messiah, than that they clothe themselves in the garb of piety while rejecting him!

Knowledge Restored

The reality of a host of doctrines that the world has long since relegated to the stature of spiritual metaphors has enjoyed a physical resurrection with the restoration of the gospel. For instance, "John 14:23—The appearing of the Father and the Son, in that verse," Joseph Smith tells us, "is a personal appearance; and the idea that the Father and the Son dwell in a man's heart is an old sectarian notion, and is false" (D&C 130:3). In like manner we learn that the promise of the Savior in the Sermon on the Mount that the pure in heart shall see God is also literal and is to be understood as taking place in this life. "Sanctify yourselves," states one of the many scriptural texts so teaching, "that your minds become single to God, and the days will come that you shall see him; for he will unveil his face unto you" (D&C 88:68). Another text states "that every soul who forsaketh his sins and cometh unto me, and calleth on my name, and obeyeth my voice, and keepeth my commandments, shall see my face and know that I am" (D&C 93:1). Similarly, we learn that the promise in the Sermon on the Mount that the meek shall inherit the earth is also literal, for this earth is destined to be exalted and be the abiding place of celestial beings (D&C 88:17—18).

Another of the great doctrines to regain its physical reality in the Restoration was that of the gathering of Israel. "We believe in the literal gathering of Israel," Joseph Smith said (Article of Faith 10). Also restored was a knowledge of the promises made to the "literal seed" of Abraham (Abraham 2:11), and the knowledge that we "are the children of Israel, and of the seed of Abraham" (D&C 103:17), and that as such we "are lawful heirs, according to the flesh" (D&C 86:9).

16

History of Bible Interpretation

Having seen the havoc wreaked by the twisting winds of misinterpretation, as figurative has been made literal and literal made figurative, we now trace the prodigal wanderings of Bible interpretation. We shall see the prophetic teachings shackled and imprisoned by rabbinic legalism; stripped of meaning by Greek philosophers; robbed again by the Latin fathers; starved in the ecclesiastical dungeon of the popes; finally to be rescued by the Reformers, emancipated by courageous translators, and reunited with the family of revelation through the restoration of the gospel. Yet for long years the Bible was lost in a Babylon of allegory where it was a conscripted servant of philosophers and armor bearer for suppressors. Like Samson, shaved of his hair and blinded, the Bible without prophets or revelation to sustain it, having lost its heaven-given strength, has been forced to grind the corrupt wheat of Philistines.

IDOLATRY OF TRADITION

The religion of the Jews at the time of Christ consisted of scripture, fable, legend, and allegory tied together with the bonds of tradition. Of his nation Christ said, they worship in "vain," preferring the commandments of men to those of God—whose commandments they have made of "none effect" by their traditions (Matthew 15:3, 6, 9). Paul frequently warned the church of his day against "Jewish fables, and commandments of men, that turn from the truth" (Titus 1:14; 1 Timothy 1:4; 4:7; 2 Timothy 4:4). Peter emphasized that in the doctrine taught by the Apostles they avoided these "cunningly devised fables" (2 Peter 1:16).

Such was the spiritual status of a nation in which rabbis had replaced prophets and traditions had replaced revelations. "The wise man (that is, the rabbi) is greater than the Prophet," their law held. Prophecy had ceased because "it was no longer esteemed a necessity" (Farrar, p. 51). The office of a priest had dwindled to a point of insignificance—the likes of John's father, Zacharias, were known as the "idiot priests" because they had no formal theological schooling (*Life and Times* 1:141).

According to the Jewish view, God gave Moses both the written and the oral law on Sinai. That is, Moses had revealed to him at that time all that would subsequently be expounded by their scholars. In answer to the obvious question as to why so much was left unwritten, it was said that Moses wanted to write down all that was revealed to him but the Lord could not allow it. The reason for this was that God knew that other peoples would claim divine support from the Bible—thus the unwritten or oral traditions would remain the exclusive province of the Jews and would act to keep them separate from the Gentiles.

Tradition took this a step further and placed the oral law above the written law. "The sayings of the elders have more weight than those of the prophets," stated one Jewish source. Another source stated it thus: "An offence against the sayings of the Scribes is worse then one against those of Scripture" (*Life and Times*, 1:97–98, footnotes). The thread of justification required to bear the entire weight of the oral tradition is Exodus 34:27, which reads, "And the Lord said unto Moses, Write thou these words: for after the tenor of these words I have made a covenant with thee and with Israel." The phrase "after the tenor of these words" was interpreted by ancient Jews as meaning that the covenant was founded on the spoken rather than the written word.

The legends of the Jews hold that when Moses went up to heaven to receive the Torah he found God in the process of adding various symbols and ornaments to it. Moses, wondering why that was necessary, asked, "Isn't the Torah rich enough in meaning, and sufficiently obscure?" In response he was told that many generations thereafter, a man called Akiba, son of Joseph, would seek and discover "a gigantic mountain of Halakot [oral tradition] upon every dot of these letters." Moses asked to see the man and was directed to where he was. Rabbi Akiba was in the act of teaching Talmud. Moses listened but was unable to understand a single thing the rabbi taught. He then heard one of Akiba's pupils ask, "What proof do you have that your views on the subject are correct?" And the master, Rabbi Akiba, replied: "I have it from my Masters, who had it from theirs, who for their part claimed Moses as their teacher. What I am telling you is what Moses heard at Sinai." (*Messengers*, pp. 155-56; *Legends* 3:115.)

So strong were the traditions of the fathers that we are told that the great Rabbi Hillel would mispronounce a word because his teacher before him had done so (*Life and Times*, p. 98). Yet the classic illustration of the hold of tradition came in the debate between Rabbi Eliezer and Rabbi Joshua over the possibility of a revelation being given that would add to the law. After exhausting every possible argument to no avail, Eliezer, to sustain God's right to continue to speak, called upon the carob tree to prove it—whereupon we are told that the carob tree was torn from the ground and hurled a hundred and fifty cubits away. This sign was rejected on the grounds that no proof can be brought from a carob tree. So Eliezer called upon the stream of water to prove it, whereupon the stream started to flow backwards, to which the objection was, "What sort of demonstration does a stream afford?" Eliezer then said, if the oral tradition agrees with me, let the walls of the schoolhouse prove it, whereupon the walls inclined to fall. Rabbi Joshua rebuked them, for when scholars were engaged in a debate over the law the school had no right to interfere. Hence the walls did not fall but remained on an angle or incline. Seeking an irrefutable witness, Rabbi Eliezer then called on the heavens to speak for themselves, whereupon a heavenly voice sounded forth and said, "What have ye against Rabbi Eliezer after whose opinion the law is always to be framed?" At which Rabbi Joshua arose and said, "The Torah declares concerning itself, 'It is not up in heaven'; that is to say, once the Torah was given on Mount Sinai, we pay no heed to heavenly voices but, as the Torah ordains further, we follow the opinion of the majority." (*Judaism*, pp. 68—69.)

Farrar aptly describes the effect of tradition on the nation of Israel:

> Tradition shifted the centre of gravity of the moral system. A minute ritual had become the sole possible fence of national holiness. The consequence was the gradual material-ising of spiritual conceptions; the depreciation of righteous-ness in comparison with ceremonialism and the theological opinion. Just as in the middle ages a suspicion of heresy was avenged by the stake, while heinous moral offences were easily condoned, so among the Rabbis, if a man were but an orthodox casuist his sins were recorded with unblushing indifference. The Talmud abounds in narratives which detail without the slightest blame the impurity of the Rabbis. Their hedge about the Law made no pretense of keeping out the wild boars of Pride and Lust, though it might exclude the little foxes of irregular ceremonial. (Farrar, p. 57.)

Returning from their Babylonian exile, the nation of the Jews lost little time returning to idolatry — a more subtle idolatry, but idolatry nonetheless. Idols of wood and stone were replaced with images of words and professions of reverence for the law. So rigid did the literal and ceremonial become that righteousness was overshadowed by legalism and salvation became the reward for outward conformity. Pharisaism and scholasticism ruled supreme. God himself was said to spend three hours a day in the study of law.

> All liberty of thought was abrogated; all Gentile learning was forbidden; no communion was allowed with the human intellect outside the Pharisaic pale. Within the circle of Rabbinism the Jew was "the galley-slave of the most rigid orthodoxy." The yoke of the Romans was not so exacting as that of the Rabbis, which dominated over a man's whole existence and intruded itself into the most trivial actions of life. The weak were tortured by the knowledge that they could not so much as wash their hands or eat a meal without

running the risk of deadly offences. The "ordination" of the Rabbis made them oracles for every subject and every action, from the cleaning of the teeth to the last prayer in which the dying commended their souls to God. (Farrar, pp. 60–61.)

"The hedge was made; its construction was regarded as the main function of Rabbinism; it excluded all light from without and all egress from within; but it was so carefully cultivated that the shrine itself was totally disregarded. The Oral Law was first exalted as a necessary supplement to the Written Law; then substituted in the place of it; and finally identified with the inferences of the Rabbis." (Ibid., p. 62.) "The Jews were a stiff-necked people," Jacob said, "and they despised the words of plainness, and killed the prophets, and sought for things that they could not understand. Wherefore, because of their blindness, which blindness came by looking beyond the mark, they must needs fall; for God hath taken away his plainness from them, and delivered unto them many things which they cannot understand, because they desired it. And because they desired it God hath done it, that they may stumble." (Jacob 4:14.)

The oral traditions were used first to explain the written law, and then to explain it away. Thus the understanding of the words of the prophets became lost to them. "Search the scriptures," the Savior told them, "for in them ye think ye have eternal life: and they are they which testify of me" (John 5:39).

Not only did they tamper with the meaning of the law, they tampered with and destroyed scriptural texts as it was necessary to sustain their traditions. "Woe unto you, lawyers!" Christ said, "for ye have taken away the key of knowledge, the fulness of the scriptures; ye enter not in yourselves into the kingdom; and those who were entering in, ye hindered" (JST, Luke 11:53).

For Scripture History we find the gross substitution of the fictions that Israel is sinless, and holy, and never committed idolatry; that Rebecca, and Rachel, and Leah were never actuated by any but the purest motives; that Reuben never committed incest; that Judah took the daughter of "a merchant," not of a "Cannaanite;" that the Twelve Patriarchs were all immaculate; that they never meant to murder their brother Joseph until he tried to lead them into Baal-worship;

that Tamar was a daughter of Shem, and was perfectly innocent; that it was only the Proselytes, not the Israelites, who worshipped the golden calf; that neither Aaron's sons, nor Samuel's sons, nor Eli's sons, were really guilty. David, Bathsheba, Josiah, are all excused from blame, and so step by step by the aid of an exegesis which begun in fetish worship and ended in casuistry, Scripture was first placed upon an idol's pedestal and then treated with contumely by its own familiar priests. (Farrar, p. 63.)

ALEXANDRIAN ALLEGORISM

In contrast with the Talmudic idolatry of Palestine in which the letter of the law was worshipped in the place of God, came the Alexandrian system of scriptural interpretation in which the literal meaning of virtually every passage was supplanted with a spiritual or allegorical meaning. The Pharisees smothered the fire and light of the scriptures with a blanket of legalism, while the Alexandrian Jews used the blanket of Greek philosophy to extinguish the flame. The first sought to interpret the law to exclude the world, the other to embrace it. The one lost itself in ceremony and isolation and the other in allegory and assimilation.

When Jerusalem fell in 587 B.C. the Jewish Diaspora began. Though a great many Jews returned to Judea after the Babylonian exile, the greater part of them continued to live outside of Palestine in the nations around the Mediterranean. Following the destruction of Jerusalem, a large number of Jews had migrated to Egypt. When Alexander the Great founded the city of Alexandria in 332 B.C., Jews constituted an important part of its population. Alexandria came to be the chief home of Jewish dispersion and of Hellenistic culture. Greek being its language, its Jewish population found it necessary to embrace the language and much of the Greek culture in order to carry on commerce with their neighbors. In the course of a few generations the knowledge of Hebrew was lost to them. The desire to retain their heritage created the need to translate the Hebrew scriptures into Greek. The version thus created became known as the Septuagint, meaning "seventy," so named according to tradition because it was translated by seventy-two men, six from each tribe, and the work of translation, it is said, was accomplished in seventy-two days. The legend is that each translator labored in a separate cell independent of all others. At the end of the seventy-two days they compared their work and discovered that all seventy-two of them had translated the Bible exactly the same—an obvious sign of divine approval.

The Septuagint reflected its Greek culture and freely departed from the Hebrew manuscripts. Chief among these departures was the repugnance exhibited toward references to Deity as an anthropomorphic being. These phrases, explained away as allegory in earlier ages, were softened or altered in the Septuagint. (See Farrar, pp. 119–20.) Also added to this translation were the fifteen Apocryphal books we now know as a part of the Catholic Bible. This included such works as Bel and the Dragon, the Story of Susanna, and some legendary additions to Ezra and Esther. Farrar suggests that this was a manifestation "that the Jews had felt the charm of Greek romance, and desired that something which resembled it should exist among themselves" (ibid., p. 127). This was also the age that produced many of the pseudepigraphical works, books bearing the names of such notables as Enoch, Solomon, Jeremiah, and Baruch. It was an era in which forgery and fiction sought acceptance in the name of religious piety.

The Septuagint was not just a translation of the scriptures, it was a corrected edition that weeded out things causing social embarrassment. Philo, a Jew of Alexandria (and a contemporary of Christ, though there is no evidence that he ever learned of Him), erased all differences between the two cultures with his voluminous writings in which he systematically allegorized everything in the books of Moses. The essential thesis of his works was that those of a higher mind would see that the literal reading of scripture was but its earthly body, while the allegorical was its soul. The greater meaning was to be found in allegory, which, as it happened, proved to be in harmony with Greek philosophy. Though Philo completely diluted the Jewish faith, it ought to be observed that in contrast with the legalism of the rabbis he placed the spirit above the letter and morality above formalism.

Josephus (A.D. 37–100), the Jewish priest turned Roman citizen after his surrender to the Roman army in Galilee, was also among the articulate writers who abandoned the defense of the law in its literal meaning to find its true light in allegorical interpretation. Everything in the tabernacle in the wilderness would, to those "without prejudice, and with judgment," be simply an "imitation and representation of the universe." For instance,

> When Moses distinguished the tabernacle into three parts, and allowed two of them to the priests, as a place accessible and common, he denoted the land and the sea, these being of general access to all; but he set apart the third division for God, because heaven is inaccessible to men. And when he ordered twelve loaves to be set on the table, he denoted the year, as distinguished into so many months. By branching out the candlestick into seventy parts, he secretly intimated the Decani, or seventy divisions of the planets; and as to the seven lamps upon the candlesticks, they referred to the course of the planets, of which that is the number. The veils, too, which were composed of four things, they declared the four elements; for the fine linen was proper to signify the earth, because the flax grows out of the earth; the purple signified the sea, because that colour is dyed by the blood of a sea shell-fish; the blue is to signify the air; and the scarlet will naturally be an indication of fire." (Josephus, p. 75.)

Such was the art of the allegorists who created a Bible of their own, a Bible endowed with claims and interpreted by methods unseen and unhinted at in its pages. In grasping for shadows the allegorists lost the substance as surely as the rabbis had buried it in their sepulchre of tradition.

THE APOSTOLIC FATHERS

The history of scriptural interpretation thus far has been one of aberration. The apostolic Fathers continued that tradition. It should be noted that these writers of the first few centuries of the

Christian era were beset with nearly insurmountable difficulties. It was not until the end of the fourth century that the canon of the New Testament was finally established, while the matter of what constituted the Old Testament was left unsettled until the sixteenth century (Farrar, p. 164). In the place of revelation, the gift of the Holy Ghost, and the Church established by Christ, they were "surrounded by Paganism, Judaism, and heresy of every description," along with a faulty Bible translation. "The earliest Fathers and Apologists add little or nothing to our understanding of Scripture" (ibid., p. 165). For the most part they clothed themselves in the threadbare garments of Philo and the rabbis.

> The only Bible used by the Apostolic Fathers was the Septuagint, and they rely on its supposed inspiration even when it differs widely from the original Hebrew. But while they proclaim the words of the Bible to be the very words of the Holy Spirit, they treat them with the strongest freedom. They alter; they misquote; they combine widely different passages of different authors; they introduce incidents borrowed from Jewish ritual and Jewish legend; they make more use of the Old Testament than of the New; they not only appeal to apocryphal writings as of inspired authority, but build arguments upon them. In matters of interpretation they show so little title to authority that their views have been abandoned by the whole Christian world. (Ibid., pp. 165–66.)

The apostolic Fathers turned to allegory to find a witness for Christ in the Old Testament. Once they started they didn't know where to quit. Clement of Rome established the pattern of using the Phoenix as a sign of the resurrection, and was the first to endow Rahab, the prostitute of Jericho, with the gift of prophecy — the scarlet cord hung out of her window being the symbolic announcement that redemption could come only by the blood of the Lord to all that believe and have hope in God (ibid., p. 166).

The epistle of Barnabas, reputed to have been written by Paul's missionary companion, was another oft-quoted second-century source used to sustain the typical nature of the Old Testament as foreshadowing the New Testament. Though strongly anti-Judaic in tone, it was very Judaic in method. It uses the mystical kabalistic system of the rabbis in which each letter of the alphabet is given a number value and then great truths are deduced by playing with the numbers. Noting that Abraham circumcised his 318 servants and that the letter value of the number 318 is TIH, the book of Barnabas proudly announces that the *T* stands for the cross and *IH* represents the name of Jesus in Greek. So by two letters he signified Jesus, and by the third the cross, and proudly concluded, "I never taught to any one a more certain truth; but I trust you are worthy of it" (Barnabas 8:11—14). The system attributes to Abraham a knowledge of the mystic processes of numerical values of letters of an alphabet that did not exist in his day. Still the system was eagerly adopted by many of the writers of the day with results every bit as enlightening.

Barnabas also provides us with the earliest of Christian attempts to give a mystic reason to the clean and unclean animals of the Mosaic code. The Israelites were forbidden to eat swine to remind them that they were not to join with people living in pleasure and forgetting God. (Barnabas 9:3.) They were to refrain from eating the hare as a reminder that they were not to commit adultery. Neither were they to eat the hyena, to show that men must not be corrupted, since it changes its sex from male to female every year. (Barnabas 9:7—8.)

Justin Martyr was another of the apostolic fathers who wrote with the idea that the Old Testament prophets always spoke in mysteries and allegories. He explained away the problem of polygamy in the Old Testament with the use of allegory, as he did such other problems as Judah's immorality and David's adultery. Noah, he held, was saved by wood and water, showing that Christians are delivered from sin by the cross and baptism (*Law*, p. 149.) So fully was he able to find Christ in the Old Testament that one of his critics observed, "He applied all the sticks and pieces of wood in the Old Testament to the cross." He would also freely add details to Bible stories to sustain his types. Samples include his conclusion that there were twelve bells on the high priest's robe, symbolizing the twelve Apostles, and the fact that the ass at Bethphage was tied to a vine. (Ibid.)

Another of the great teachers of the day was Clement of
Alexandria, who was also an avid proponent of the doctrine that
all scripture was allegorical. According to Clement, the literal
reading of the word was the milk, the esoteric vision the meat.
These secret and private doctrines, he held, were taught by Christ
to Peter, James, and John only after his resurrection. They were
transmitted orally but were not to be written.

The master allegorist was Origen, whose commentaries, it is
said, were "the common mine in which all his successors dug"
(Farrar, p. 189). Origen shared many views with Philo, Barnabas, Justin, and Clement of Alexandria. He believed the Bible to
be supernaturally perfect and thus found hidden and mysterious
meanings even in its obvious errors. He also accepted the
Aopcrypha as having been divinely dictated. Like his predecessors he realized that the position that scripture was inerrant could
not be maintained if it were accepted at face value. He saw much
in the Bible that taken literally seemed absurd, unworthy, unjust,
or just impossible, and found answers to each and every such
difficulty in allegory.

Origen did not oppose the literal reading of scriptures. He felt
that all had value; even physical scriptural sounds might act akin
to a magical formula. Still, such a thing should not go un-
checked, he warned, for it could easily lead to immorality,
unbelief, and heresy—not the least of which might be a "carnal
view of God" (ibid., p. 194).

Two samples of his scriptural interpretation must suffice.
First, Rebecca's going to the well to draw water and meeting
Abraham's servant tells us that we must daily come to the well of
scripture in order to meet Christ. And of Christ sending two of
his disciples to fetch the ass upon which he made his triumphant
entry from Bethphage to the temple, we are told that the ass represented the letter of the Old Testament. Its foal, which was
gentle and submissive, represented the New Testament, and the
two Apostles typified the moral and mystic senses. (See Farrar, p.
200.)

What Origen was to the Eastern Church and Philo to the Jews
of the Diaspora, Jerome, the hermit of Bethlehem, was to the
western branch of Christianity. He penned volume after volume

of commentary on the scriptures, though his monumental work was the Vulgate Bible, which became the authorized version for the Roman Catholic Church. This labor, which spanned twenty-three years (A.D. 382—405), provided the opportunity to expose the fables referred to in the Septuagint. He also made a clear distinction between the aprocryphal books and the Old Testament, and rejected outright the New Testament apocrypha that had gained much popularity (ibid., p. 225).

Jerome did much in his writings to develop and defend the literal and historical sense of scripture. Yet his great failing was that of vacillation—he was consistent only in his inconsistency. He praised and then repudiated Origen; quoted the Septuagint as inspired and then rejected it with contempt; treated Jews with tolerance and then with blind hatred. Farrar accused him of bringing to scriptural study "a thousand years of retardation," which if nothing else is a tribute to his influence (ibid., pp. 229—30). Thus there is no surprise at finding him at complete variance with himself on the matter of allegory. He filled books with allegorical interpretations as arbitrary as Origen's and on other occasions rejected it as "mere cloud and shadow" (ibid., p. 232). In his hands the book of Joshua became an allegory about the Church and the heavenly Jerusalem. He developed a type for each character in the book of Judges. Kings became a description of the struggle of heretics against the Church. The Ethiopian wife of Moses was also identified as representing the Church. The adultress in Hosea represented Mary Magdalene and Rahab. The last chapter of the book of Joel is explained as referring to the day of Pentecost and the fall of Jerusalem, but as to the locusts, Jerome gives a liberal choice, for he said, "they may be Assyrians and Babylonians, Medes and Persians, or Greeks, or Romans." (Ibid. pp. 232—33.)

No writer was more emphatic in establishing rules of scriptural interpretation than St. Augustine. He insisted that allegory be based on the historical sense (ibid., p. 234). "He laid down the rule that the Bible must be interpreted with reference to Church Orthodoxy and that no Scriptural expression can be out of accordance with any other" (ibid. p. 236). He warned against the fraud of distorting the meaning of isolated verses; then, having established these rules, he systematically violated them. He adopted the Philonian and rabbinic rule that everything in scripture that appeared to be unorthodox or immoral must be interpreted mystically, and determined that there are passages written by the Holy Ghost which are objectionable if taken in their obvious sense. Thus in the established tradition he gave us such interpretations as the fig leaves in the story of the Fall representing hypocrisy, the coats of skins mortality, and the four rivers of Eden the four cardinal virtues. In the story of the Flood, the ark, he said, was pitched within and without to show the safety of the Church from inward and outward heresies. The drunkenness of Noah became a "figure of death and passion of Christ" (ibid., p. 238).

THE DARK AGES

The birth of papal supremacy marked the death of theological originality. With it came the long winter's night of history known as the Dark Ages, when the Bible was bound "with the double chains of dogma and allegory" (ibid., p. 299). The church eclipsed all light in the name of the Bible and tradition. The pope became the infallible interpreter of both. All education became ecclesiastical and all authority papal priesthood. One of the great advantages of a system of infallibility is that it frees its people from the responsibility of individual thought. It was for the pope and his priests to attend to all matters of salvation. "The system, besides saving the trouble of much study, was advantageous to hierarchic usurpations. It made of Scripture an Apocalyptic book with seven seals, which only priests and monks were able to unlock. It made a standing dogma of the 'obscurity' of Scripture, which was thus kept safely out of the hands of the multitude. It made the Pope the doorkeeper of Scripture, not the Holy Spirit. It placed at the disposal of the hierarchy an indefinite number of flaccid symbols which might be oracularly applied to prove whatever they desired." (Ibid., pp. 296—97.)

Thus the scriptures responded to the papal call:

The eighth Psalm was used by Antonius, Bishop of Florence, to mean that God put all things under the feet of the

Pope, —sheep, i.e., Christians; oxen, i.e., Jews and heretics; beasts of the field, i.e., pagans; and fishes of the sea, i.e., souls in purgatory. "Thou hast broken the heads of the dragon in the waters" (Ps. 74:13) proved the expulsion of demons by baptism. The celibacy of priests was supported by the comparison, in Canticles, of the cheeks of the beloved to doves. The root of the tree in Daniel's vision (Daniel 4:12) furnished a proof of the Immaculate Conception of the Virgin. The two rods of Zechariah (11:7) are types of the Dominicans and Franciscans. The papal canonisation of saints was maintained by a reference to the putting of a lamp on a lampstand. (Matthew 5:15; ibid., pp. 297.)

THE REFORMATION

By the sixteenth century the whole papal system had, by the admission of its own historians, "sunk into a formalism and corruption which made it a curse to mankind" (ibid., p. 308). The dark winter of suppression had ruled the minds and souls of men too long. Theological fires that gave no warmth were abandoned as the Bible itself rose like the summer sun to give warmth and light to all who chose to stand in its rays. It was a time of courageous men who dared to go beyond the towering walls of tradition, and the polluted moat called sacraments, and free themselves of the prison of papal infallibility. And such men there were: Luther, Calvin, Wycliff, Tyndale, and others, each doing his divinely appointed part that the light of the scriptures might freely shine.

It was John Wycliffe (1328-1384) who gave English-speaking people the first Bible they could read. Excommunicated from the church of Rome for his opposition to pardons, indulgences, and masses for the dead, Wycliffe secreted himself from his enemies and translated Jerome's Latin Bible into English. He died before his enemies could make a martyr of him— yet forty years after his death his bones were dug up and burned, and the ashes flung into a river. It was another excommunicant, Martin Luther (1483—1546), equally opposed to indulgences and the host of corruptions in the Catholic Church, who gave the German people the Bible in their native tongue. His was not the first

German translation, but it was by far the best. Luther announced that "christianity has ceased to exist among those who should have preserved it" (John Todd, *Martin Luther: A Biographical Study*, p. 188). Having lost faith in the power of the priesthood allegedly bequeathed by apostolic succession and the sacraments as they had been perverted, Luther found refuge only in the scriptures. There he chose to rest his case. "A layman who has Scripture," he said, "is more than Pope or council without it" (Farrar, p. 326). "I have observed," said Luther, "that all heresies and errors have originated, not from the simple words of Scripture, as is so universally asserted, but from neglecting the simple words of Scripture, and from the affectation of purely subjective tropes and inferences" (ibid., p. 327).

Like most of the Reformers, Luther rejected the validity of allegory. "Allegories are empty speculations, and as it were the scum of Holy Scripture," he held (Farrar, p. 328). Where his predecessors had handled the difficult and embarrassing problems of the Bible as allegory, Luther took a more direct approach. He simply demoted the book from the list of the canon. He saw "hay and stubble as well as gold and precious stones in the superstructure" of the Bible. He held Paul's epistles to be of greater value than the synoptic Gospels. John, Romans, and 1 Peter were, he said, "the right kernel and marrow of all books." Chronicles was historically inferior to Kings; the book of Solomon he rejected. Jude he thought to be "unnecessary, second-hand, and non-apostolic." And the epistle of James, which seemed to contradict so many of his conclusions from Romans and Galatians, he saw as a "right strawy epistle" and of questionable worth. (Farrar, pp. 335–36.) In ordering his New Testament translation, Luther put Hebrews, James, Jude, and Revelation in the back. He dared not exclude them, but he put them together at the end, separating them from the rest in numbering so that they appeared almost like an appendix. He numbered the others from one to twenty-three, giving no number to these final four books.

Ulrich Zwingli (1484–1531), also a Catholic priest, independently arrived at many of the same conclusions as Luther in his scriptural study and rejection of the mother church. He did so choosing Matthew, Acts, and Timothy as his primary text. He did not share Luther's preoccupation with justification by faith. From Zwingli the Reformation in Switzerland passed to John Calvin.

John Calvin (1509—64) was another of the great voices echoing the theme that the Bible was the sole source of God's law. Calvin, who may have been the finest and yet most unpopular theologian of the Reformation, had no use for allegory. A good cause, he felt, should not be sustained by bad reasoning. He saw the writings of the psalmists and the prophets as primarily applicable to the events of their day. As to the manner in which they were quoted and applied by New Testament writers, he saw them as "illustrative references; as skillful adaptations; as admissible transferences; as metaphoric allusions; as fair accommodations; as pious deflections," but not as actual fulfillment of prophecy (ibid., p. 374). He would not hold to the legitimacy of an interpretation in which a passage could not have been understood by those to whom the prophets addressed their words.

For all his discipline and rules, Calvin, like the others, had difficulty in abiding by them. He also freely read into scripture what he wished to find there.

The Restoration

A review of the history of Bible interpretation gives greater meaning to the message of the First Vision. In response to Joseph Smith's question as to which church he should join, Joseph was answered that he "must join none of them, for they were all wrong." Their creeds, he was told, were "an abomination" in the sight of God, and their professors corrupt. For doctrines they taught " 'the commandments of men, having a form of godliness, but they deny the power thereof.' " (JS—H 1:19.) No more apt summary of Christian history could have been given. During that period in which Joseph struggled to bring forth the Book of Mormon, the Lord said to him, "Satan doth stir up the hearts of the people to contention concerning the points of my doctrine; and in these things they do err, for they do wrest the scriptures and do not understand them" (D&C 10:63).

Later a more experienced Joseph Smith, while being held prisoner for his own religious views, wrote of the tyranny and oppression to which he and his people had been subjected. It represented the "influence of that spirit which hath so strongly riveted the creeds of the fathers, who have inherited lies, upon the hearts of the children, and filled the world with confusion, and has been growing stronger and stronger, and is now the very mainspring of all corruption, and the whole earth groans under the weight of its iniquity. It is an iron yoke, it is a strong band; they are the very handcuffs, and chains, and shackles, and fetters of hell." (D&C 123:7—8.)

In our concluding chapter we will turn our attention to the revelations of the Restoration and the teachings of the Prophet Joseph Smith to establish as nearly as we can those principles that should guide us in the interpretation of scripture.

17

Interpreting Scripture

John records an incident in which God audibly responded to a public prayer offered by Christ. Among those present, some said it thundered, others that an angel spoke to him. (See John 12:28–29.) Apparently few both heard and understood the heavenly voice, as John did. Thus it has always been; when the heavens speak some give it one interpretation, others another.

There is a remarkable divergency of views among those professing the Bible as the source of their doctrine, practices, and authority. Declaring the Bible to be the "sole norm of faith" has resulted in everything but a unity of the faith. Borrowing the language of Jacob's allegory, "All sorts of fruit did cumber the tree . . . and there is none of it which is good" (Jacob 5:30, 32). Many have struggled to suggest rules or standards by which the scriptures should be interpreted, though none have ever followed the rules they established. Like their pharisaical fathers before them, "They say, and do not" (Matthew 23:3). Wary of the dangers of such an undertaking, we now take up that same quest, not with the idea of marking the sure and infallible path, but in the hopes of identifying those high peaks given to us as correct principles, so that the honest might find their way and properly govern themselves.

The Bible Fraud

The Bible is the most misused and misunderstood book ever written. It has been used to justify all manner of impropriety, wickedness, and falsehood. Every spiritual fraud ever perpetrated in the history of Judaism or Christianity has claimed support from the Bible. It has been quoted as often by devils as it has by Saints. It has served as an instrument of suppression as often as it has served as a source of inspiration.

A knowledge of what the Bible does and does not claim for itself is important in protecting against its misrepresentations. The following paragraphs deal with things falsely claimed for the Bible which it does not claim for itself.

1. The Bible makes no claim to infallibility. The infallibility of the Bible is a fundamental doctrine among Bible cultists, though by their own admission they cannot find a book, chapter, or verse within the Bible to sustain this doctrine. Infallibility and mortality are incompatible. We no more have infallible books than we have infallible men. Such a belief quickly leads to the ridiculous. It was in the name of infallibility that Galileo was condemned by the church in Rome for saying that the earth moved around the sun. The idea, it was held, contradicted scriptural passages that spoke of the sun's rising and setting.

The Book of Mormon, which is a much more perfect translation than the Bible, not only makes no pretense of infallibility but specifically addresses the inevitability of errors existing in it. "Whoso receiveth this record," Moroni said, "and shall not condemn it because of the imperfections which are in it, the same shall know of greater things than these." He also said, "if there be faults they be the faults of a man." (Mormon 8:12, 17.) This principle and spirit apply to the reading of all scripture.

2. The Bible makes no claim to having been supernaturally dictated. It is not inerrant. "Whoever was the first dogmatist to make the terms 'the Bible' and 'the Word of God' synonymous, rendered to the cause of truth and of religion an immense disservice. The phrase in that sense has no shadow of Scriptural authority. It occurs from three to four hundred times in the Old Testament, and about a hundred times in the New; and in not

one of all those instances is it applied to the Scriptures." (Farrar, p. 396.)

3. By disposing of the divine dictation fraud we can also dispose of the unfortunate idea that everything in the scriptures is of equal worth. It is hard to imagine that the Song of Solomon, even if someone can concoct some meaningful allegory, could be thought of as having equal value with the Sermon on the Mount. And it is difficult to suppose that the account of the Levite cutting the dead body of his wife into twelve pieces and sending them to the tribes of Israel to arouse their anger against those who killed her (Judges 19) is of the same spiritual merit as the Savior's bread of life discourse. Leviticus is hardly as valuable to us as the Gospel of John, and the Nephite wars as recorded by Alma hardly compare with the visit of Christ in 3 Nephi.

"All scripture is given by inspiration of God, and is profitable for doctrine, for reproof, for correction, for instruction in righteousness" (2 Timothy 3:16), but all is not of equal worth. The Proverbs, for all their wisdom, do not compare with the knowledge received in the vision on the degrees of glory (D&C 76) or with the vision of the redemption of the dead (D&C 138).

4. The Bible makes no claim that its prophets are infallible. James wrote of Elijah, one of the greatest of the Old Testament prophets, that he was "a man subject to like passions as we are" (James 5:17). Paul corrected Peter (Galatians 2:11—14), and Peter said of Paul that he wrote things "hard to be understood" (2 Peter 3:16). Jonah misunderstood his own prophecy (Jonah 4); Jeremiah got so discouraged that he said the Lord had "deceived me" and swore that he would speak in the name of the Lord no more (Jeremiah 20:7, 9); and Noah got drunk (Genesis 9:21). Balaam had his head turned by the promise of riches and was destroyed with the wicked (Numbers 31:8); Judas, a member of the Twelve, betrayed the Son of God.

Again, there is no need to multiply examples. Prophets are mortal and are, as James said, "subject to like passions as we are." Christ warned the Nephite Twelve that they "must watch and pray always" lest they be tempted and taken captive by the devil (3 Nephi 18:15), and he told Peter that Satan desired to sift him as wheat (Luke 22:31). As a warning to Joseph Smith, the Lord said,

"For although a man may have many revelations, and have power to do many mighty works, yet if he boasts in his own strength, and sets at naught the counsels of God, and follows after the dictates of his own will and carnal desires, he must fall and incur the vengeance of a just God upon him" (D&C 3:4).

It was Joseph Smith who taught us that "a prophet was a prophet only when he was acting as such" (*Teachings*, p. 278). Yet nowhere is the principle more beautifully taught than by Moroni, who after having penned scripture humbly pleaded, "Condemn me not because of mine imperfection, neither my father, because of his imperfection, neither them who have written before him; but rather give thanks unto God that he hath made manifest unto you our imperfections, that ye may learn to be more wise than we have been" (Mormon 9:31).

5. The Bible makes no pretense to having answers to all the questions needing answers, nor does it pretend to be a composite of all revelation ever given. In fact, the Bible continually directs its readers to implore the heavens for knowledge and understanding beyond what it contains, and often quotes statements and books that are now lost to it. Further, nowhere does the Bible purport to give its readers either authority or commission to preach the gospel or to perform gospel ordinances.

Notwithstanding the fact that it contains the fulness of the gospel (see D&C 42:12), the Bible is not the source to which we as Latter-day Saints properly turn to establish doctrine, determine truth, or prove authority. This is one of the most important lessons the Prophet Joseph Smith ever sought to teach us. Of his own struggles to find the truth he said, "The teachers of religion of the different sects understood the same passages of scripture so differently as to destroy all confidence in settling the question by an appeal to the Bible" (JS—H 1:12). The Book of Mormon was given for the purpose of "confounding of false doctrines and laying down of contentions, and establishing peace" (2 Nephi 3:12). It is the Book of Mormon that has been given to prove the Bible true (D&C 20:8—12). All meaningful understanding of the Bible must come by revelation.

6. One of the greatest of Bible frauds is the idea that the canon of scripture is complete and that revelation has ceased. Again, the

announcement cannot be sustained by the Bible itself. As Joseph Smith said, "We have what we have, and the Bible contains what it does contain: but to say that God never said anything more to man than is there recorded, would be saying at once that we have at last received a revelation; for it must require one to advance thus far, because it is nowhere said in that volume by the mouth of God, that He would not, after giving, what is there contained, speak again; and if any man has found out for a fact that the Bible contains all that God ever revealed to man he has ascertained it by an immediate revelation, other than has been previously written by the prophets and apostles" (HC 2:18).

ACCEPTING THE BIBLE FOR WHAT IT IS

Farrar insightfully observes: "The Scriptures never claim for themselves as a whole the supernatural dictation or miraculous infallibility which from the days of the Rabbis have been claimed for them. They do not even furnish any test of their own canonicity; nor do they protect themselves from grievous mistranslation; nor do they give any definition of the nature of their own inspiration; nor do they lay down any of its limits or degrees; nor has their text been kept free from numberless variations; nor do they furnish any rules whatever as to the manner in which their difficulties should rightly be explained." (Farrar, p. 162.)

The New Testament church was led by Apostles and prophets and governed by the spirit of revelation. The life-giving force of the Church was the Holy Ghost, not some scriptural record that no member of that church ever read. The New Testament did not exist until some considerable time after the apostasy was complete.

The spirit of revelation must be as much a part of the true church today as it was in the time when the events of the New Testament occurred. Every significant issue in the Bible that has been confused as to whether it was literal or figurative, whether it was allegorical or factual, has been clearly answered by the coming forth of the Book of Mormon and the revelations contained in the Doctrine and Covenants. Every saving truth and necessary ordinance has clearly been spelled out.

JOSEPH SMITH AND THE BIBLE

There has never been a man on the face of the earth that had greater faith in the Bible than the Prophet Joseph Smith, and save Jesus only there has never been a man who knew more about it. A library containing everything the world knows about the book would not rival his understanding. It is one thing to read the book and quite another to be instructed by its authors. Who among the world's scholars can boast of having stood face to face with Adam, Noah, a messenger from Abraham's dispensation, Moses, Elijah, John the son of Zacharias, Peter, James, and John? While religious leaders were claiming the heavens to be sealed to them, Joseph Smith was being personally tutored by these ancient prophets and had their hands laid upon his head that they might bless him and confer upon him the power, keys, and authority they held.

Joseph Smith claimed the Holy Ghost as his textbook (*Teachings*, p. 349) and made his translation of the Bible from the original language—the language in which all the revelations were originally given—the language of revelátion. By that same power and from that same language he restored the contents of a parchment written and sealed up by John the Beloved (D&C 7) and part of another written by John the Baptist (D&C 93:6—20), and by it he translated a parchment written by Abraham. Who but Joseph Smith could tell us that Seth was the perfect likeness of his father (D&C 107:43), or give a detailed description of Paul (*Teachings*, p. 180)? Joseph Smith knew the Bible, he knew its prophets, he knew its message, and he knew its central character—the Lord Jesus Christ—with whom he also stood face to face and by whom he was instructed.

Joseph Smith spoke as one having authority. He was a living Bible, and in restoring the Book of Mormon and giving us the revelations in the Doctrine and Covenants he has done more to enhance the world's understanding of the Bible than any man who ever lived in it.

The Contradictory, Unbelievable, and Unworthy

To establish tranquillity in the kingdom of scriptural belief we must venture through the dark valley of confusion and face the dragons of faith, those elusive ghosts of contradiction, those texts that make God, his prophets, or his word appear quite unworthy. The dangers are plentiful even to the well-meaning and zealous, and so we carefully dress ourselves in the full armor of faith, taking with us the sword of common sense and reason. Knowing that all scripture is dependent on the Spirit for proper interpretation, we must have as companions on such a venture the light of revelation, the wise counsel of living prophets, and such trusted allies as the Book of Mormon and the Doctrine and Covenants. Doing so we can conclude the following:

1. Omissions. Many great truths and revelations that were once a part of the Bible are now lost to it. "I believe the Bible as it read when it came from the pen of the original writers," said Joseph Smith. "Ignorant translators, careless transcribers, or designing and corrupt priests have committed many errors." (*Teachings,* p. 327.) Let us first give examples of translation errors due to carelessness and then consider the matter of deliberate corruptions of the text.

Consider this text from Deuteronomy: "Ye shall not eat of any thing that dieth of itself: thou shalt give it unto the stranger that is in thy gates, that he may eat it; or thou mayest sell it unto an alien: for thou art an holy people unto the Lord thy God" (14:21). In the JST the Prophet simply restored the "not" that had been lost by a careless transcriber so that the text directs Israel "not" to give or sell bad meat to strangers. In 1 Samuel we read of "an evil spirit from the Lord" which troubled Saul. The JST assures us that this spirit "was not of the Lord."

The Bible went forth from the hands of its writers "in purity," but it fell into the hands of spiritual thieves who took from it "many parts which are plain and most precious; and also many covenants of the Lord have they taken away. And all this have they done that they might pervert the right ways of the Lord, that they might blind the eyes and harden the hearts of the children of men." (1 Nephi 13:24–27.) Moses was told that much that he would write would be taken from the scriptural record by those who esteemed not the word of God (Moses 1:41). Jeremiah wrote of scribes who with "lying pens" had falsified the scriptural record even in that day (NEB, Jeremiah 8:8). Christ similarly accused the scribes of his day of having tampered with and taken truths from the scriptural text (JST, Luke 11:53). Examples could be multiplied, but in lieu thereof we simply ask, Could not a people who mocked, scourged, imprisoned, and killed the prophets find it within the grasp of their own conscience to tamper with what those hated men had written?

If a simple illustration is desired of the manner in which the Bible text has been perverted, one need only compare Moses chapters 1 through 8 with their Bible counterpart. The entire first chapter of Moses is a restoration of a scriptural text written by Moses. Among other things of great interest, its absence from the Bible leaves out Moses' confrontation with Satan, who desired to be worshiped as the Only Begotten. Also missing are the doctrines of faith in Christ, repentance, and baptism, as taught by Adam, Enoch, and Noah (Moses 6:57—59, 64; 7:11). The reference to God repenting is also corrected (Genesis 6:6 versus Moses 8:25) and much of interest is restored.

2. Additions. Just as things have been taken from the Bible, so others have been added. Not all Bible interpolations were malicious—often scribes would give way to temptation to improve the text, or to write comments in the margin that were later incorporated into the text. Most modern English versions do not have verse 4 in John 5. It is the explanation for the moving of the waters of the pool of Bethesda. Some scribe, it is believed, explained in the margin that an angel came down at certain times to trouble the waters, and a later scribe incorporated it into the text. It is argued that the better manuscripts do not have it. Scholars have in the course of years developed a set of rules that they use to detect additions to the text as they compare various manuscripts, though there would never be universal agreement on such matters.

The authenticity of the apocryphal books which are a part of the Catholic Bible has been argued for centuries. By revelation Joseph Smith was told that there is much in the Apocrypha that is true and that the translation was "mostly" correct. Yet he was cautioned that it also contained "interpolations," or things added by overzealous scribes and translators. (See D&C 91.) This raises the question to what extent the Bible in like manner has been embellished with interpolations. Surely men who would take from the sacred book would not hesitate to add to it. We are left in some instances wondering what in the Apocrypha is biblical and what in the Bible is apocryphal.

3. Translation errors. An example of a poor translation is found in Exodus 23:3, which reads, "Neither shalt thou countenance a poor man in his cause." In the JST Joseph Smith renders it, "Neither shalt thou countenance a wicked man in his cause." Similarly, 1 Corinthians 10:24 reads, "Let no man seek his own, but every man another's wealth." Hardly good doctrine, this passage is changed in the JST to read "Let not man seek therefore his own, but every man another's good."

A mistranslation that makes one Bible character appear quite depraved is that of Lot offering his two daughters for the sexual pleasure of the men of Sodom if they would but leave his guests unharmed (Genesis 19:8). From the Joseph Smith Translation we learn that Lot refused both his daughters and his visitors to the pleasures of his debased and lecherous neighbors (JST, Genesis 19:10–14).

Along with the errors that are a result of the ignorance or carelessness on the part of scribes are the errors that are the result of theological bias on the part of translators. We have already observed the Septuagint aversion to an anthropomorphic God. A more obvious bias, one universal to all translation, is the rendering of the plural "Elohim" or Gods as the singular *God*. The justification for this is simply that the translators "know" that there is only one God and not a plurality of Gods. They then turn around and cite the thousands of "Elohim" passages as evidence of the three-in-one Holy Trinity (Girdlestone, pp. 19–22), for which there is no scriptural justification.

The concept of salvation as espoused by Luther and Calvin had an obvious influence on the King James Bible. This can be easily demonstrated by comparing the way it uses the word *saved* with its translation in the New English Bible.

King James Version

The New English Bible

Acts 11:14.
"Who shall tell thee words,
whereby thou and all thy
house shall be saved."

Acts 11:14.
"He shall speak words that
will bring salvation to you
and all your household."

Romans 10:1.
"Bretheren, my heart's desire
and prayer to God for Israel
is, that they might be saved."

Romans 10:1.
"Brothers, my deepest desire
and my prayer to God is for
their salvation."

Romans 10:9.
"That if thou shalt confess
with thy mouth the Lord
Jesus, and shalt believe in
thine heart God hath raised
him from the dead, thou shalt
be saved."

Romans 10:9.
"If on your lips is the con-
fession, 'Jesus is Lord,' and in
your heart the faith that God
raised him from the dead,
then you will find salvation."

1 Corinthians 1:18.
"For the preaching of the
cross is to them that perish
foolishness; but unto us which
are saved it is the power of
God."

1 Corinthians 1:18.
"This doctrine of the cross is
sheer folly to those on their
way to ruin, but to us who
are on the way to salvation it
is the power of God."

1 Corinthians 15:2.
"By which also ye are saved,
if ye keep in memory what I
preached unto you, unless ye
have believed in vain."

1 Corinthians 15:2.
"On which you have taken
your stand, and which is now
bringing you salvation."

2 Corinthians 2:15.
"For we are unto God a sweet
savour of Christ, in them that
are saved, and in them that
perish."

2 Corinthians 2:15.
"We are indeed the incense
offered by Christ to God,
both for those who are on the
way to salvation, and for
those on the way to perdition."

Translated correctly, Paul consistently spoke of salvation as a
process that continued throughout life. "Paul would say 'you

have been justified,' or 'you have been reconciled to God,' but not 'you have been saved,' rather 'you await salvation' " (IB 10:645). An appropriate representation of Paul's intent is found in Romans 13:11, which reads, "now it is high time to awake out of sleep: for now is our salvation nearer then when we believed."

4. Not all scripture is the word of God. Paul's statement to Timothy rendered in the King James Version as "all scripture is given by inspiration," is corrected by the Prophet to read, "all Scripture given by inspiration of God, is profitable . . . "(JST, 2 Timothy 3:16). Clearly the Prophet is telling us that not all scripture is scripture. Responding to the claim that every word in the Bible is divine, Brigham Young said: "I believe the words of men and the words of angels are there; and that is not all—I believe that the words of a dumb brute are there. I recollect one of the prophets riding and prophesying against Israel, and the animal he rode rebuked his madness." (JD 14:280.)

The classic illustration of the unscriptural is the Song of Solomon, which Joseph Smith left out of his translation of the Bible. Similarly, the Qumran community rejected the Book of Esther from their canon because it does not mention God and contributes nothing to the understanding of eternal truths. Luther in like manner spoke of the "canon within the canon" and rejected the Song of Solomon.

The idea of unscriptural scripture is easier to illustrate with the Doctrine and Covenants than the Bible because it stands so much closer to us historically. Doctrine and Covenants 134 was written by Oliver Cowdery, along with an article on marriage, both of which were included in the 1835 edition. Neither were understood to be revelations. In 1876 the article on marriage was dropped from the Doctrine and Covenants. The article on governments and laws has been retained and has informally assumed the status of revelation.

The Doctrine and Covenants includes two official declarations: the first announcing that plural marriages would no longer be practiced, the second announcing that the privilege of holding the priesthood was to be extended to worthy males of all races. These are not actual revelations—they are announcements that a revelation has been received on the matters involved. Much in the scripture that is held to be "the word of God" would likewise more accurately be described as an announcement that the "word" has been received, rather than as the actual word itself.

In some instances even that which is correctly recorded identifies itself as unscriptural. For instance, Alma offers his "opinion" on the order of the resurrection (Alma 40:20). Similarly, we have an instance in which Paul gives a "commandment, not of the Lord, but of himself" (D&C 74:5), to which we would not accord the same respect as that which has been divinely given.

ERRORS OF INTERPRETATION

Latter-day Saints are as subject to the law of gravity as other people. Among our number there are those who have crowded the edge and unwittingly slipped where many have fallen before us. That we might not be numbered among the "unlearned and unstable" who "wrest . . . scriptures, unto their own destruction" (2 Peter 3:16), the following cautions are suggested:

1. When protective walls are built too high they block out the light. Such was the experience of the nation of Jews who in the name of loyalty to the law of Moses rejected the Savior. To them he said, "Do not think that I will accuse you to the Father: there is one that accuseth you, even Moses, in whom ye trust" (John 5:45). Such is also the case with those who out of a false sense of loyalty to the "word of God" as they perceive it in the Bible, have announced it the "sole norm of faith" and closed their minds and ears to a God who desires to speak to them through living prophets. Such is the case with food faddists who would do to the Word of Wisdom what the Pharisees did to the law of the Sabbath, and some who claim "special" relationships with God and who can match the misguided zeal of our "saved by grace" friends who have no need for the fulness of the gospel. We do not strengthen a principle by overprotecting it; we only pervert it by isolating it from appropriate association with the congregation of principles that constitute the fulness of the gospel.

2. The plain and obvious meaning of any passage can be rejected and lost by declaring it to be figurative or allegorical. This is a dangerous affliction, the only antidote for which is honesty, a commodity particularly hard to find among people priding them-

selves on their objectivity. Those most susceptible to this error of interpretation are usually defending some scientific theory or unusual and speculative view.

Admitting the validity of allegory is something like the introduction of cheat grass or the starling—beautiful and useful in their place, they can quickly spread to become more of a menace than a help. In some instances a more apt illustration would be to liken them to a vaccine that gives immunity to some and a deathly disease to others. Nonetheless, some passages are allegorical. The account of the birth of Adam from the dust of the earth and the birth of Eve from the rib of Adam are examples. Yet, as with this illustration, significant doctrines are not given in allegorical form unless some scriptural explanation is also given.

3. Caution must also be used in the interpretation of figures and symbols like those used in the visions of Ezekiel, Daniel, and the book of Revelation. On this matter Joseph Smith has assured us that "whenever God gives a vision of an image, or beast, or figure of any kind, He always holds Himself responsible to give a revelation or interpretation of the meaning thereof, otherwise we are not responsible or accountable for our belief in it. Don't be afraid of being damned for not knowing the meaning of a vision or figure, if God has not given a revelation or interpretation of the subject." (*Teachings*, p. 291.) This principle holds for the interpretation of allegories, parables, or imagery of any kind.

4. There is also a danger, especially among those whose minds are already made up, of squelching the spirit of revelation. The counsel to "deny not the spirit of revelation" (D&C 11:25) was given to the faithful, not to the unbelievers in the world. A characteristic of the spirit of revelation is that it expands our understanding beyond the literal reading of scripture. It does not deny the literal reading, nor does it become an excuse to give some unrelated meaning to it, but it carries us beyond that which is immediately and obviously apparent to the mind and to the naked eye. There is no difference between saying, "A Bible! A Bible! We have got a Bible, and there cannot be any more Bible," (2 Nephi 29:3) and saying "A Verse! A Verse! We have got a Verse, and there cannot be any more to this Verse."

5. A knowledge of the gospel comes only by our growing into it. No one, Christ included, receives a fullness at first (D&C

93:6—18). Too often we expect Joseph Smith to have had all the answers when he came out of the Sacred Grove. He did not. Like all prophets before him, he had to learn the gospel line upon line and precept upon precept. This principle becomes important in scriptural study, for one revelation may depend on another for its correct interpretation. For instance, in February of 1832 Joseph Smith received the revelation on the degrees of glory. In his description of those who will inherit the terrestrial kingdom he wrote, "these are they who died without law." No intimation is given in this section that the gospel is to be taught to all in the world of the spirits and that those who would have accepted it in this life, living true and faithful to the end, will have the opportunity to gain those same blessings in the spirit world. That revelation came, in its time, some four years later (see D&C 137). We can assimilate only so much at once, and it would be foolish to be critical of Joseph Smith and the revelations because they do not attempt to reveal all things to us at once.

6. Revelation does not come without the trial of our faith. The Lord has promised understanding to the "faithful line upon line, precept upon precept," but not without trials and tests (D&C 98:12). This is the very principle that has dictated the manner in which we will receive the records of the Nephites. We now have a fragment of that ancient record, which we are told is expedient that we should have first, to try our faith, and if we believe what is contained therein "then shall the greater things be made manifest" unto us. And conversely, we are told that "if it so be that they will not believe these things, then shall the greater things be withheld from them, unto their condemnation" (3 Nephi 26:9—10).

It was not intended that we have all the answers. Revelation marks the path, but the journey must still be one of faith.

CHRIST AND SCRIPTURAL INTERPRETATION

Christ's example as a teacher is itself a revelation on how scriptures are to be interpreted. Our most perfect example of his scriptural exegesis is found in 3 Nephi. The following principles are clearly illustrated in that text:

1. He made application of the principle first suggested to us by Nephi of likening or applying the scriptures to those to whom he spoke (1 Nephi 19:23). He did this by reminding the Nephites that they were "a remnant of the house of Joseph" (3 Nephi 15:12) and as such were the seed of Abraham (3 Nephi 20:27). He then applied to them prophetic promises made initially to all the house of Israel by the prophets of the Old Testament. He quoted the prophecies of Micah (3 Nephi 16:15; 20:16—19; 20:12—19), Isaiah (3 Nephi 16:17—20; 20:11—15, 32—46), and Habakkuk (Habakkuk 1:5; 3 Nephi 21:9) to that end. He also quoted prophecies of Moses (3 Nephi 21:11) and Malachi (3 Nephi 24, 25).

2. He illustrated the principle of multiple fulfillment of scripture by taking an Isaiah passage fulfilled by him in his Old World ministry and applying it anew to the Prophet Joseph Smith 3 Nephi 20:43—45; 21:10—11).

In his reapplication of prophecies fulfilled by himself he illustrated that prophecies are not always limited in their intent to events within the range of understanding of those to whom they were first addressed. It also suggests that their fulfillment may go well beyond the understanding of the prophet by whom they were spoken. Habakkuk's prophecy about one who would do a work that would not be believed (Habakkuk 1:5; 3 Nephi 21:9), and Malachi's prophecy about the messenger who would prepare the way for Christ (Malachi 3:1; 3 Nephi 24:1), in their multiple fulfillments are examples.

3. If Christ gave the Nephites a full explanation of the passages just cited, it has not yet been given to us. The Micah prophecy about the remnant of Jacob who will be "as a lion among the beasts of the forest" who both "treadeth down and teareth in pieces" is an example. He thus establishes the doctrine of ambiguity or the idea that not all things will be understood at once. The manner in which this passage, like many others, is to be fulfilled is simply not clear to us at the present time.

MORONI AND SCRIPTURAL INTERPRETATION

Moroni used Bible prophecies as the basis of his instruction to Joseph Smith. Considerable insight can be obtained about scriptural interpretation from Moroni's example. His amplified rendering of the Malachi prophecy about the return of Elijah (D&C 2) is a classic example. Moroni took a passage of scripture (Malachi 4:5—6) correct in its translation, as evidenced by its rendering in the Book of Mormon (3 Nephi 25:5—6), and gave it a more detailed and specific interpretation. In so doing he illustrated that there are levels of understanding and levels of interpretation. His interpretation takes us well beyond the literal reading of Malachi's words. It also demonstrates that no passage of scripture can contain more than a fragment of the mind of God, and that the standard works contain only portions of the eternal truths known to Deity. The Bible and Book of Mormon give us an accurate translation of "content," whereas Moroni gave us a translation of "intent."

The principle being established in this instance is that the Spirit sustains the literal reading of scriptures and then, as we are prepared and as the time is appropriate, it takes us beyond that reading to even greater understanding. This is why the Lord gave Joseph Smith the gift of the Holy Ghost in preference to manuscripts in order that he might give us the Joseph Smith Translation of the Bible. As with Moroni, it was that Spirit which took him beyond what could be obtained from manuscripts and languages. This is why when a Moroni or a Joseph Smith translates the Bible it takes on the spirit and clarity of the Book of Mormon. Scholars speak of getting back to the original documents; prophets take us back to the original source and meaning.

CORRECT PRINCIPLES

Faith coupled with "a sincere heart" and "real intent" are the requisites of spiritual understanding (Moroni 10:4). The source of that understanding must always be the Spirit. "That which is born of the flesh is flesh; and that which is born of the Spirit is spirit" (John 3:6). The law of tithing serves as an example. Ten thousand questions could be asked about what and how we should tithe, yet the Lord simply said that his people should "pay one-tenth of all their interest annually" (D&C 119:4). Unlike our tax laws, the principle is not a contest with laws and loopholes but rather a measure of loyalty and honesty. So it is with scriptural interpretation. Beyond the obvious announcement that truth is always in harmony with itself, there are no rules or guarantees of infallibility. Our interpretation of the scriptures becomes a measure of our honesty, wisdom, and maturity.

If we are to be honest in scripture study we cannot claim for the scriptures what they do not claim for themselves. The scriptures do not claim infallibility or inerrancy. They do not claim to have all the answers, and they do not claim to be all of equal worth. They do not claim prophets to be infallible. They do not convey authority, remit sin, or call to offices. They are in all things subject to the living oracles. Such is the testimony they bear of themselves.

Honesty in scriptural study requires of us that we stay in context. The context of every saving truth that we as Latter-day Saints have is the revelations of the Restoration. We are out of context to argue our doctrines from the Bible, for that is not where we learned them. If the Bible is the answer, there was no need for a Restoration. If there is a need for Joseph Smith, and those prophets, seers, and revelators that have followed in his stead, if there is a need for the Book of Mormon and its truths, if there is a need for the Doctrine and Covenants, then we should admit it and identify it as our context. To do so is to enter the environment of the Spirit; to do otherwise is to enter the arena of debate and confusion.

Parley P. Pratt illustrated this principle with a story from the life of Joseph Smith. When he, Sidney Rigdon, and others had gone east to seek redress from the federal government for the driving of the Saints out of the state of Missouri, a large church building was opened for them in which to preach. Some three thousand people were in attendance. Elder Pratt records:

> Brother Rigdon spoke first, and dwelt on the Gospel, illustrating his doctrine by the Bible. When he was through, brother Joseph arose like a lion about to roar; and being full of the Holy Ghost, spoke in great power, bearing testimony of the visions he had seen, the ministering of angels which he had enjoyed; and how he had found the plates of the Book of Mormon, and translated them by the gift and power of God.

He commenced by saying: "If nobody else had the courage to testify of so glorious a message from Heaven, and of the finding of so glorious a record, he felt to do it in justice to the people, and leave the event with God."

The entire congregation were astounded; electrified, as it were, and overwhelmed with the sense of the truth and power by which he spoke, and the wonders which he related. A lasting impression was made; many souls were gathered into the fold. And I bear witness, that he, by his faithful and powerful testimony, cleared his garments of their blood. Multitudes were baptized in Philadelphia and in the regions around; while, at the same time, branches were springing up in Pennsylvania, in Jersey, and in various directions. (*Autobiography of Parley P. Pratt*, pp. 298—99.)

If we are to be honest in our scriptural study, we will not be found creating doctrines from Bible dust or creating bodies for that which has no spirit. This is most often done by establishing a doctrine from an allegory or parable. Doctrines are not revealed in allegories or parables. An allegory or parable can be used to illustrate or sustain a clearly revealed doctrine, but not to originate it. Nor will those who are spiritually honest seek to avoid the clear and factual meaning of scripture using the tag of allegory or parable.

To be spiritually honest is to listen for and accept the quiet whisperings of the Spirit. Although the Ten Commandments were thundered from the mountaintop, the more sacred doctrines are manifest in temples, closets, and quiet places. Describing the spirit of revelation, the Lord said, "I will tell you in your mind and in your heart, by the Holy Ghost, which shall come upon you and which shall dwell in your heart" (D&C 8:2). As both "mind" and "heart" are involved in the receipt of revelation, so they must be used in growing into an understanding of the revelation. Both mind and heart are to be sensitive to all that is about us, for as we observed in the first chapter, "all things have their likeness," and as Christ said, "All things are created and made to bear record of me, both things which are temporal, and things which are spiritual; things which are in the heavens above, and things which are on the earth, and things which are in the earth, and things which are under the earth, both above and beneath: all things bear record of me" (Moses 6:63).

There are few if any stories in the scriptures that do not cast a shadow, that are not types or illustrations of greater principles or events. Virtually every passage of scripture is layered with meaning, and its full interpretation need not be limited to our present understanding. "That which is of God is light; and he that receiveth light, and continueth in God, receiveth more light; and that light groweth brighter and brighter until the perfect day" (D&C 50:24). For us to begin to see those countless types and shadows, the endless symbolic representations of Christ, is for us to be ever assured of the reality of his gospel and the blessings enjoyed by those who choose to live it.

Glossary of Symbols

Aaron. (1) As the high priest, Aaron was a type for Christ. (2) Aaron was the illustration or symbol of one properly ordained to the priesthood (Heb. 5:4).

Abel. Adam's son, a prophet, seer, and revelator, whose innocent blood was shed at the hands of Cain, who is Perdition (Gen. 4:8; *Teachings*, p. 169). As such he was a type for Christ.

Ablutions. An act of washing; a cleansing or purification by water. Paul refers to the ablutions associated with the Levitical order as "baptisms" and "divers washings" (Heb. 6:2, 9:10). It was in imitation of such a ritual that Pilate "washed his hands before the multitude, saying, I am innocent of the blood of this just person" (Matt. 27:24).

Abraham. (1) The father of the faithful and thus a type for what all men must be and do to gain salvation (D&C 84:34; 132:32). Through eternal marriage every man becomes as Abraham to his family and obtains the promise of eternal seed (D&C 110:12; 132:30–31). (2) In his willingness to offer Isaac as a sacrifice he was a type for our eternal Father (Gen. 22).

Abraham's bosom. A symbol for paradise, the place where the righteous spirits await the day of their resurrection (Luke 16:22–23).

Adam. (1) Abraham tells us the name means "first father" (Abr. 1:3). (2) New Testament writers typically use Adam as a symbol of all humankind (as in 1 Cor. 15:21–22; Rom. 5:12–21). (3) Christ is referred to as the Second Adam because through the Resurrection he was the firstborn into immortal life (1 Cor. 15:45).

Adultery. A frequent characteristic of Hebrew prophecy is the description of apostasy through the metaphor of adultery. God's covenant with Israel is referred to as a marriage. Having made a sacred covenant with Christ, those who turned from it in their lust and love for the things of the world are called adulterous. (See also Fornication.)

Allegory. An extended metaphor in which people, places, or things are given a symbolic meaning. Classic scriptural illustrations are Zenos's allegory of the tame and wild olive trees (Jacob 5); Paul's comparison of the two covenants to Sarah and Hagar (Gal. 4:21–31); and the story of Eve being created from the rib of Adam (Gen 2:21–25).

Almond. A symbol of divine favor, as demonstrated by the flowering of Aaron's rod and its bringing forth fruit (Num. 17:1–8). That chosen of God is identified by its fruit.

Alpha and Omega. The first and last letters of the Greek alphabet are used as name-titles for Christ. Figuratively they represent the timeless and eternal nature of the attributes of Deity (D&C 76:4).

Altar. A place of worship, most frequently associated with making sacrifices and entering into or renewing covenants. Always found in temples, altars are a place of the divine presence. Anciently, they were built on raised ground so that there was a ritual ascent as one approached the place of worship. Among the Book of Mormon peoples they were a place where one called upon God and confessed sins (Alma 17:4). In the Bible they are clearly seen as the place from which prayers were to ascend to heaven and to which angels descended bringing heavenly messages (Luke 1:9–20).

Amen. A term derived from a Hebrew word whose root suggests "so be it." Typically used as a confirmation (1 Kgs. 1:36), it implies agreement, as at the conclusion of a prayer (Matt. 6:13; 1 Cor. 14:16). In Revelation 3:14, "the Amen" is a synonym for Jesus Christ, who affirms the divine purpose.

Ancient of days. Name-title for Adam, "the first and oldest of all, the great, grand progenitor" (D&C 27:11; *Teachings*, p. 167). The title is incorrectly thought by the sectarian world to refer to God.

Angels. Messengers of God. They may be pre-earth spirits, translated beings, disembodied spirits, resurrected beings, or even righteous mortal men. Angelic symbols included flaming swords, trumpets, and scepters.

Anointing. Anointing with oil is associated with healing (James 5:14–15) and with consecrating or designating of something as holy (Ex. 29:36). The oil is a symbol of the outpouring of the Holy Spirit. The words *Messiah* and *Christ* signify Anointed One. The anointing of prophets, priests, and kings made of each a type for the Christ.

Antitype. That which the type or symbol represents—for instance, a New Testament event prefigured in the Old Testament. Christ was the antitype of the sacrificial lamb of the Old Testament.

Apron. The fig leaves used by Adam and Eve to cover their nakedness after they had partaken of the forbidden fruit are called aprons (Gen. 3:7).

Ark of the Covenant. Signified the divine presence and as such was the most sacred symbol in ancient Israel. It was made of incorruptible wood covered with gold. The wood symbolized the unchanging nature of God, the gold his glory and power.

Arm. (1) The upraised arms denote supplication, prayer, surrender. (2) The arm "made bare" (Isa. 52:10) represents the strength or power of God. (3) Those on the Lord's errand are the arm of the Lord (D&C 35:14).

Armageddon. A Greek transliteration of the Hebrew *Har Megiddon*, or "Mountain of Megiddo," a famous battlefield in the Plain of Jezreel in ancient Israel (Judg. 5:19, 2 Kgs. 9:27; 23:29). The name is used only once in the scriptures (Rev. 16:16), where it becomes the symbol for the gathering place of all nations for the final great battle preceding the return of Christ.

Armor. Used by Isaiah, Paul, and Joseph Smith as a symbol of protection against evil (Isa. 59:17; Eph. 6:11–17; D&C 27: 15–18).

Asherah (Ashtoreth, Astarte). A fertility goddess made of a tree trunk. Referred to in the KJV as a grove, or groves (Deut. 16:21; 1 Kgs. 14:15; Isa. 17:8).

Atonement, Day of (Yom Kippur). The annual day upon which the high priest made the sin offering to effect a reconciliation between God and Israel. The ritual included the banishment of a "scapegoat" to which the priest had symbolically transferred the collective guilt of the nation. The Day of Atonement marked the once-yearly entrance of the high priest into the Holy of Holies. Paul explains this is a symbolic representation of Christ's sacrificial death and ascension to the heavenly sanctuary (Heb. 9).

Babylon. As the archetypal enemy of God's people, Babylon is used as a symbol for the idols of false religious, philosophical, and political systems that seek to destroy true religion and enslave God's people in worldliness (Rev. 17:5; D&C 1:16).

Baptism. A ritual immersion in water which symbolizes the death and burial of sins and a rebirth or resurrection into a newness of life (Rom. 6:3—6).

Bee. A symbol of industry. (See Deseret.)

Bethel. An ancient site, meaning "house of God," associated with Abraham (Gen. 12:8) and Jacob (Gen. 28:19).

Blood. (1) Represents life—"the life of the flesh is in the blood" (Lev. 17:11). In scriptural language the shedding of blood is the taking of life. The atoning power of animal sacrifice came from the shedding of the animal's blood, which represented the life of the animal, as a type for the atoning sacrifice of Christ. Christ literally shed his blood both in Gethsemane and on Calvary. (2) Thus, the blood also symbolizes an atoning sacrifice. Moses said, "It is the blood that maketh an atonement for the soul" (Lev. 17:11). Through the blood of the Savior we are both redeemed and sanctified (D&C 27:2; Moses 6:60). (3) Blood is also a symbol of sin; by raising the warning voice we rid ourselves of the blood or sins of others (2 Ne. 9:44). (4) As the corruptible element in the body, blood represents mortality, or that which is earthly. "Flesh and blood cannot inherit the kingdom of God" (1 Cor. 15:50), while resurrected beings have bodies of "flesh and bone" (D&C 129:1—2).

Bosom. (1) Figuratively used to describe a position or place of special intimacy. The bosom is naturally associated with the idea of embracing in love and fellowship. In the East it had an extended meaning associated with the manner of dress. Long, flowing garments bound at the waist by a girdle provided a convenient carrying place, like a bag, in the fold of material over the breast. Thus the bosom became a carrying place used by shepherds to carry helpless lambs (Isa. 40:11). Latter-day scripture draws upon this imagery, speaking of Zion being taken into the bosom of the Lord (D&C 38:4), and of God sitting upon his throne "in the bosom of eternity" (D&C 88:13).

Branch. (1) Posterity: for instance, Ephraim and Manasseh are the branches of Joseph (Gen. 49:22) and those left with neither "root nor branch" will be those without family ties in the world to come (Mal. 4:1). (2) Christ is called the Branch of David (Jer. 23:5). (3) Groups of people over the centuries who have been grafted into the House of Israel, that is, have come to the knowledge of the true Messiah (1 Ne. 10:14) or been pruned from the mother tree (Jacob 5:8; Rom. 11:17).

Brazen Sea. In Solomon's Temple a large molten sea of brass placed on the backs of twelve brazen oxen (1 Kgs. 7:23—26). It was a baptismal font. Similar fonts, though not made of brass, are found in Latter-day Saint temples for the purpose of performing baptisms for the dead.

Brazen Serpent. The lifting up of the brazen serpent on a pole in the wilderness was likened by Christ to his death on the cross (John 3:14—15; Num. 21:6—9; 1 Ne. 17:41; Hel. 8:15).

Bread. (1) A symbol of life and the source of nourishment— Christ is known as the Bread of Life. As manna was showered down from heaven to save Israel anciently, so Christ came down from heaven as the living bread by partaking of which all men may gain everlasting life (John 6:31—65). (2) In the ordinance of the sacrament the bread is a symbol of the body of Christ (Matt. 26:26).

Bride and Bridegroom. One of the seven figures used to set forth the relationship of the Church to Christ: the branches and the Vine (John 15:1—11), the sheep and the Shepherd (John 10), the stones and the Chief Cornerstone (1 Pet. 2:4—8), the priest and the High Priest (Heb. 2:17), Adam and the Second Adam (1 Cor. 15:45—50), the parts of the body and the Head of the Body (1 Cor. 12), the bride and the Bridegroom. Ultimately, the Bride (the Church) will reign with her Husband (Christ) over the new earth (Rev. 21:2,9—10).

Candlestick. (1) The seven-branched candelabrum of the tabernacle was part of the furniture of the holy place. It was not lit by candles but rather by pure olive oil in cup-shaped containers resting on the head of each of its branches (Ex. 25:31—40). The light thus given was a type of the Holy Spirit illuminating all the things of God. The seven branches or stems represented the fullness and completeness of the revelations of the Spirit. The pure beaten gold of which it was made represented Christ and may allude to his role as the suffering servant. The candlestick is an appropriate representation of the tree of life. (2) The seven golden candlesticks seen by John in his revelation represent the seven churches of Asia (Rev. 1:20). (3) The two candlesticks spoken of in Rev. 11:4 "are two prophets that are to be raised up to the Jewish nation in the last days, at the time of the restoration" (D&C 77:15).

Cedar. Strength; nobility; incorruptibility. The sacred wood of Solomon's Temple.

Censer. A vessel used for the burning of incense (Lev. 16:12—13). Those used in the tabernacle were made of brass (Num. 16:39), while those used in the temple were of gold (1 Kings 7:50). The smoke rising from the vessel was a symbol of the prayers of Israel rising to God (Ps. 141:2).

Cherub, Cherubim (pl.). Angels of God who guarded the tree of life after the Fall (Gen. 3:24). The images of two cherubim were placed over the mercy seat of the ark in the Holy of Holies. They were made of gold and fashioned so that they faced each other and had wings that covered the mercy seat (Ex. 25:18—20). Their images were also embroidered on the veil of the temple (2 Chr. 3:14) and sculptured on a frieze around the walls of Solomon's Temple and on the bases of the "molten sea" (1 Kings 7:29). The cherubim are obviously so stationed to see that the holiness of God is not violated by those in transgression or those who have not complied with the proper rituals (see D&C 132:19). The Semitic peoples pictured them as winged lions and bulls, having human faces, and Ezekiel so describes them in his vision (Ezek. 1:5—28; 10:20). These are symbolic representations. Cherubim are angels and, as such, independent of their heavenly glory, are no different in their appearance than Christ or other men. (See also Eye, Wings.)

Circumcision. An operation in which the foreskin of eight-day-old males was removed as a ceremony of initiation into God's covenant with Israel. By it they knew that the children were not accountable before God until eight years of age (JST, Gen. 17:4—20). "When a child was circumcised he was consecrated to God by the fact that his life (i.e., under the symbol of blood) was offered to God" (DCG, p. 331). Thus this covenant, sealed in the flesh, typified the subjugation of passion and the consecration of the body to God, or a putting away of the sins of the flesh (Col. 2:11). The imagery is frequently drawn upon as those who would be acceptable to the Lord are told to circumcise their hearts, their ears, and their lips.

Clay. (1) Represents the mortal body (Mosiah 3:5). (2) A symbol of limited mortal vision (John 9:6; Moses 6:35—36).

Clouds. (1) A symbol of the veil between God and man, as with the cloud on Mt. Sinai and on the Mount of Transfiguration (Ex. 24:15; Matt. 17:5). (2) In her wilderness wanderings ancient Israel followed "a pillar of a cloud" by day and the "pillar of fire" by night, which signified the presence of the Lord (Ex. 13:21—22). (3) A cloud as a symbol of the Lord's glory will rest upon the temple in the New Jerusalem in the future (D&C 84:5).

Colors. Often have symbolic meaning in the scriptures. Those most often used in this way are: white, black, purple, red, blue, gold, and silver. White signifies spotless purity, chastity, sanctification, righteousness, and sinlessness. God and heavenly beings are always clothed in white. It is also associated with transcendent perfection, simplicity, light, the sun, illumination, innocence, holiness, and sacredness. It is a statement of triumph of the spirit over the flesh, of good over evil. Black and darkness are often a symbol of evil or wickedness. Black is also associated with mourning. Purple (or scarlet) is the color of royalty, imperial and sacerdotal power. Red (or scarlet) naturally associates itself with blood and suffering and hence with the blood of atonement. Blue as the color of the heavens becomes associated with the idea of revelation and its source. Gold is the color of the sun; it represents divine power, the splendor of enlightenment; radiance, and glory. Because of its great value, and its radiance, gold is known to us as the possession of kings and great kingdoms. It is a symbol common to scriptural descriptions of God and the heavenly kingdom. Silver, like gold, is of great value and hence is associated with Christ. Traditionally, it is associated with the idea of a Reconciler, Savior, and Redeemer.

Cross. (1) Because of its association with the Lord, the cross has come to represent the Atonement (1 Cor. 1:17). (2) The trials of mortality that we are called upon to endure are commonly referred to as the cross we must bear. (3) Those committed to the gospel cause are called upon to take up their cross and follow him. "And now for a man to take up his cross, is to deny himself all ungodliness, and every worldly lust, and keep my commandments," Christ said (JST, Matt. 16:25–26; 3 Ne. 12:30).

Crown. An ornamental head covering symbolic of royalty, victory, or great honor. The official headpiece of the high priest of the Israelites, and later of their kings, was called the "crown of the annointing oil" (Lev. 21:12). *Nezer,* the Hebrew root for such a crown, means "consecrate" or "set apart." Numerous passages speak of the Saints receiving the "crown of eternal life" (D&C 20:14).

Deseret. The Jaredite word for the honeybee (Ether 2:3). A symbol for industry and diligence.

Devil. The English word used to translate two Greek words with different meanings: (1) *diabolos,* "the accuser," which is synonymous with the Old Testament *Satan* (Zech. 3:2); (2) *daimonion,* a demonic being, or evil spirit (Matt. 9:32).

Diadem. "Royal power; sovereignty; the circle of continuity; endless duration" (ETS, p. 51).

Dove. "The sign of the dove was instituted before the creation of the world, a witness for the Holy Ghost, and the devil cannot come in the sign of a dove. . . . The dove is an emblem or token of truth and innocence." (*Teachings,* p. 276).

Ear. A figure for spiritual understanding (Moses 6:27).

East. As the direction of the dawn and the rising sun, it becomes a symbol of light, truth, and Christ. The orientation of the East Gate of the Temple at Jerusalem was such that on the days of the spring and fall equinoxes the first rays of the rising sun, heralding the advent of the glory of God, could penetrate into the Holy of Holies. Joseph Smith said that the coming of the Son of Man will be as the light of the morning coming out of the east (*Teachings,* p. 287).

Eden, Garden of. The events associated with the Garden of Eden make it the archetype of our temples. Here Adam received the priesthood, here Adam and Eve walked and talked with God; here our first parents were eternally married by God himself; here they learned of the tree of good and evil and of the tree of life; here they were taught the law of sacrifice and clothed in garments of skin; and from here they ventured into the lone and dreary world that they and their posterity might prove themselves worthy to return again to that divine presence.

Egypt. To dramatize the wickedness of Jerusalem in the last days, John the Revelator called it a spiritual "Sodom and Egypt" (Rev. 11:8).

Ensign. The standard of a king or prince, providing a rallying point in battle. "I have sent mine everlasting covenant into the world, to be a light to the world, and to be a standard for my people, and for the Gentiles to seek to it, and to be a messenger before my face to prepare the way before me," the Lord said (D&C 45:9).

Eve. The first woman, whose name means "mother of all living" (Gen. 3:20).

Eye. The lamp of the body. The eye is thought of as the source of light, enlightenment, and knowledge to the soul. Those laboring in the Lord's cause are to do so with "an eye single to the glory of God" (D&C 4:5). The eyes of the beasts seen in the revelation by John represented "light and knowledge" (D&C 77:4).

Fable. A fictitious story that draws its moral through the use of plants or animals endowed with human characteristics. Only two fables appear in the Bible: Jotham's fable of the trees choosing a king (Judg. 9:8—15) and Jehoash's fable of the thistle and the cedar (2 Kgs. 14:8—10). In the New Testament the word has reference to Jewish myths espoused to sustain falsehood (1 Tim. 1:4).

Famine. Symbolizes a period in which the word of the Lord is not heard (Amos 8:11—12).

Fire. (1) A symbol of the presence of the Lord. God dwells in "everlasting burnings" (*Teachings*, p. 367). (2) On the head of or surrounding a person, fire represents divine power, glory, and holiness (Ezek. 8:2). Angels or ministering spirits are so presented (Heb. 1:7). (3) The act of purification as in baptism by fire (3 Ne. 9:20). It is a symbol of the burning out of the dross of sin. (4) A metaphor for the word of God (Jer. 23:29). (5) The feeling associated with testimony or the witness of the Spirit (Jer. 20:9). Fire is associated with spiritual power, illumination, inspiration, and enlightenment.

Firstborn. To Moses the Lord said: "Sanctify unto me all the firstborn, whatsoever openeth the womb among the children of Israel, both of man and of beast: it is mine" (Ex. 13:2). By destroying the firstborn sons of Egypt and sparing those of Israel, God acquired a special ownership over the latter. Each belonged to the sanctuary, the firstborn son to serve as a priest, and the firstborn of the beasts, if a clean animal to be offered as a sacrifice, if unclean, then to be redeemed with a lamb. Later the firstborn sons excepting those of the tribe of Levi were redeemed from this obligation by the payment of a redemption tax (Num. 3:12—13). The consecration of the firstborn to the Lord as priest or as a sacrificial offering was a type for Christ, who as the firstborn in the spirit of all the Father's children was chosen in the heavenly council to be our priest or mediator and "the Lamb slain from the foundation of the world" (Rev. 13:8).

Firstfruits. The Mosaic code required the Israelites to bring the firstfruits of their harvest to the sanctuary. This included grain, wine, and oil, which was to be used to support the priests. Thus, the Lord's people are spoken of as "the firstfruits," meaning those dedicated to him and his service (D&C 88:98).

Fornication. Is used with adultery to describe apostasy, particularly when it involves idolatry. The term is fitting because the idolatrous fertility cult worship of the Canaanites as well as of the Greeks often involved fornication with "sacred" prostitutes or priestesses (Jer. 2:20—37; Ezek. 16; Hosea 1—3).

Fountain. Christ is the fountain of all righteousness (1 Ne. 2:9; Jer. 2:13).

Frankincense. (See Incense.)

Gardens. Three sacred gardens are central to the whole plan of salvation: the Garden of Eden, the place of the Fall; the Garden of Gethsemane, with Golgotha the place of the Atonement; and the Garden of the Empty Tomb, the place of the Ressurection.

Gate. Shares the symbolism of the threshold or place of entrance, also the idea of protection or shelter. Anciently gates were commonly guarded by symbolic animals such as lions, dragons, bulls, or some strange beast. Kings sat in judgment at gates and they were also thought of as a place of communication between the living and the dead (ETS, pp. 72—73).

Gehenna. The Greek form of the Hebrew *Hinnom*, rendered *hell* in the New Testament. Gehenna is the deep narrow glen on the south and west of Jerusalem where children were burned to Molech and other pagan gods (Jer. 7:31; 1 Kgs. 11:7). Later used as a dump in which garbage was continually being burned, it became a symbol of punishment in the after life (Matt. 5:22; 10:28).

Gethsemane. Meaning garden of the "oil press," this is the garden across the brook Kidron, apparently near the foot of the Mount of Olives. Here Christ and his disciples frequently met and here Christ, pressed with the sins of all mankind, sweat great drops of blood (Luke 22:44).

Girdle. To put on one's girdle, or to gird oneself, was to prepare for, or be bound to, some action or to go forth on a mission. To gird up one's loins was to prepare for battle or some other activity (1 Kgs. 18:46). Since the girdle carried a man's weapon, it was also associated with power and strength (Isa. 11:5).

Gog and Magog. The terms *Gog* and *Magog* are used to represent the nations Satan will gather about him to attack the forces of the Messiah. Two great battles will be fought with these forces of evil: the battle that ushers in the Second Coming (Ezek. 38–39), and the final great battle at the end of the millennium when Satan and his forces have been loosed again (Rev. 20:7–9).

Gold. Often used in the scriptures as an emblem of what is divine, pure, precious, incorruptible, or glorious.

Grain. All grains are a symbol of renewal of life, the resurrection and fertility.

Grove. (See Asherah).

Hagar. Paul uses Hagar as a symbol of the Mosaic law in contrast to Sarah, who he said symbolized the fulness of the gospel (Gal. 4:22–31).

Hallelujah. A Hebrew word meaning "praise ye Jehovah," or as anglicized, "praise ye the Lord."

Hands. One of the most symbolically expressive parts of the body. (1) In Hebrew, *yad*, the root word, means either "hand" or "power." Thus hands signify power, strength, providence, or blessings. Priesthood, keys, ordinations, offices, blessings, and so on, are granted by the laying on of hands. This symbolizes the placing of God's hand or power upon the one so blessed (see D&C 36:1–2). It also provides an orderly, observable, and documentable way of conveying offices and authority (see D&C 42:11). (2) The extended open hand or clasped hands are a sign of friendship, confidence, and trust.

Head. Since the head is to rule the body, Christ is spoken of as the head of the Church (Eph. 4:15). Two examples illustrate the variety of ways the head is used as a scriptural type: (1) It is a type for the utter defeat that shall be brought upon Satan by Christ (Gen. 3:15). (2) The placing of dirt on the head was a sign of deep grief, sorrow, shame and humiliation (see 2 Sam. 15:32).

Heart. Has a host of usages in the scriptures. Three of the more prominent are: (1) The place of affections and emotions such as joy, fear, or hatred (Isa. 65:14). (2) An expression of spiritual receptivity or the lack of it, such as a hardening of the heart (1 Ne. 15:10). (3) True gospel understanding is to take place in the heart (Matt. 13:15).

High Priest. An obvious type for Christ, who is the great Prophet, Priest, and King (Heb. 4:14).

Honey. (1) In the Mosaic ritual, like leaven, it represented that which was corruptible (Lev. 2:11). (2) In John's revelation it represented the sweetness of the divine word (Rev. 10:9).

Horn. A symbol of power and strength (Ps. 75:10). Moses likened Ephraim and Manasseh to the horns of unicorns who would "push" or gather Israel from the ends of the earth in the last days (Deut. 33:17). Their horns or power is that of the priesthood.

Hyssop. A small plant of Egypt and Palestine, used by Israel for the ritualistic sprinkling of blood and water (Lev. 14:4,6,51–52). It is thus associated with purification and could be likened to the acts of faith that bring a remission of sins. "The addition of this herb to the vinegar or sour wine on the sponge would aid in alleviating the suffering of one on the cross. A bunch of hyssop may have accompanied the sponge upon the reed." (WDB, p. 415.)

Idumea. The name given to Edom by the Greeks and Romans. Since Israel had to pass through it to obtain their promised land it became a symbol of the world or that which is wordly (D&C 1:36).

Incense. A fragrant substance burned in religious services of the Israelites (Ex. 25:6). The burning of the incense or frankincense was a symbol of the rising of prayers to heaven (Rev. 8:3—4).

Isaac. (1) A type for Christ when his father Abraham was commanded to offer him as a sacrifice (Gen. 22).

Israel. Is the new name given to Jacob after he wrestled with the angel at Bethel (Gen. 35:10). As the name means prince or soldier of God, it symbolizes that those of the house of Israel are of royal blood and are called upon to be soldiers or defenders of the faith.

Jacob's ladder. Jacob dreamed a dream in which he saw a ladder which joined heaven and earth which angels ascended and descended. The Lord standing above it renewed with Jacob the Abrahamic covenant. Jacob named the place of his dream Bethel, or house of God (Gen. 28:12—14, 19). Joseph Smith said, "Paul ascended into the third heavens, and he could understand the three principal rounds of Jacob's ladder —the telestial, the terrestrial, and the celestial glories or kingdoms" (*Teachings*, pp. 304—5).

Jehovah. The anglicized form of the Hebrew YHWH (Yahweh), the God of Israel. Generally, references to Jehovah were translated as Lord or God (printed in small capitals) in the KJV. The meaning conveyed by the name is that of an unchanging, ever-living God, who is faithful to his word throughout all generations of time.

Jesus. Is the Greek form of the Hebrew name *Joshua*. The name means "Jehovah saves."

Jordan River. Crossing over the Jordan is a metaphor for entering heaven, because the children of Israel were miraculously enabled to go over it dryshod on their way to the Promised Land (Josh. 3).

Joseph of Egypt. A type for: (1) Christ; (2) Joseph Smith; (3) The tribe of Joseph (Ephraim and Manasseh) in the latter-day gathering of Israel. (See Chapter 12.)

Joshua. An Old Testament type for Christ. (See Jesus.)

Jot. Derived from *Iota*, the smallest letter in the Greek alphabet. Figuratively, it signifies a matter of small moment (Matt. 5:18).

Key. (1) From the days of Adam the term *key* has been used by inspired writers as a symbol of power and authority. Keys are the right of presidency, and the one holding them holds the reigns of government. The keys given by Christ to Peter and the Twelve represented the authority to bind or loose all gospel ordinances and covenants both in heaven and on earth (Matt. 16:19; John 20:23). It was these same keys that were restored to the Prophet Joseph Smith (D&C 132:45—47). (2) Keys also denote the idea of liberation; knowledge; the mysteries; and initiation (ETS, p. 90). That is, they are the means provided whereby things are revealed or made manifest (D&C 107:18—19; 128:11).

Kings. In the Old Testament they were intended to be a type for Christ, and as such those properly assuming their thrones were anointed by the Lord's prophet (1 Sam. 9:16; 10:1).

Kneeling. Represents homage, supplication, and submission.

Lamb. (1) The gentleness of the lamb is a natural symbol of innocence, meekness, purity, and uncomplaining submissiveness. (2) A common metaphor for Israel with Christ as the good Shepherd (3 Ne. 15:21). (3) The lamb without blemish was the sacrificial victim for the sins of Israel. This was a type for Christ who is the "Lamb of God" and who offered himself as a sacrifice for all (Isa. 53:7; John 1:36).

Lamp. A symbol of enlightenment, knowledge, and guidance. The lamp represents the word of the Lord, the light by which all men are invited to walk (Ps. 119:105). (See also Olive Oil.)

Laver. In Solomon's Temple an enormous bronze bowl mounted on twelve oxen used for cleansing rituals by the priests and obviously for baptisms. (See also Brazen Sea.)

Leaven. (1) As an agent which causes fermentation, it symbolically represents any corrupting influence. Since the leaven itself has undergone corruption, and since it has a tendency to spread, it is a most apt figure. Only unleavened bread was acceptable as a sacrificial offering (Lev. 2:11); and only unleavened bread was to be eaten during the period of the Passover (Ex. 13:7). In speaking of the leaven of the Pharisees and the Sadducees, the Savior had reference to their corrupt doctrines (Matt. 16:6, 12). (2) Leaven is also used as a metaphor to depict those influences that cause a thing to raise and expand (Matt. 13:33).

Light. Is a symbol for revelation, knowledge, truth, the gospel, or the word of God (see D&C 45:9; 84:45). Christ is the "light of the world" (John 8:12), which light gives life to all things. The light of Christ is the power by which all things are created and governed (D&C 88:7—13).

Lucifer. (1) A name of honor once held by Satan when he held high position in the pre-earth kingdom of God (D&C 76:25—27). The name means "shining one" or "lightbearer." (2) By analogy this name is given to the king of Babylon by Isaiah (Isa. 14:12—22).

Manna. The food miraculously supplied the Israelites during their wilderness wanderings (Ex. 16). Commonly referred to as "bread" from heaven (Deut. 8:3), manna typified the spiritual salvation that can be had only through Christ, who is the Bread of Life.

Mantle. Was an emblem of authority. Elijah's placing of his mantle upon Elisha symbolized both a call and the conferring of spiritual power (1 Kgs. 19:19; 2 Kgs. 2:14).

Meggiddo. The ancient Palestinian city that overlooked the Valley of Jezreel, also referred to as the Plain of Esdraelon or Armageddon. It is the symbolic focal point of the last great war.

Melchizedek. A priest and king of the ancient city of Salem. His name means king of righteousness. Melchizedek was one of the most perfect types for Christ. From the JST it appears that he ascended to heaven with his righteous followers (JST, Gen 14:34).

Mercy Seat. The golden lid of the ark of the covenant. The name comes from the Hebrew *kapporeth,* which in turn comes from the root *kaphar,* meaning to cover, expiate, make an atonement, cleanse, forgive, or be merciful.

Messiah. A Hebrew term meaning anointed one; prophets, priests, and kings were so designated. Each were types of what the Messiah would be.

Moon. A metaphor used to contrast the glory of the terrestrial with that of the telestial (stars) and the celestial (sun) kingdoms (D&C 76:97).

Moses. As prophet, redeemer, mediator, and lawgiver of Israel, he was another of the perfect Old Testament types for Christ.

Mountains. Nature's temples. So often the place where God and man met, when there was no temple, that temples have become known as "the mountain of the Lord's house" (Isa. 2:2). They are the high place, the place to which one must ascend to commune with God. They were thought of as the summit of paradise, the place of passage from one plane to another.

Offering. All the offerings described in the scriptures are connected with Christ. Most of them picture the Savior as our offering or the propitiation for our sins.

Olive Leaf. A symbol of peace, particularly when associated with the dove. Joseph Smith designated the revelation known to us as D&C 88 as the "olive leaf . . . plucked from the Tree of Paradise, the Lord's message of peace to us."

Olive Oil. Was valued among the ancients as a source of light (Matt. 25:3), nourishment (1 Kgs. 17:12), and for its healing powers (Isa. 1:6). It is natural therefore that symbolically it be associated with enlightenment, nourishing the spirit, and the healing of the sick. The outpouring of consecrated olive oil was a symbol of the outpouring of the Spirit (1 Sam. 16:13). In the scriptures, it is associated with acts of consecration, dedication, and the infusing of new life. As the olive branch was a symbol of peace, so olive oil was a symbol of that peace which comes by the Spirit—that is, the comforting influence of the Holy Ghost (Isa. 61:3; Ps. 23:5).

Olive Tree. An emblem of peace and purity. The ancients frequently used the olive tree as an allegorical representation of Israel (Rom. 11:17—24; Jacob 5).

Palm Leaf. The palm leaf was a symbol of peace, also of triumph and victory (John 12:13; Rev. 7:9). 2 Esdras (one of the apocryphal books) captures the imagery: "I, Ezra, saw on Mount Zion a great multitude, which I could not number, and they all were praising the Lord with songs. In their midst was a young man of great stature, taller than any of the others, and on the head of each of them he placed a crown, but he was more exalted than they. And I was spellbound. Then I asked an angel, Who are these, my lord? He answered and said to me, These are they who have put off mortal clothing and have put on the immortal, and they have confessed the name of God; now they are being crowned and receive palms." (2 Esdras 2:42—45.)

Parable. Comes from the Greek word *parabole* ("a placing beside," "a comparison"). As used by Christ, parables were short narratives that compared something familiar to a spiritual truth. Parables were used both to unfold and to withhold spiritual truths, depending on the spiritual receptivity of those who heard them. (See Chapter 2.)

Passover, The. The commemoration of Israel's last night of bondage in Egypt when the Angel of Death "passed over" Israelite homes marked with the blood of a sacrificial lamb and destroyed the firstborn of every Egyptian household and the firstborn of their animals (Ex. 12). All that was associated with the Passover was a type of the atoning sacrifice of Christ. The Last Supper was the Passover meal. In this ritual meal with his Apostles, Christ introduced the ordinance of the sacrament, which was to replace the Passover among those who accepted him as the Christ.

Pearl. The value of the pearl was not so much in its commercial worth but in the beauty inherent in it. This made it an especially appropriate jewel to represent the word of God (Matt. 7:6; 13:46).

Perfume. Its fragrance is thought to represent the character of Christ rising in sweetness and fragrance to the heavens (Ex. 30:35).

Phylacteries. Small cases made of leather worn by Jewish men on the forehead and the left arm during prayers. Within these small cases are copies of four scriptural passages: Exodus 13:1—10, 11—16; Deuteronomy 6:4—9; 11:13—21. Christ was offended by this ostentatious display of piety (Matt. 23:5).

Pomegranate. An emblem of fruitfulness because of its many seeds.

Priest. In function and dress the priests of the Aaronic Order were types of Christ. Similarly today the priest in the Aaronic Priesthood in administering the sacrament represents Christ at the Last Supper.

Prince of Peace. A name-title of Christ signifying that eternal and abiding peace known only in him (Isa. 9:6). Melchizedek and Abraham, both prophetic types of Christ, also bore this title (JST, Gen. 14:33; Abr. 1:2).

Psalm. A sacred song or poem used in praise or worship of God.

Rain. Is a symbol of revelation or heavenly blessings (Deut. 32:2).

Rainbow. (1) In a revelation to Joseph Smith the Lord said: "In the days of Noah I set a bow in the heavens as a sign and token that in any year that the bow should be seen the Lord would not come; but there should be seed time and harvest during that year: but whenever you see the bow withdrawn, it shall be a token that there shall be famine, pestilence, and great distress among the nations, and that the coming of the Messiah is not far distant" (*Teachings*, pp. 340–41). (2) The rainbow is the token of the Lord's promise that he will never again destroy the world by flood (Gen. 9:8–17). (3) The rainbow was also the sign of the covenant that the Lord had promised Enoch and his city that they would return to live on the earth during the millennial era (JST, Gen. 9:21–25).

Rend or Rent. (1) In biblical times the rending of clothes was a token of grief (Gen. 37:34). (2) The rending of a garment was also a way of dramatizing horror at what was deemed blasphemous or impious (Matt. 26:65; Acts 14:14). (3) It was also associated with the making of an irrevocable decision.

Rest of the Lord. Where mortals are concerned, the rest of the Lord is enjoyed by those whose spiritual knowledge and confidence shield them from the poisonous darts of doubt constantly hurled at them by those seeking to destroy their faith. In the eternal sense it is to gain the fulness of the Father (D&C 84:24).

Ring. (1) A symbol of eternity, because it is without beginning and without end. (2) Anciently, it was also a symbol of authority (Gen. 41:42).

River. (1) A symbol of divine life (Rev. 22:1–2). (2) A metaphor for the words of eternal life (John 7:38). (3) In the dream seen by Lehi and Nephi the river represented the filthiness of the world (1 Ne. 15:26–27).

Robe. A garment of distinction or majesty. Works of righteousness in which we must be clothed (Rev. 19:8).

Rock. An often-used metaphor conveying such ideas as permanence, solidity, steadfastness, strength, refuge, reliability and so on. In these and similiar senses both God and Christ are spoken of as the Rock (Ps. 42:9;1 Cor. 10:4). The Church is built on the rock of revelation (Matt. 16:13–18).

Rod. (1) An emblem of authority sharing the symbolism of a staff (Jer. 48:17). (2) The rod of Aaron is also associated with the ability to receive revelation (D&C 8:6). (3) The rod is also a symbol of chastisement (D&C 19:15). (4) Rod is used as a metaphor by Isaiah to describe a prophet of the Restoration (Isa. 11:1; D&C 113:3—4).

Rod of Iron. The word of God (1 Ne. 15:23—24; JST, Rev. 19:15).

Root. (1) Christ is the Root of David (Rev. 5:5;22:16). (2) The root of Jesse spoken of in Isaiah 11:10, is "a descendant of Jesse, as well as of Joseph, unto whom rightly belongs the priesthood, and the keys of the kingdom, for an ensign, and for the gathering of my people in the last days" (D&C 113:6). This is probably the Prophet Joseph Smith. (3) As the source of nourishment to a plant, the root also becomes a natural symbol for the heart or the source of life. Destruction is described as plucking up the root or the ax being laid to the root (Matt. 13:29).

Sabbath. (1) Comes from the Hebrew *shabbat*, meaning "rested." On the seventh day God commanded men to rest from the toil of the six days in commemoration of his having rested after the six days of creation. He blessed the seventh day and sanctified it (Gen. 2:1—3). After the Exodus it became a memorial for his having delivered Israel from their Egyptian bondage (Deut. 5:12—15). The day now sanctified to the Lord is the first day of the week, it having been the day of Christ's resurrection (Acts 20:7). (2) Anciently, other sacred days and periods were also called sabbaths, such as the Day of Atonement, the sabbatical year, and the year of jubilee.

Sackcloth. A coarse, dark cloth made of goat or camel hair worn by mourners, and thus a symbol of mourning, repentance, and humiliation.

Sacrifices. True sacrifices were gospel ordinances, given to man by revelation and performed by the authority of the priesthood. Their purpose was to typify the coming sacrifice of the Son of God for the sins of the world. From the day of Adam to the death of Christ sacrifices were offered by the Saints. No sacrifices were acceptable to God unless they were attended by personal righteousness if a personal sacrifice, or by group righteousness if a group sacrifice.

Salt. (1) Is an emblem of preservation from corruption. Salt was so essential to the sacrificial ordinance that it was the symbol of the covenant being made (Lev. 2:13). (2) The faithful in keeping covenants are spoken of as the salt of the earth. Covenant breakers are as salt that has lost its savor (D&C 101:39—40).

Satan. The name depicts the devil's role as an "adversary" in the Old Testament (Zech. 3:1—3), or as an "accuser" in the New Testament (Rev. 12:9). In all things he stands opposite God and righteousness.

Scapegoat. (1) A sacrificial goat upon whose head the high priest placed the collective sins of the people. This was done each year on the Day of Atonement, after which the goat was sent out into the desert. The scapegoat was a symbol of Christ, who would take upon himself the sins of the world. (2) In colloquial usage the term has come to mean anyone who bears the blame of others.

Scepter. A symbol of divine or royal power. (1) A prophetic figure representing the Messiah (Gen. 49:10;Num. 24:17). (2) The power of righteousness through which one obtains an everlasting dominion (D&C 121:46).

Seed. (1) Those who hearken unto the words of the prophets are the seed of Christ (Mosiah 15:10—14); similarly, those who honor the priesthood are the seed of the prophets (D&C 84:33—34). (2) Paul identifies Christ as the seed promised to Abraham (Gal. 3:16).

Serpent. A metaphor for cunning, craftiness, evil, guile, slyness, subtlety and so on. (1) Satan is known to us in the scriptures as the "old serpent" or "great dragon" (Rev. 12:9). (2) In contrast to our first definition, the serpent raised on the pole (Num. 21:9) was a prototype of Christ raised on the cross for the healing and salvation of the world.

Sheep. The flock of Christ. (See also Lamb.)

Shepherd. (1) Christ is the good shepherd (John 10). (2) The leader or protector of any flock, thus anyone serving in any capacity in the Church in which he is responsible for the spiritual or temporal well-being of others (Jer. 23:1–4).

Shewbread. The literal meaning is "bread of the presence." Twelve loaves, one representing each of the twelve tribes, were placed on the table in the holy place of the sanctuary each Sabbath. The bread was eaten in a symbolic ritual by the priests (Lev. 24:9).

Shield. A symbol of protection. "Above all," Paul said, we must take "the shield of faith" to protect ourselves from "all the fiery darts of the wicked" (Eph. 6:16).

Sleep. Used as a metaphor for death (1 Cor. 15:6).

Smoke. Represented prayer ascending to heaven.

Sodom. (1) The city forever associated with unnatural sex perversions, which God destroyed by fire, can properly be seen as a type for the destruction of all practicing such perversions today. (2) Used as a name for peoples and cities given up to wickedness (Ezek. 16:48, Rom. 9:29, Rev. 11:8).

Stake. In prophetic imagery, Zion is pictured as a great tent upheld by cords fastened securely to stakes (Isa. 54:2–7). That imagery finds its fulfillment in the eccelesiastical units called stakes in the Church today (D&C 101:21).

Star. (1) Christ is the "bright and morning star" (Rev. 22:16). (2) Pre-earth spirits are frequently referred to as stars (Job 38:7, Rev. 12:4; Abr. 3). (3) Those obtaining the celestial kingdom are also called stars (Dan. 12:3; Rev. 12:1). (4) By way of contrast with the sun and the moon the stars are used to represent the glory of the telestial kingdom (D&C 76:98).

Stem of Jesse. Christ (Isa. 11:1–5; D&C 113:1–2).

Stone. A metaphor for Christ (Ps. 118:22). (See also Rock.)

Sun. Is used to represent the glory of the celestial kingdom (D&C 76:96).

Sword. Associated with protection and strength. Paul calls the "sword of the Spirit" the "word of God" (Eph. 6:17). The word of the Lord, we are told, is "sharper than a two-edged sword" (D&C 6:2).

Symbol. From the Greek *symbolon*, a "token" or "sign," and *symballein*, to "throw together" or "compare." In the broad sense, anything that stands for something else. Synonyms include: type, sign, image, emblem, and representation.

Tabernacle. (1) The portable temple used by the children of Israel in their wilderness wanderings. Used in both the Old and New Testaments as a symbol of God's presence (Ps. 15:1; 43:3; 61:4; Rev. 21:3). (2) The physical body is also referred to as a tabernacle of clay (Mosiah 3:5).

Tares. Noxious weeds that resemble wheat in its early stages. They can only be clearly distinguished when the grain has started to mature. They represent the spiritual tares who masquerade as faithful Saints within the Church yet fail to produce good fruits (Matt. 13:24–30, 36–43; D&C 86:1–7).

Temple. (1) A true temple is the house of the Lord. It is the place where God and man meet both symbolically and literally. Within the temple, ordinances of salvation are performed. The significance of these ordinances is taught in the language of symbols. They are the most sacred places of worship on earth. (2) To dramatize the sacred and holy nature of the human body it is called a temple (1 Cor. 3:16–17; 6:19; D&C 93:35). (3) In a figurative sense, Jesus referred to himself as the temple (John 2:19). (4) Paul used the temple as a representation of the Church (Eph. 2:21).

Thorns. A figure for the enemies of Israel (Num. 33:55; Ezek. 28:24).

Tittle. A small mark made to distinguish one Hebrew letter from another. The English equivalent would be the stroke of the "t" or the dot of the "i". Figuratively, it means any trifling matter (Matt. 5:18).

Tree of Knowledge. The tree in the Garden of Eden from which Adam and Eve ate to bring upon themselves mortality (Gen. 3:3; 2 Ne. 2:15; Alma 12:21–26).

Tree of Life. Spoken of in the creative account as that tree in the midst of the Garden of Eden, the fruit of which contained the power of everlasting life (Gen. 2:9; 3:22–24). Writing to the seven churches in Asia, the Revelator said, "To him that overcometh will I give to eat of the tree of life, which is in the midst of the paradise of God" (Rev. 2:7). Partaking of that fruit in his dream, Lehi described it as "most sweet, above all that I ever before tasted. Yea, and I beheld that the fruit thereof was white, to exceed all the whiteness that I had ever seen." (1 Ne. 8:10–12.) Such is the fruit that all who obtain eternal life will partake (Rev. 22:14).

Trees. Represents men: green trees the righteous, dry trees the wicked (Luke 23:31; D&C 135:6). (See also Asherah.)

Trumpet. Anciently the sound of the trumpet summoned the congregation of Israel before the Lord at the door of the tabernacle. Their response represented a people assembled in a public acknowledgment of Jehovah as their King. This is but the type for the trumpets which will sound calling forth the elect on the day of his coming (Matt. 24:31), and not only the living but those who have died (1 Cor. 15:52; D&C 88:92).

Type. A person, event, or ritual with likeness to another person, event, or ritual of greater importance which is to follow. The term *antitype* describes the future fulfillment, while typology is the study of types. True types will have noticeable points of resemblance, show evidence of divine appointment, and be prophetic of future events.

Veil. (1) A covering for a person or sacred object. (2) That which conceals, protects, or separates (Ether 3:6, 19–20). (3) When the minds of men are veiled they are darkened by ignorance, wickedness, or unbelief (Ether 4:15; D&C 38:8; 67:10). (4) Passing through the veil denotes degrees of initiation or the gaining of sacred knowledge. (5) A passing from this life to the next is commonly spoken of as passing through the veil. (6) The wearing of a veil by a bride, or the veiling of one's face, is an ancient custom indicating modesty and subjection. (See Clouds.)

Veil of the Temple. The thick curtain separating the Holy of Holies from the holy place in the Jerusalem temple is known to us as the veil of the temple. In Luke's account of the crucifixion, from the sixth to the ninth hour (12 noon to 3 P.M.), darkness covered the land, the sun's light failed, "and the veil of the temple was rent in the midst" (Luke 23:45). The rending of the veil symbolized the removal of the barrier between man and God, for man was thus enabled "to enter into the holiest by the blood of Jesus" (Heb. 10:19).

Vine. A symbol of Christ, who said, "I am the true vine" (John 15:1), meaning that he is the source of life to the branches (the Apostles) and that only as they are associated with him can they bring forth fruit (John 15:5).

Vineyard. (1) A type which represents any field of labor to which God may call his servants (Matt. 20:1), (2) Often in a parable or metaphor the vineyard was used to represent Israel (Isa. 5:1—7; Matt. 21:33). (3) Also used as a metaphor for the world (Jacob 5, 6).

Water. Always associated with rituals of cleansing, purification, and rebirth. (2) Water is also a symbol of the word of God as the source of eternal life (John 4:1—14; D&C 63:23).

Wind. An emblem of the power of the Spirit and the glory of God (see Acts 2:2). Dedicating the Kirtland Temple, Joseph Smith prayed, "Let thy house be filled, as with a rushing mighty wind, with thy glory" (D&C 109:37).

Winepress. The device used to press the juice from grapes is figuratively used to represent the vengeance the Lord will take upon the wicked (Isa. 63:3—4; Rev. 19:15; D&C 133:50—51).

Wings. (1) Joseph Smith declared, "An angel of God never has wings" (*Teachings*, p. 162). As seen in visions, the wings on angels "are a representation of power," the ability to move, act, and so on (D&C 77:4). (2) Christ has "healing in his wings," meaning his extremities, i.e., his hands (Mal. 4:2).

Word. A title for Christ. God speaks his word, which the Son by the power of the Spirit, puts into operation, and thereby becomes himself the Word (Moses 2:5, JST, John 1:1).

Yoke. (1) A symbol of obedience (Matt. 11:29). (2) Also an emblem of bondage and servitude (Jer. 27:2). In the New Testament church, those Jews who accepted Christ but could not let go of the traditions of the Mosaic system lived under an unnecessary "yoke of bondage" (Acts 15:10; Gal 5:1).

Zion. Used to describe both a pure people and those places consecrated for sacred events (Moses 7;18; Isa. 2:3; D&C 84:1—4; 133:18).

Bibliography

Adams, Lamar L. *The Living Message of Isaiah*. Salt Lake City: Deseret Book Co., 1981.

Ad de Vries. *Dictionary of Symbols and Imagery*. Amsterdam-London: North Holland Publishing Co., 1974.

Anderson, Richard Lloyd. *Understanding Paul*. Salt Lake City: Deseret Book Co., 1983.

Bible Dictionary. LDS Edition of the King James Version of the Bible. Salt Lake City: The Church of Jesus Christ of Latter-day Saints, 1983.

Brentel, Lancelot C. L. *The Septuagint with Apocrypha: Greek and English*. Grand Rapids, MI: Zondervan Publishing House, 1982.

Brieg, James. "Hell: Still a Burning Question?" *U. S. Catholic,* Nov. 1977, pp. 6—10.

Bruce, F. F. *Commentary on the Book of Acts*. Grand Rapids, MI: Wm. B. Eerdmans Publishing Co., 1983.

Bucke, Emory Stevens, ed. *The Interpreter's Dictionary of the Bible, an Illustrated Encyclopedia*. Nashville: Abingdon Press, 1962.

Butteric, George Arthur, ed. *Interpreter's Bible*. 12 vols. Nashville: Abingdon Press, 1971.

Caird, G. B. *The Language and Imagery of the Bible*. Duckworth Studies in Theology. London: Gerald Duckworth and Co. Ltd., The Old Piano Factory, 1980.

Charles, R. H., ed. *The Apocrypha and Pseudepigrapha of the Old Testament in English*. Vol. I & II. Oxford: Clarendon Press, 1913, 1965.

Clarke, Adam. *Clarke's Commentary*. 3 vols. Nashville: Abingdon Press, no date given.

Comay, John, and Ronald Browning. *Who's Who in the Bible*. New York: Bonanza Books, 1980.

Cooper, J. C. *An Illustrated Encyclopedia of Traditional Symbolism*. London: Thames & Hudson, 1978, 1982.

Cope, Gilbert. *Symbolism in the Bible and the Church*. New York: Philosophical Library, no date given.

Cruden, Alexander. *Cruden's Complete Concordance to the Old and New Testaments.* Grand Rapids, MI: Zondervan Publishing House, 1977.

Dummelow, J. R. *The One Volume Bible Commentary by Various Writers.* New York: Macmillan Publishing Co., 1908.

Edersheim, Alfred. *Bible History, Old Testament.* Grand Rapids, MI: Wm. B. Eerdmans Publishing Co., 1890.

Edersheim, Alfred. *The Life and Times of Jesus the Messiah.* Grand Rapids, MI: Wm. B. Eerdmans Publishing Co., 1971.

Edersheim, Alfred. *The Temple: Its Ministry and Services as They Were at the Time of Christ.* Grand Rapids, MI: Wm. B. Eerdmans Publishing Co., 1982.

Encyclopedia Judaica, First Edition. Jerusalem.

Farbridge, Maurice H. *Studies in Biblical and Semitic Symbolism.* London: Kegan Paul, Trench, Trubner and Co., Ltd., 1923.

Fairbain, Patrick. *The Typology of Scriptures.* Vols. I and II. Edinburgh: T & T Clark, 1800, 1975.

Farrar, Frederic W. *History of Interpretation.* Grand Rapids, MI: Baker Book House Co., 1961.

Freeman, James M. *Manners and Customs of the Bible.* Plainfield, NJ: Logos International. Reprinted 1972.

Gardner, Joseph L., ed. *Atlas of the Bible.* Reader's Digest Assoc., 1981.

Garner, David H. "The Tabernacle—A Type for the Temples." Paper presented at the Religious Educators Symposium, Provo, UT: Brigham Young University Press, 1979.

Gaster, Theodore H. *Myth, Legend and Customs in the Old Testament.* New York: Harper and Row Pub., no date given.

Ginzberg, Louis. *On Jewish Law and Lore.* Philadelphia: The Jewish Publication Society of America, no date given.

Ginzberg, Louis. *The Legends of the Jews.* 7 vols. Philadelphia: The Jewish Publication Society of America, 1909.

Girdlestone, Robert Baker. *Synonyms of the Old Testament.* Grand Rapids, MI: Wm. B. Eerdmans Publishing Co., reprinted 1978, 1897.

Habershon, Ada R. *The Study of the Parables.* Grand Rapids, MI: Kregal Publications, 1957, 1975.

Habershon, Ada R. *The Study of the Types.* London: Morgan and Scott Ltd., 1907.

Haran, Manahem. *Temples and Temple-Service in Ancient Israel.* Oxford: Clarendon Press, 1978.

Harris, Stephen L. *Understanding the Bible: A Reader's Guide and Reference.* Palo Alto, CA: Mayfield Publishing Co., 1980.

Hastings, James, ed. *A Dictionary of Christ and the Gospels,* New York: Charles Scribner's Sons, 1908.

Hengstenberg, E. W. *Christology of the Old Testament.* Grand Rapids, MI: Kregal Publications, 1970, 1981.

Hennecke, Edgar. *New Testament Apocrypha.* Wilhelm Schneemelcher, ed., R. Mel. Wilson, trans., Vol. II. Philadelphia: The Westminster Press, 1964.

Herbermann, Charles G., ed. *Catholic Encyclopedia.* 15 vols. New York: Appleton Co., 1907.

Jerusalem Bible, The. First Edition. Doubleday & Co., 1966.

Josephus. *Complete Works.* William Whiston, trans. Grand Rapids, MI: Kregal Publications, 1960.

Jukes, Andrew. *The Law of the Offerings.* Grand Rapids, MI: Kregal Publications, 1980.

Jukes, Andrew. *The Name of God.* Grand Rapids, MI: Kregal Publications, 1974.

Jukes, Andrew. *Types in Genesis.* Grand Rapids, MI: Kregal Publications, 1976, 1981.

Keil, C. F., and F. Delitzsch. *Biblical Commentary on the Old Testament.* Vol. II, Grand Rapids, MI: Wm. B. Eerdmans Publishing Co., no date given.

Kiene, Paul F. *The Tabernacle of God in the Wilderness of Sinai.* Grand Rapids, MI: Lamplighter Books, Zondervan Publishing House, 1977.

Klotz, John W. "The Vine, the Fig Tree, and the Olive: A Study in Biblical Symbolism." *Concordia Journal,* Nov. 1980, 6:6.

Lost Books of the Bible and the Forgotten Books of Eden, The. Cleveland and New York: World Publishing Co., 1926.

Loughead, Flora Haines. *Dictionary of Given Names with Their Origin and Meanings.* Glendale, CA: The Arthur H. Clark Company, 1934.

Lundquist, John M. "The Common Temple Ideology of the Ancient Near East." In *The Temple in Antiquity*, BYU Religious Studies Center. Salt Lake City, UT: Bookcraft, Inc., 1984.

McConkie, Bruce R. *Doctrinal New Testament Commentary*. Vol. 1. Salt Lake City, UT: Bookcraft, Inc., 1973.

McConkie, Bruce R. *Mormon Doctrine*. Salt Lake City, UT: Bookcraft, Inc., 1966.

McConkie, Bruce R. *The Mortal Messiah*. 4 vols. Salt Lake City: Deseret Book Co., 1981.

McConkie, Bruce R. *The Promised Messiah*. Salt Lake City: Deseret Book Co., 1978.

McConkie, Joseph Fielding. *His Name Shall Be Joseph*. Salt Lake City: Hawkes Publishing Co., 1980.

Messenger and Advocate, Vols. I and II. Salt Lake City: Modern Microfilm Co.

Metford, J. C. J. *Dictionary of Christian Lore and Legend*. London: Thames and Hudson, 1983.

New Analytical Bible and Dictionary of the Bible. Chicago: John A. Dixson Publishing Co., 1931, 1973.

New English Bible with the Apocrypha, The. New York: Oxford University Press, 1971.

Nibley, Hugh. *Abraham in Egypt*. Salt Lake City: Deseret Book Co., 1981.

Nibley, Hugh. *Lehi in the Desert*. Salt Lake City: Bookcraft, Inc., 1952.

Nibley, Hugh. *The Timely and the Timeless*. Provo, UT: Religious Studies Center, Brigham Young University Press, 1978.

Nibley, Hugh. *What Is a Temple? The Idea of the Temple in History*. Provo, UT: Brigham Young University Press, 1968.

Old Testament: Gospel Doctrine Teacher's Supplement. Part I & II. Published by The Church of Jesus Christ of Latter-day Saints, 1980.

Packer, J. I., Merrill C. Tenney, and Wm. White, Jr., eds. *The Bible Almanac*. Nashville: Thomas Nelson Publishers, 1980.

Parry, J. H. and Company, trans., *The Book of Jasher*. Salt Lake City: 1887, 1973.

Pfeiffer, Charles F., Howard F. Vos, and John Rea, eds. *Wycliffe Bible Dictionary*. Vol. 2. Chicago: Moody Press, 1976.

Pink, Arthur W. *Gleanings in Genesis.* Chicago: Moody Press, 1950.

Porter, William, ed. *The Jewish Encyclopedia.* New York: Funk and Wagnalls Co., 1901—06.

Pratt, Parley P. (son). *Autobiography of Parley P. Pratt.* Salt Lake City: Deseret Book Co., 1950.

Rapaport, Samuel. *A Treasury of the Midrash.* New York: KTAV Publishing House Inc., 1968.

Smith, Joseph Fielding. *Doctrines of Salvation.* Vol. 2. Salt Lake City, UT: Bookcraft Inc., 1954.

Smith, Joseph. *History of the Church of Jesus Christ of Latter-day Saints.* Salt Lake City: Deseret Book Co., 1927 (published by the Church).

Smith, Joseph. *Teachings of the Prophet Joseph Smith.* Joseph F. Smith, comp. Salt Lake City: Deseret Book Co., 1976.

Smith, Joseph Fielding. *Answers to Gospel Questions.* Salt Lake City: Deseret Book Co., 1963.

Smith, Joseph Fielding. *Origins of the Reorganized Church,* pamphlet. Salt Lake City: The Deseret News, 1909.

Smith, William. *Dictionary of the Bible.* Vols. 1—4. New York: Hurd and Houghton; Cambridge: Riverside Press, 1870.

Soltan, Henry W. *The Tabernacle: The Priesthood and the Offerings.* Grand Rapids, MI: Kregal Publishers, 1972.

Speiser, E. A. *The Anchor Bible: Genesis.* New York: Doubleday and Co., 1964.

Stark, Rodney and Charles Y. Glock. *The Nature of Religious Commitment.* Berkeley: University of California Press, 1968. Table 7.

Steinberg, Milton. *Basic Judaism.* New York: Harcourt, Brace, and World, Inc., 1947.

Stranberg, Victor. "A Hell for Our Time." *The Christian Century,* Sept. 4, 1968.

Strong, James. *Strong's Exhaustive Concordance.* Nashville: Regal Publishers, Inc., n.d.

Todd, John M. *Martin Luther: A Biographical Study.* Westminster, MD: Newman Press, 1965.

Trent, Kenneth E. *Types of Christ in the Old Testament.* New York: Exposition Press, 1960.

Vine, W. E. *An Expository Dictionary of New Testament Words.* Old Tappan, NJ: Fleming H. Revell Co., 1960.

Wiesel, Elie. *Messengers of God, Biblical Portraits and Legends.* New York: Random House, 1976.

Wilson, Walter Lewis. *Wilson's Dictionary of Bible Types.* Grand Rapids, MI: Wm. B. Eerdman's Publishing Co., 1975, 1983.

Wilson, William. *Old Testament Word Studies.* Grand Rapids, MI: Kregal Publications, 1978.

Wouk, Herman. *This Is My God.* New York: Pocket Books, Simon & Schuster, Inc., 1959.

Young, Brigham. *Journal of Discourses,* Vols. 1–26. Liverpool: F. D. and S. W. Richards, 1854.

Zimmerli, Walther, *Ezekiel 1.* Philadelphia: Fortress Press, 1979.

Index

— A —

Aaron, 21, 57—58, 62, 64, 72—73, 108
  meaning of name, 185
  Melchizedek Priesthood held by, 79
  Passover instituted by, 48
  rebellion of, 69—70
  rod of, 46, 73
  type for Christ, 249
  vision of God, 207
Aaronic Priesthood, 3, 61, 71—72, 76, 77
Abel, 249
  meaning of name, 180—81
  type for Christ, 147—48
Abihu, 72, 207
Abinadi, 171
Abiram, 71—72
Abraham, 7—8, 61, 121—22, 149, 223, 249
  book of, 126—27, 137—38, 179, 181, 236
  bosom of, 249
  endowment of, 202
  garment of, 138
  meaning of name, 182
  type for Christ, 151—53
Absolutism, 19—20, 22—23
Ablutions, 249
Acacia wood, 109
Adam, 92, 121, 127, 179—81, 196
  coat of skins, 137, 138, 140
  creation of, 211—12, 243
  first principles taught by, 238
  garment of, 110—11, 138, 202
  meaning of name, 179, 250
  sacrifices offered by, 86
  type for Christ, 146—47
Adam-ondi-Ahman, 120, 187
Administration of angels, 77
Administration to the sick, 198, 202
Adultery, symbolism, 250
Agag, 161
Ahab, 17—18
Ahijah, 162
Ai, 151
Akiba, Rabbi, 216
Allegory, 14—17, 135, 137, 169—70, 242—43, 250
  misuse of, 205, 209—10, 220—29
  of wild and tame olive trees, 231

Alexandrian Jews, 219—21
Alma, 242
  on law of Moses, 79
  on Melchizedek, 150
  on pure garments, 142, 144, 202—3
  on sanctification, 197
Almonds, symbolism, 73
Alpha and Omega, 250
Altar of burnt offering, 103—4, 116
Altar of incense, 106, 108, 117
Altars, 2, 63, 250
Amalekites, 54—55, 57—58, 175
Ambrose, 149
Amen, 250
Amos, 90
Amulek, 81
Anchor Bible, Genesis, 31
Ancient of days, 179, 251
Angels, 65—66, 68, 100, 108, 134—35, 137, 198. 251
Animals, as symbols for Christ, 3
Anointings, 3, 61, 79, 120, 114—15, 134, 201, 251
Anti-Mormons, 208
Antitypes, 251
Apocalypse, 173
Apocryphal writings, 159, 220, 225, 238—39
  Ascension of Isaiah, 135
  epistle of Barnabas, 222—23
  Esdras, 134, 159
  Jasher, 139
  Odes of Solomon, 145n
  Secrets of Enoch, 134, 136
  Testament of Levi, 134—35
Apologists, 222
Apostasy, 127, 214—27
Apostles, 125
Apostolic Fathers, 221—26
Apron, symbolism, 251
Ark of the Covenant, 69, 73, 83, 109—10, 117, 251
Arm, symbolism, 251
Armageddon, 173, 252, 265
Armor, symbolism, 252
As a Driven Leaf, 18
Asaph, 38, 193
Ascension of Isaiah, 135
Asenath, 140
Asher, 184

Asherah, 252
Ashes, 94, 95
Assyria, 163
Astronomy, 7
Atonement, 2, 3, 49, 50, 81—84, 96—97,
    100—15, 196, 209—10
  by Moses, 65
  Day of, 82—84, 108, 110, 133, 201,
    252
  law of Moses based on, 81—84
  sacrament in memory of, 198
  Tabernacle of Moses a symbol for,
    100—15
Augustine, 15
Authority, 20—21, 197
Azazel, 82

                    — B —

Baal, priests of, 2
Babel, 174
Balaam, 233
Babylon, 163—65, 167, 186, 252
  king of, 264
Baptism, 5, 101—2, 104, 185, 196,
    201—2, 252
  for the dead, 120, 253
  of fire, 196—97
  of the earth, 148—49
  practiced in Moses' time, 61, 77, 80, 83
  Red Sea a symbol for, 52
  taught in Old Testament, 238
Baptismal fonts, 253
Barnabas, epistle of, 222—23
Basic Judaism, 217
Bee, symbolism, 252
Beer, meaning of name, 174
Beersheba, 123, 152, 174
Beetles, 47
Bells, 111
Belshazzar, 187
Ben-hadad (Syrian king), 17—18
Benjamin, meaning of name, 184
Beth, meaning of name, 74
Bethel, 123, 151, 154, 252
Bethesda, pool of, 238
Bethlehem, 2, 6—7, 190
Bible, additions to, 238—39
  Catholic, 220, 238
  clarified by Book of Mormon and
    Doctrine and Covenants, 235
  fallibility of, 231—41
  history of, 222—29
  history of interpretation, 214—30

Joseph Smith Translation, 64—65, 66,
    133, 150, 182, 191, 193, 211, 218,
    229, 234, 236—41, 246, 255, 268
  loss of texts, 79—80
  New English, 239—40
  omissions from, 237—38
  translation errors, 239—42
  understood by Joseph Smith, 236
  Vulgate, 225
Bible History, Old Testament, 31,
    50—51, 56, 65, 98
Biblical Commentary on the Old
    Testament, 61, 111
Bilhah, 183—84
Birds, used in sacrifice, 95—96
Birth, symbolism, 93
Birthright, 31, 32, 38, 139, 183
Bishops, 95
Bitter herbs, 48—49, 50
Black, symbolism, 256
Blood, 103—4, 108—9, 110
  Nile River turned to, 46, 47
  sprinkled on doorway, 48—50
  symbolism, 252—53
Blue, symbolism, 102, 111, 112, 256
Boils, Egyptian plague, 47
Book of Abraham, 126—27, 138, 179
Book of Esther, 241
Book of Mormon, 22, 44, 141—42, 157,
    232
  altars, 250
  Bible clarified by, 234—35
  on coat of many colors, 139—40
  sacrament meeting, 106
  symbolism in, 8—9
Book of Moses, 179, 180, 212
Book of Revelation, 179, 243
Book of the Covenant, 63
Bosom, symbolism, 253
Branch, symbolism, 253
Brass, 103
Brazen Sea, 253
Brazen serpent, 75, 254
Bread, 106—7, 134
  at Pentecost, 85
  eaten by Ezekiel, 165—66
  of life, 4, 35, 42, 55—56, 136
  sacrament, 8—9, 198
  symbolism, 254
  unleavened, 48—49, 50, 106—7
Breastplate, 112, 134
Bride and Bridegroom, 254
Broidered coat, 110—11
Bullocks, used in sacrifice, 82

Bulls, used in sacrifice, 86
Burning bush, 118
Burnt offerings, 63–64, 86–87, 97,
   103–4
   See also Sacrifice

— C —

Calmet, 149
Cain, 147, 180, 249
Calf, Golden, 64–65
Calvin, John, 229, 239
Canaan, 71, 123, 151–52
Cancer, 91
Candlestick, symbolism, 254
Carmel, meaning of name, 174
Carnal law, 109
Catholic Bible, 220, 238
Cattle, cursed in Egypt, 47
Cedar wood, 94–96
   symbolism, 254
Celestial kingdom, 25, 123
Censer, 255
Cephas, 190
Cherubim, 105, 108, 109, 255
Children of Israel, dietary code, 91–92,
   223
   led out of Egypt, 48–51
   rebellion of, 64–73
   wanderings in wilderness, 52–75
   See also Israel
Christ, meaning of title, 3
   See also Jesus Christ
Christians, 4
Church, primitive, 235
Circumcision, 49, 255
Clarke's Commentary, 66, 132, 136
Clay, symbolism, 256
Cleanliness, in law of Moses, 91
Cleansing, 61
Clement of Alexandria, 224
Clement of Rome, 222
Clothing, of high priest, 110–13
   of priests, 113–14
   See also Coat of many colors;
     Garments
Cloud, on Mount of Transfiguration,
   124
   on Sinai, 62–63, 108
   symbolism, 68–69, 225–56
Coat of many colors, 29, 30–33, 39,
   139–40, 172
   remnant of, 36–37, 38
Coats, 110–11

Coats of skins, 32
Colors, symbolism, 256
   See also individual colors
Commandments, carnal, 76–77
Consecration, 3, 91–92
Constantine, 137
Contrasts, 19–20, 25
Corn, bruised, 88
Council in heaven, 7, 51
Covenants, 53, 60–61, 168, 198
   of children of Israel, 62–63
   renewal of, 83, 89
   sacrifices as, 104
Cowdery, Oliver, 4, 69, 78, 241
Creation, account of, 30, 209, 211–12
Crocodiles, 59
Cross, 223, 256
Crowns, 113, 134, 257
*Cruden's Complete Concordance to
   the Old and New Testaments*, 181
Cush, 138
Cyrus, King of Persia, 159, 189

— D —

Dan, 183–84
Daniel, 179, 207, 243
   meaning of name, 186–87
Dark Ages, 226–27
Darkness, Egyptian plague, 47
Dathan, 71–72
David, Old Testament king, 17, 21,
   100, 122, 201
   anointing of, 6–7, 114–15
   meaning of name, 188
   type for Christ, 158
Day of Atonement, 82–84, 108, 110,
   133, 201, 252
Dead Sea, 174
Death, spiritual, 70, 95–97
   symbolism, 93–95
Degrees of glory, 22, 123, 244
Delitzsch, F., 61, 111
Deseret, 129, 257
Deuteronomy, 237
Devil, 192, 210–11, 257
   See also Lucifer; Perdition; Satan
Diadem, 112–13, 135, 257
Diaspora, Jewish, 219
Dictionary of the Bible, 94–95, 199
Dietary laws, 91–92, 223
Dinah, 184
Doctrine and Covenants, 9, 61, 66–67,
   235–36, 241–42

Dothan, 33
Doves, sacrifice of, 93
  symbolism, 257
Dreams, 29, 33, 34, 42
Dummelow, J. R., 47

— E —

Ears, 97
  symbolism, 257
East, symbolism, 102, 257
Eden, Garden of, 110—11, 137, 138,
  140—41, 257, 259
  meaning of name, 173
Edersheim, Alfred, *Bible History, Old
  Testament*, 31, 50—51, 56, 65, 98
  Life and Times of Jesus the Messiah,
  215, 216
  *Temple: Its Ministry and Services
  as They Were at the Time of Christ*,
  84—85, 93, 94, 199
Egypt, 34, 42, 135, 156, 163
  Israel led out of, 45—51
  Jews in, 219—21
  symbolism, 258
Egyptus, meaning of name, 181
Elements, symbols for Christ, 5
Eliab, 6
Eleizer, meaning of name, 185
Elijah, 2, 100, 160, 233
  appearance of Joseph Smith, 236
  mantle of, 136—37, 162
  on Mount of Transfiguration, 124
Elim, 53
Elisabeth, meaning of name, 189—90
Elisha, call to prophetic office, 162
Elohim, 239
  See also God; God the Father
Emmanuel, meaning of name, 190
  See also Jesus Christ
Endowment, 124—25, 200
  See also Temple ordinances
Enoch, 121—22, 134, 136, 196, 206
  city of, 120
  first principles taught by, 238
  garment of, 138
  rainbow sign to, 268
  type for Christ, 148—49
Ensign, 258
Ephod, 111, 112, 134
Ephraim, 193
  stick of, 168
Epiphanius, 149
Epistle of Barnabas, 222—23

Esau, 139
  meaning of name, 182—83
Esdraelon, Plain of, 265
Esdras, 134, 159
Esther, book of, 241
Eternal progression, 123
Ether, 142
Ethiopia, 163
Euphrates, 164
Eve, 110—11, 180, 243, 258
  creation of, 211—12
  coat of skins, 137, 138, 140
  garment of, 202
  meaning of name, 180
Events, symbols for Christ, 3—4
Evil speaking, 70
Ewes, used in sacrifice, 96
Eye, symbolism, 258
Ezekiel, 121, 165—68, 178, 207, 243,
  255
  allegory of, 61
  meaning of name, 186
Ezra, 134

— F —

Fables, 14, 258
Faith, 1, 21, 77, 80, 116, 238
Fall of Adam, 209—10
Families, sealing of, 39
Famine, symbolism, 258
Farrar, Frederic W., 217—19, 220, 222,
  224—28, 233
Fasting, 155
Fathers' blessings, 198
Feelings, symbols for Christ, 4
Feet, 97
  washing of, 105, 201
Fig tree, cursing of, 10—11
Fire, 49, 100, 103—4
  baptism by, 196—97
  symbolism, 258
Firstorn, 49, 51, 259
Firstfruits, 84—85, 259
First Presidency, 9, 130
First principles, taught in Old Testament,
  238
First Vision, 24, 229
Flies, Egyptian plague of, 47
Flood, 181, 209
Flour, 88, 96, 159
Foods, symbols for Christ, 4
  See also Dietary laws
Foreordination, 155

Forgiveness of sins, 36, 84, 89
Fornication, 259
Fountain, symbolism, 259
Fowls, used in sacrifice, 86, 89
Frankincense, 88, 107, 158
    See also Incense
Freeman, James W., 199
Frogs, Egyptian plague of, 46, 47

— G —

Gabriel, 32, 140, 190
Gad, meaning of name, 184
Galileo, 232
Garden of Eden, 110—11, 137, 138,
    140—41, 257, 259
Garden of Gethsemane, 176, 259—60
Garden of the Empty Tomb, 260
Garments, 133—45
    of Adam, 32
    of high priest, 110—13
    of priesthood, 116, 137—41
    of priests, 113—14
    parable of, 131—33
    rending of, 161—62, 171—72
    temple, 202—3
    See also Coat of many colors; Coats
        of skins
Garner, David H., 120
Gaster, Theodore, 31
Gate, symbolism, 260
Gathering of Israel, 193, 213
Gehenna, 176, 260
Genealogical work, 78
Genesis, book of, 28
    meaning of name, 173
Gershom, meaning of name, 185
Gethsemane, Garden of, 176, 259—60
Gibeah, meaning of name, 173
Gideon, 4, 21, 100
Ginzberg, Louis, 32, 53, 61, 138—40,
    216
Girdle, 134, 260
    of high priest, 112
Girdlestone, Robert Baker, 239
Gleanings in Genesis, 30
Goats, used in sacrifice, 82, 86
God, meaning of name, 176—79
    nature of, 206—9
    "special" relationships with, 242
    visions of, 63, 206—7, 213
    voice of, 231
    See also Jehovah; Jesus Christ

God the Father, Christ a representation
    of, 172
    See also Elohim
Godhead, 9
Gods, plurality of, 239
Gog and Magog, 260
Gold, beaten, 158
    symbolism, 105, 256, 260
Golden calf, 64—65
Golden candlestick, 106, 107, 116—17,
    158
Goliath, 21, 158
Gomer, 169—70
Good Samaritan, parable of, 15
Grain, symbolism, 260
Greed, 53—55
Greek philosophy, 219—21

— H —

Habakkuk, prophecies of, 245
Hagar, 63, 182, 261
Hail, Egyptian plague, 47
Hair, of Ezekiel, 166
Hallelujah, 261
Ham, son of Noah, 138
    meaning of name, 181
Hananiah, 164
Hands, symbolism, 261
Hannah, 186
Har Megiddon, 252
Haran, 123, 151
Harmony, Pennsylvania, 78
Head, symbolism, 261
Health laws, 91
Heart, symbolism, 261
Heifers, used in sacrifice, 93
Hell, existence of, 210—11
Hermon, meaning of name, 174
Herod, 13, 137
    temple of, 109
Hezekiah, 159
High priest, clothing of, 110—13
    sacrifices offered by, 82—83
    type for Christ, 261
    See also Priests
Hinnom, Valley of, 176
History of Interpretation, 217—19,
    220, 222, 224—28, 233
Holy Ghost, 14, 88, 91, 115, 236
    anointing a symbol of, 201—2
    gift of, 196—97, 246
Holy of Holies, 82—84, 103, 108—10,
    115, 133, 252, 257

Holy Place, 105—8, 115
Honesty, in scriptural study, 247—48
Honey, symbolism, 88, 261
Horeb, Mount, 66
  meaning of name, 174
Horns, symbolism, 103, 261—62
Hosea, 169—70
Hur, 57—58
Hyperbole, 12, 22—23
Hypocrisy, 10—11
Hyrum, meaning of name, 193
Hyssop, 48, 94, 96, 262

— I —

I AM, 176—78
Idolatry, 46—47, 64—65, 163, 164, 217
Idols, of sophistry, 205—6
Idumea, 262
Incense, 109, 135, 158, 262
  altar of, 108
  See also Frankincense
Isaac, 121—22, 182
  type for Christ, 151—53, 262
Isaiah, 88, 159, 163
  anointing of, 115
  garment of, 138
  meaning of name, 186
  on garments of salvation, 133, 135
  on Jerusalem, 141
  on mountain of the Lord's house, 119,
    126, 129
  prophecies of, 144, 245
  visions of, 207
Ishmael, 152
  meaning of name, 182
Israel, children of, 48—75
  firstfruits of the Lord, 85
  gathering of, 36, 193, 213
  history of, as prophecy, 45
  meaning of name, 183, 262
Israelites, dietary code, 223

— J —

Jackson County, Missouri, 122
Jacob (Old Testament patriarch), 28,
    30—39, 121
  garment of, 139
  ladder of, 123, 262
  meaning of name, 182—83
  prophecy on seed of Joseph, 172
  type for Christ, 153—54
  vision of God, 123, 206

Jacob (Book of Mormon prophet), 142,
    218, 231
James, 124—25, 233, 236
Japheth, meaning of name, 181
Jared, brother of, 121—22
Jasher, book of, 139
Jealousy, 69—70
Jedediah, meaning of name, 189
Jehoiachin, 159
Jehoshaphat, Valley of, 176
Jehovah, 82
  meaning of name, 177, 263
  See also God; Jesus Christ
Jehovah-jireh, 122
Jehovah-nissi, 57—58, 175
Jehovah-shalom, 4
Jeremiah, 85, 126, 159, 176, 233, 238
  meaning of name, 186
  prophecies of, 163—65, 178—79
  vision of God, 207
Jericho, 167
Jeroboam, 162
Jerome, 149, 224—25, 227
Jershon, 151
Jerusalem, 132, 163, 164, 186
  beautiful garments of, 141—42
  compared to Joseph of Egypt, 29
  meaning of name, 175
  seige of, demonstrated by Ezekiel,
    165—66
  temple, 257
  See also New Jerusalem
Jesus, meaning of name, 190, 263
Jesus Christ, Aaron a type for, 249
  Abel a type for, 147—48
  Abraham a type for, 151—53
  Adam a type for, 146—47
  anointing a type for, 6—7, 203
  atonement, 2, 3, 49, 50, 81—84,
    96—97, 100—15, 196, 209—10
  authority of, 20
  betrayal of, 33—34
  brazen serpent a type for, 75
  consecrated in council in heaven, 51
  crucifixion, 111
  cursing of fig tree, 10—11
  David a type for, 158
  death purification a type for, 94—95
  Enoch a type for, 148—49
  firstborn a type for, 259
  High Priest a type for, 261
  intercessor, 108
  Isaac a type for, 151—53, 262
  Jacob a type for, 153—54
  Joseph of Egypt a type for, 28—36

Joshua a type for, 57—58, 71
Kolob a type for, 7—8
Last Supper, 50, 125, 267
law of Moses a type for, 83
law of Moses fulfilled by, 81
meaning of name, 2—3, 190, 263
meat offering a representation of, 88
Melchizedek a type for, 149—51
metaphors describing, 14
miracle of loaves and fishes, 55
mortal ministry, 1
Moses a type for, 64—65, 154—57
Noah a type for, 148—49, 181
Old Testament kings a type for, 263
ordinances received by, 195
parables, 15—16, 18
Passover a type for, 48—50
preparatory years, 20
presentation in temple, 51, 93
Prince of Peace, 4
prophecies concerning, 1, 6—7
representation of the Father, 172
robe, 33, 147
sacrament given to Nephites by, 8—9
sacrament in memory of, 198, 211
scarlet wool a type for, 96
scriptural exegesis of, 244—45
Second Adam, 250
Second Coming, 45, 157
Seth a type for, 181
sin offering a type for, 89
symbols testifying of, 1—11
Tabernacle of Moses a likeness of, 100—17
taken to high mountain, 121
taking name of, 4
"the Amen" a synonym for, 251
transfiguration, 124—25
types for, numerous, 87
use of hyperbole, 22—23
use of simile and metaphor, 13
See also Jehovah
Jesse, 6
Jethro, 58—59, 156
meaning of name, 185
Jews, religion, 214—19
Jewels, 113
Jewish Diaspora, 219
Jezreel, 169
Plain of, 252
Valley of, 265
Job, 194n
Joel, meaning of name, 187
John, 21, 124—25, 231, 236
epistle of, 115

Gospel of, 4
meaning of name, 190
parchment of, 236
revelations, 13—14, 121, 142—43, 144—45, 179, 192, 203, 207, 243
John the Baptist, 13, 78, 136, 160, 186, 212
appearance to Joseph Smith, 236
clothing, 162
parchment of, 236
Jonah, 168—69, 233
Jordan River, 69, 162, 174, 263
Joseph of Egypt, 45, 50—51, 263
coat of many colors, 29, 30—33, 36—39, 139—40, 172
compared to Joseph Smith, 38—43
meaning of name, 38, 184, 193
prophecies, 185, 191, 193
stick of, 167—68
type for Christ, 28—36
Joseph, husband of Mary, 51
Josephus, 46, 137, 157, 175, 221
Joshua, 71, 79, 133, 263
meaning of name, 2—3, 190
type for Christ, 58
Josiah, 89
Jot, meaning of, 263
Judah, meaning of name, 183
stick of, 167—68
Judaism, 214—19
Judas Iscariot, 34, 233
Jude, epistle of, 148
Jukes, Andrew, 86
Justin Martyr, 223

— K —

Kadeshbarnea, 69
Kadeshi, 71
Keil, C. F., 61, 111
Kethoneth, 32
Keys, of the kingdom, 9
restoration of, 78
symbols, 263
Kibroth-hattaavah, 54, 175
Kidron, 176
Kingdom of heaven, 101, 131—33
Kings, 3, 203
types for Christ, 263
Kirtland Temple, dedication, 100, 144, 203, 275
partial endowment in, 201
Kneeling, symbolism, 263
Kolob, type for Christ, 7—8
Korah rebellion, 71—73

— L —

Ladder, Jacob's, 123
Lambs, symbolism, 264
  Passover, 48
  used for sacrifice, 3, 93, 96—97
Lamech, 181
Lamp, symbolism, 264
Language and Imagery of the Bible, 208
Last Supper, 50, 125, 267
Laver, 104—5, 116, 264
Law of Moses, 20, 52, 76—98
  type for Christ, 83
Law of sacrifice, 86—91, 202
Law of the Offerings, 86
Law of witnesses, 2, 200
Laying on of hands, 197—98, 261
Leah, meaning of name, 183
Leaven, symbolism, 50, 88, 264
Legends of the Jews, 32, 53, 61, 138—40,
  216
Lehi, 79, 170—71
Leprosy, symbol of sin, 70
  type for spiritual death, 95—97
Levi, 134—35
  meaning of name, 183
  sons of, 3, 78, 86
  tribe of, 51, 65, 77
Levitical priesthood, 61, 76
Leviticus, 97
Liahona, 170
Lice, Egyptian plague, 48
Life and Times of Jesus the Messiah,
  215, 216
Light, symbolism, 5, 107, 264
Linen, 101—2, 112
Loammi, 170
Locusts, Egyptian plague, 47
Lo-ruhamah, 169
Lot, 239
Lucifer, 48, 147, 264
  meaning of name, 192
  See also Devil; Perdition; Satan
Lundquist, John M., 126—28
Luther, Martin, 149, 227—28, 239, 241
Luz, 123

— M —

McConkie, Bruce R., *Mormon Doctrine*,
  115, 197
  Mortal Messiah, 16, 125, 157
  Promised Messiah, 50, 82, 83, 104
McLellin, William, 69
Malachi, 78, 86, 104, 159, 245, 246
  meaning of name, 188

Manasseh, 193
Manna, 4, 54—56, 59, 265
Manners and Customs of the Bible, 199
Manoah, 63, 100
Mantle, symbolism, 265
Marah, 52—53, 174—75
Mariam, meaning of name, 190
Marriage, 22—23, 127
  celestial, 182, 203—4
  of Adam and Eve, 138
Martin Luther: A Biographical Study,
  228
Massah, 56, 175
Mary, mother of Jesus, 51, 93
  meaning of name, 190, 194n
Meat offerings, 87—88, 97
Meggido, 265
  Mountain of, 252
Melchizedek, 175, 202, 265
  meaning of name, 188
  type for Christ, 149—51
Melchizedek Priesthood, 61, 66—67, 71,
  76, 79
Menorah, 107
Mercy seat, 109, 158, 265
Meribah, 56
  meaning of name, 175
*Messengers of God, Biblical Portraits
  and Legends*, 40, 216
Messiah, 6—7
  meaning of name, 265
  See also Jesus Christ
Metaphor, 12—14
  misuse of, 205, 207—8
Methuselah, 138
  meaning of name, 181
Micah, 163, 245
  meaning of name, 187
Micaiah, 207
Michael, 134, 179
  See also Adam
Midianites, 100
Millennium, 199
Miracles, 46, 156
  of Satan, 48
Miriam the prophetess, rebellion of,
  69—70
Missionaries, 20—21
Mitre, 112—13
Mizpah, 173—74
Molech, 176, 260
Moon, metaphor, 265
"More sure word of prophecy," 124
Moreh, plains of, 151
Moriah, Mount, 100, 122, 152—53, 175
Mormon, 26—27

Mormon Doctrine, 115, 197
Mormon exodus, 59
Moroni, Nephite military commander, 36, 171—72
Moroni, Nephite prophet, 24, 29, 36, 122, 141—42, 143
  instructions to Joseph Smith, 245—46
  on New Jerusalem, 203
Mortal Messiah, 16, 125, 157
Mosaic law, *See* Law of Moses
Moses, 21, 50—51, 174—75, 176—77, 215—16, 265
  appearance to Joseph Smith, 236
  as redeemer of Israel, 45
  ascension of Sinai, 62—67, 118—19
  book of, 179, 180, 212, 237—38
  brazen serpent lifted up, 75
  confrontation with Pharaoh, 45—48
  law of, 20, 52, 76—98, 152
  meaning of name, 185
  Melchizedek Priesthood held by, 79
  miracles of quail and manna, 55—56
  on judgment seat, 59
  on Mount of Transfiguration, 124
  Passover instituted, 48
  prophecies of, 245
  rebellion against, 69—73
  rod of, 57—58
  type for Christ, 64—65, 154—57
  vision of God, 120—21, 206—7
  vision of Satan, 23—24, 25
  water from rock, 56, 74
Mount Horeb, 66, 174
Mount Moriah, 100, 122, 152—53, 175
Mount of Olives, 157, 175—76
Mount of Simeon, 122
Mount of Transfiguration, 124—25, 174, 255
Mount Ophel, 176
Mount Sinai, 62—67, 118—19, 121—22, 255
Mount Zion, 144
Mountain of Megiddo, 252
Mountains, 118—26, 265—66
Murder, 103
Myth, Legend and Custom in the Old Testament, 31

— N —

Nadab, 72, 207
Names, symbols for Christ, 2—3
  significance of, 173—94
Naphtali, 184
Nathan, 17
Nativity story, 189—90

Nebuchadnezzar, 164, 187
Needle's eye, 22
Nehemiah, meaning of name, 186
Nephi, 126, 142, 143, 195, 210
  vision of, 121
Nephites, 245
  sacrament introduced to, 8—9
  sealed records of, 244
New English Bible, 110
New Jerusalem, 29, 122, 129, 144, 203, 256
New Testament, 44, 61
  history of, 222—29
  understanding, through symbolism, 10—11
Nezer, 257
Nibley, Hugh, 126, 127, 145n
Nile River, turned to blood, 46
Nimrod, 138—39, 181
Noah (Book of Mormon king), 171
Noah (Old Testament prophet), 138, 202, 233, 236, 238
  meaning of name, 181
  type for Christ, 148—49, 181
North Star, 130

— O —

Obadiah, meaning of name, 187
Obedience, 33, 83, 116
Objects, symbols for Christ, 2
Odes of Solomon, 145n
Offerings, 266
Oil, 96—97, 107, 114—15, 134, 158—59
  in meat offering, 88
Old Testament, history of, 222—29
  understanding, through symbolism, 6—7
  value, 44—45
Olive leaf, symbolism, 266
Olive oil, 3, 107, 114, 266
Olive tree, symbolism, 266
One Volume Bible Commentary by Various Writers, 47
Onyx, 112
Ophel, Mount, 176
Oral tradition, 215—18
Ordinances, 52, 66—67, 195—204
  of law of Moses, 81—98
Origen, 149, 224, 225
Oshea, 71

— P —

Palm leaf, symbolism, 266
Parables, 14—18, 267

of the garment, 131—33, 136—37
of the Good Samaritan, 15
of the king's son, 131—33, 136—37
of the wicked husbandmen, 18
Paran, wilderness of, 71
Partridge, Edward, 197
Paschal feast, 125
Paschal lamb, 50
Passover, 80, 85, 264, 267
    symbolism explained, 49—50
    type for Christ, 48—50
Patriarchal blessings, 22, 157, 193, 198
Paul the Apostle, 19—20, 21, 233, 242
    Joseph Smith's description of, 236
    on Adam, 146
    on baptism, 5, 196
    on Christ, 89, 147
    on Ishmael, 152
    on law of Moses, 83, 84
    on Melchizedek Priesthood, 149
    on ordinances, 52
    on Passover, 50
    on prophets' wardrobe, 136
    on sacrifice, 90
    on salvation, 240—41
    on symbolism of ancient Israel, 44
    on unfaithfulness of children of Israel,
        67
    on veil of temple, 109
    on water from rock, 56
    Symbolism interpreted by, x
    vision of degrees of glory, 25, 123,
        262
    vision of God, 207
    warnings against Jewish fables, 215
Peace, altars as places of, 2
    spirit of, 4
Peace offerings, 88—89
Pearl, symbolism, 135, 267
Pearl of Great Price, understanding
    through symbolism, 7—8
Peleg, meaning of name, 181
Peniel, meaning of name, 174
Pentecost, 85
Perdition, 147, 249
    meaning of name, 192
    See also Devil; Lucifer; Satan
Perfume, symbolism, 267
Persecution, 39—40
Persons, symbols for Christ, 4
Peter the Apostle, 21, 115, 124—25,
    215, 233, 236
    meaning of name, 190—92
Pharisaism, 217, 231
Pharisees, 13, 131, 192, 212, 219, 242,
    264

Pharaoh (time of Joseph), 30, 34, 42
Pharaoh (time of Moses), 21, 45—48
Philadelphia, Pennsylvania, 248
Philo of Alexandria, 220, 222
Phoenix, symbolism, 222
Phylacteries, 212, 267
Pigeons, used in sacrifice, 86, 93
Pillar of fire, 68
Pilate, Pontius, 34
Pink, Arthur W., 30
Pisgah, meaning of name, 173
Places, symbols for Christ, 2
Plagues, after Korah rebellion, 72—73
    Egyptian, 46—48
Plain of Esdraelon, 265
Plain of Jezreel, 252
Plan of salvation, 135, 209—10
Pomegranates, symbolism, 111, 267
Popes, 226—27
Potiphar's wife, 34, 41
Pratt, Parley P., 247—48
Premortal life, 7, 155
Presidency of the High Priesthood, 9
Presiding Bishopric, 130
Pride, 69
Priesthood, Aaronic, 61, 76, 77
    garment of, 137—41
    Levitical, 61, 76
    Melchizedek, 61, 66—67, 76, 79
    ordinations, 198
    received by Adam, 141
    taken away through unfaithfulness,
        66—67
Priests, 3, 267
    vestments of, 113—14
    See also High priest
Primitive church, 235
Prince of darkness, 46, 48
    See also Devil; Lucifer; Perdition;
    Satan
Prince of Peace, 4, 267—68
Promised Messiah, 50, 82, 83, 104
Prophecy, 244—45
    denied by Jews, 215—19
    history of Israel as, 45
    of Messiah, 6—7
Prophets, 3, 132
    clothing of, 136—37, 162—64
    fallibility of, 233
    living, 20
    types for Christ, 159
    See also names of individual
        prophets
Proverbs, 233
Psalms, 268
Purification, 91—92

following childbirth, 93
following contact with death, 93—95
for leprosy, 95—97
Purity, 62, 116
Purple, symbolism, 102, 106, 112, 256

— Q —

Quails, 54—55
Qumran, 22, 241
Quorum of the Twelve, 8—9

— R —

Ra the Sun-God, 47
Rabbis, 20, 215—19
Rachel, 39
  meaning of name, 183—84
Rahab, 222
Rain, symbolism, 268
Rainbow, 200
Rams, used in sacrifice, 82, 86
Rapaport, Samuel, 29
Red, symbolism, 102, 106, 256
Red Sea, symbol of baptism, 52
Reformation, 227—29
Rehoboam, 162
Rending of garments, 162—62, 171—72,
  268
Repentance, 65, 77, 80, 238
Rephidem, plain of, 56
Rest of the Lord, 268
Restitution, 89
Restoration, 20, 229—30
Resurrection, 109, 209—10
  symbolized by Jonah in the whale,
    168—69
Reuben, meaning of name, 183
Reubenites, rebellion of, 71—73
Revelation, ix-xi, 1, 4, 20—21, 177,
  242—44, 248
  book of, 142—43, 144—45, 179, 192,
    203, 207, 243
  language of, 236
  need for, 234—36
  spirit of, 243
Rigdon, Sidney, 197, 247
Righteousness, 22—23, 90—91
Ring, symbolism, 268
Rituals, symbolism, 5, 195—204
River, symbolism, 268—69
Robe, 111, 134, 269
  of Christ, 33, 137
Rock, symbolism, 269
  type for Christ, 56
  water from, 56, 174

Rod, symbolism, 269
  of Aaron, 46, 73, 269
  of Iron, 269
  of Moses, 57—58
Rods, of Egyptians, 46, 47
  twelve tribal, 73
Rome, 132
Root, symbolism, 269
Root of Jesse, 269

— S —

Sabbath, 3—4, 80, 92, 198—99, 242,
  269—70
Sacrament, 3, 83, 87, 89, 106—7, 116,
  150—51, 267
  covenants renewed through, 198
  introduced to Nephites, 8—9
Sackcloth, 163, 270
Sacrifice, 63—64, 270
  blood, 2, 3, 103—4
  by Abel and Cain, 147—48
  by Adam, 140—41
  law of, 86—91
  of Isaac, 152—53
  of firstborn, 51
  of lamb for Passover, 48
  on Day of Atonement, 82—84
  part of Priesthood, 77—79
Sadducees, 131, 192, 212, 264
St. Augustine, 225—26
Salt, symbolism, 88, 270
Salt Lake Temple, 129—30
Salem, 120, 150
  meaning of name, 175
Salvation, 35, 239—41
Samson, 21
Samaria, 17, 163
Samuel, 6—7, 161—62
  meaning of name, 186
Sanctification, of children of Israel, 61
  of firstborn, 51
  through Holy Ghost, 196—97
Sanctuary, 64
Sanhedrin, 21, 35, 45
Sarah, meaning of name, 182
Sarai, 63, 151—53
  meaning of name, 182
Satan, 46, 48, 155, 260, 264
  meaning of name, 192, 270
  metaphors describing, 14
  Moses' confrontation with, 238
  rebellion of, 7
  See also Devil; Lucifer; Perdition
Saul, 6, 158, 161—62, 237
  anointing of, 114

Scapegoat, 34, 82—83, 270
Scarlet, symbolism, 94, 102, 106, 112, 256
Scarlet wool, 96
Scepter, symbolism, 270
School of the prophets, 201
Scribes, 20
Scriptures, errors of interpretation, 242—44
  interpretation of, ix—xi, 231—49
  study, ix
  understanding through symbolism, 6—11
Sealing power, 39
Sealings, 203—4
Second Coming, 45, 157
Secrets of Enoch, 134, 136
Seed, 271
Seer stones, 44, 191—92
Septuagint, 66, 103, 137, 220—21, 222, 225, 239
Sermon on the Mount, 20, 125, 233
Serpents, 13, 75, 135, 271
  brazen, 75
  rods turned to, 46, 47, 59
Seth, 147, 202, 236
  meaning of name, 181
  type for Christ, 181
Seven, symbolism, 199
Seventy, calling of, 157
  elders under Moses, 62, 64, 79, 119, 207
  symbolism, 53
Shadows, types and, 44—45
Sharon, meaning of name, 173
Shaving, symbolism, 96
Sheaf offerings, 85
Shechem, 32, 33, 151
Sheep, symbolism, 271
Shem, meaning of name, 181
Shepherds, 30, 156, 271
Shewbread, 106—7, 159, 271
Shield, symbolism, 136, 271
Shittim wood, 103, 106—7, 108, 109
Silver, symbolism, 105, 256
Simeon, meaning of name, 183
  mount of, 122
Similes, 12—14
Simon, 190—91
Sin, desert of, 53, 56
Sin offerings, 82, 86, 87, 89, 97, 108, 110
Sinai, 118—19, 121—22, 255
  a temple, 62
  Moses' ascension of, 62—67, 118—19
Sleep, metaphor, 271

Smith, Hyrum, 143, 193
Smith, Joseph, 13, 21, 23, 143, 159
  betrayal of, 41
  Bible Translation, 64—65, 66, 133, 150, 182, 185, 191, 193, 211, 218, 234, 236—41, 246, 255, 268
  commandment to build temples, 120
  compared to Joseph of Egypt, 28, 36—43
  First Vision, 229
  instructions from Moroni, 245—46
  Kirtland Temple dedication, 100, 144, 203, 275
  learned line upon line, 243—44
  Oliver Cowdery's rebellion against, 69
  on Apocrypha, 238—39
  on apostasy, 230
  on baptism of Holy Ghost, 196
  on degrees of glory, 262
  on eternity, 204
  on gathering of Israel, 213
  on interpretation of scriptural imagery, 243
  on Jacob's ladder, 123
  on kings and priests, 203
  on Melchizedek Priesthood, 76, 79
  on "more sure word of prophecy," 124
  on nature of God, 206, 213
  on New Jerusalem, 129
  on offering by sons of Levi, 86
  on ordinances, 195
  on redemption of Israel, 141
  on revelation, 235
  on sacrifice, 77—79
  on Second Coming, 257
  on the Bible, 237
  on the Father and the Son, 147, 172
  on white stone, 55, 193
  persecutions against, 39—40
  Priesthood keys restored to, 78
  prophecies concerning, 193, 245
  revelations, 144, 198, 201, 229, 233—34, 244, 268
  root of Jesse, 269
  testimony, 247—48
  type of Christ, 160
  understanding of the Bible, 236
  vision of degrees of glory, 25
  vision of Satan, 24
Smith, Joseph, Sr., 193
Smith, William, 95, 199
Smitten rock, miracle of, 56
Smoke, symbolism, 271
Snakes, 13, 75, 135, 271
  rods turned to, 46, 47, 59

Sodom, 271
Solomon, temple of, 2, 100, 253, 254, 264
  type for Christ, 188—89
Solten, Henry W., 111, 113
Song of Solomon, 241
Sons of Levi, 3, 78, 86
Sophistry, 205—13
Speiser, E. A., 31
Spirit of God, communicated through anointing, 114—15
Spirit prison, 41
Spiritual death, 70, 95—97
Stakes, 271—72
Stars, 7—8, 272
Steinberg, Milton, 18, 217
Stem of Jesse, 272
Stephen, 21, 45, 35—36, 207
Stick of Joseph, 167—68
Stick of Judah, 167—68
Stone, symbolism, 272
Stranberg, Victor, 210
Suffering servant, 158—59
Sun, symbolism, 272
Susquehanna River, 78
"Sweet savor" offerings, 87, 88, 89
Sword, symbolism, 272
Symbols, 1, 272
  interpretation of, ix—xi
Synonyms of the Old Testament, 239

— T —

Tabernacle of Moses, 66, 83, 119—20, 124, 272
  cloud in, 68—69
  description, 99—117
  likeness of Christ, 100—17
  pattern for, revealed, 64
  temple ordinances in, 79
Tabernacle: The Priesthood and the Offerings, 111, 113
Table of shewbread, 106—7, 116
Talmud, 216
Tares, symbolism, 272
Targums, 149
Taylor, John, 13, 20
Teachings of the Prophet Joseph Smith, 76, 77—79, 86, 195, 196, 234, 236, 237, 243, 257, 268
Telestial kingdom, 25, 123
Temple: Its Ministry and Services as They Were at the Time of Christ, 82, 84—85, 93, 94, 199

Temple Mount, 175
  See also Mount Moriah
Temple ordinances, 78, 79, 124—25, 199—204
Temple worship, in ancient Near East, 126—28
Temples, 118—30, 272—73
  clothing, 110—14
  Herod's, 109
  Kirtland, 100, 144, 201, 203, 275
  Jerusalem, 257
  modern, 99—100, 116
  Salt Lake, 129—30
  Sinai, 62
  Solomon's, 2, 100, 253, 254, 264
  symbols of true religion, 128
Ten Commandments, 63, 66
Ten tribes, 42
Tent of the Testimony, 99
Terrestrial kingdom, 25, 123
Testament of Levi, 134—35
Testimony, symbols the language of, 1
This Is My God, 91
Thorns, symbolism, 273
Tithing, 246—47
Title of liberty, 37, 171
Titles, symbols for Christ, 3
Tittle, meaning of, 273
Todd, John, 228
Tongues, 100
Torah, 215—17
Transfiguration, Mount of, 124—25, 174, 255
Transubstantiation, 211
Treasury of the Midrash, 29
Tree, symbolism, 273
Tree of knowledge, 273
Tree of life, 127, 273
Trespass offerings, 89, 97
Trinity, 239
Trumpet, 273
Turtledoves, used in sacrifice, 86
Twelve, calling of, 157
  Nephite, 172
  spies, 71
  symbolism, 53
Types, 274
Types and shadows, 6, 44—45

— U —

U.S. Catholic, 210—11
Unleavened bread, 48—49, 50, 106—7
Urim and Thummim, 7, 55, 112

Utah, meaning of name, 129—30
Uzziah, 159

— V —

Valley of Hinnom, 176
Valley of Jehoshaphat, 176
Valley of Jezreel, 265
Veil, 274
    of Tabernacle of Moses, 105, 108—9
    of temple, 117, 274
Vine, symbolism, 274
Vineyard, 274
Vulgate Bible, 225

— W —

Washing of feet, 105, 201
Washings, 61, 79, 96, 104—5, 113, 114,
    120, 134, 200—1
Water, symbolism, 136, 200—1, 274
    from rock, 56, 74
Wave offerings, 85, 97
White, symbolism, 101, 105, 256
White stone, 55, 193
Wiesel, Elie, 40, 216
Wind, symbolism, 275
Wine, 107, 134
    sacrament, 8, 198
Winepress, 275
Wings, 275

Word, title for Christ, 275
Word of Wisdom, 91, 242
Words, power of, 13
    symbols for Christ, 4
Wouk, Herman, 91
Wycliffe Bible Dictionary, 149, 201
Wycliffe, John, 227

— Y —

Yoke, symbolism, 275
Yom Kippur, 252
Young Brigham, 59, 130, 200, 212, 241

— Z —

Zacharias, 189—90, 215
Zaphnath-paaneah, 30, 34, 42
Zebulun, 184
Zechariah, 133, 162
    meaning of name, 187
Zedekiah, 163, 167
Zephaniah, 133
    meaning of name, 187
Zerubbabel, 133, 159
    meaning of name, 189
Zilpah, 184
Zion, 29, 129, 275
    meaning of name, 174
    Mount, 144
Zipporah, 59
Zwingli, Ulrich, 228—29